"These are the best stories to come out of Latin America in some time."

—Gregory Rabassa, National Book Award winner

STRANGE THINGS HAPPEN HERE
Twenty-Six Short Stories and a Novel
by Luisa Valenzuela

Argentina's leading writer confronts the absurd and insane violence of her native country with sensitivity, wit, and power. Valenzuela uses the themes of sex, psychoanalysis, masks, and mirrors to create a brilliant picture of political reality and life in Argentina today. **"There is true brilliance, there is true love, there is true freedom and liberty in each one of her pages."—Julio Cortázar**

"There's something more to Valenzuela's art than just mastery... she may be divinely inspired."— Saturday Review

$9.95

Translated by Helen Lane

HARCOURT BRACE JOVANOVICH
757 Third Ave. NYC 10017

The Poetry of Pablo Neruda

René de Costa

"René de Costa guides us intelligently through a range of styles and subjects. North Americans can be grateful for a serious, extended study of Neruda."—*The New Republic* $12.50

Distributed by the Press

Art Inscribed

Essays on Ekphrasis in Spanish Golden Age Poetry

Emilie L. Bergmann

Bergmann discusses the poetic tradition of ekphrasis — the description of visual works of art — from Garcilaso de la Viega to Sor Juana Ines de la Cruz. She demonstrates that ekphrasis exposes the boundaries between the arts and the limitations of artistic imitation, while using that limitation as a source of poetic wit.
Harvard Studies in Romance Languages, 35 $12.00

Harvard University Press
Cambridge, Massachusetts 02138

 STUDIA HISPANICA EDITORS

Review 25/26 Contents

Focus

Texts

Topics

continued

Review 25/26 Contents _{continued}

Reviews

Editor	Ronald Christ
Managing Editor	Gregory Kolovakos
Circulation and Advertising	Pamela Zapata
Art Director	Dennis Dollens For Lumen, Inc.
Editorial Assistants	Donna Hildreth
	Alison Peake
	Wilfredo Corral
Contributing Editor	Luis Harss
	Jo Anne Engelbert
Poetry Editor	Octavio Armand
Advisory Board	Anna Balakian
	John Bierhost
	José Guillermo Castillo
	Zunilda Gertel
	Edith Grossman
	Ivan Van Sertima

Cover Photo:
Abraham Guillen

REVIEW gratefully acknowledges a grant from the Coordinating Council of Literary Magazines.

Review is published three times a year by the Center for Inter-American Relations. The Center, a non-profit, membership corporation financed by foundation support, membership dues and corporate as well as individual gifts, conducts educational programs in the visual and performing arts, literature and public affairs. Subscription rates for Review: $7.00 yearly within the United States; $9.00 foreign; $10.00 institutions. Past issues available. All subscriptions should be addressed to Review, Center for Inter-American Relations, 680 Park Avenue, New York, N.Y. 10021. Unsolicited manuscripts in English are welcome but will not be returned unless accompanied by a stamped, self-addressed envelope. All translations must be accompanied by the original Spanish or Portuguese. Neither the editors nor the Center can be responsible for damage or loss of such manuscripts. Opinions expressed in Review are those of the individual writers and not necessarily of the editors or the Center. Copyright © 1980 by the Center for Inter-American Relations, Inc. Library of Congress Cat. No. 74-86354. All rights reserved. Microfilms of issues 1-23 available from University Microfilms, Inc., 300 N. Zeeb Road, Ann Arbor, Mich. 48106.

Olga Luna

Death of the Dancer

LUIS HARSS

He was the stranger (*forastero*) and, at the same time—in a country of strangers—the embodiment of a national conflict.

Like the ritual dancer, Rasu-Ñiti, who danced his own death and mythic rebirth in the River of Blood (*yawar mayu*), he knew: "The world will never sing that way again."

As a child, in the mountain village, because of a heartless stepmother (and a wandering father), he lived with the Indian servants who "saw me as one of them."

There is a portrait (almost a self-portrait) of the father—a smalltown lawyer and judge—in *Deep Rivers:* "impulsive and generous"; a dreamer, lover of harp music (*huaynos*), Cuzcan by birth; blue eyes, blond beard, refined manners—the marks of racial estrangement; a solitary, voiceless figure "trotting along between stones and bushes," on his endless journeys in search of work (or mere restless movement), lost in memories of when Cuzco was "the center of the world, chosen by the Inca" and the rivers were speaking gods, and the world a place of joy, whose "shadow"—when they traveled together—"passed from him to me."

Another, much beloved, father figure: the often mentioned don Felipe Maywa, "that great Indian"—the sagest of household servants—who knew, "from birth and long years of experience, the nature of the immense mountains, their language and that of the insects, the rivers and waterfalls, small and large," and watched over him as he stood "facing the huge depths and heights of the Andes, where the trees and flowers wound you with a beauty that concentrates all the loneliness and silence of the world."

His first and only childhood language: Quechua, "the legitimate expression of the man of this land, the man born of this landscape and under these skies." As for the *Inca* Garcilaso, three centuries before, the "mother tongue" from which he later had to translate into the "foreign" tongue, Spanish, which he bent and tortured into new meanings, a new syntax that could only approximate, he said, but never really touch, the "depths that speak of the soul and the light of this land as a sense of beauty and a place of residence."

Quechuan, too, was the flight to the *ayllu* (tribal community, with its "maternal cornfields")—in a period of political disgrace for the father—where he seems to have found the only true happiness of his life, remembered ever afterwards as a lost paradise.

It was the community Indians who once "took twenty-eight days to build a highway from the provincial capital to the coast, in an effort that involved ten thousand men working almost twenty-four hours a day, to show the local authorities that they were capable of feats that no doubt only they could perform," so that "when the highway was inaugurated, at the moment of handing it over to the authorities, the Indian mayors of the four communities of the town of Puquio came and said in Quechua: 'Here is the highway. If the community decided, it could build a tunnel through the mountains, from here to the sea.'"

The same Indians who, in *Deep Rivers,* take over the provincial capital (another remembered childhood incident), defying rifles and machine guns (as, in *Yawar Fiesta,* they defied bulls and condors), in a spontaneous mass movement, to force the priest to say Mass against an epidemic that feeds on the diseased social fabric of a country oblivious to the presence of mountain valleys where "you raise your head, look two thousand meters up, and the length and depth of those two thousand meters you see hundreds of terraces, some abandoned today, but which were all farmed in ancient times and where there are still villages, trees and crops."

And Quechuan, too, at the opposite pole of experience (debased reality), the hacienda Indian, the pongo (who rotates as unpaid household serf): a wretch "who even the Indians of the communities regard with utter contempt," a tongue fed to the dogs. In *Deep Rivers,* the humble Christ-like figure of the first chapter, identified with the suffering crucifix tree, in which the boy recognizes himself.

Then there was the church school in a "captive" hacienda town (Abancay), ironically named after a wildflower (*amank'ay*) and the "soaring flight" (*awankay*) of large birds gliding, "gazing into the deep." A prison, as portrayed in *Deep Rivers,* enclosed in several circles of Hell, the innermost being a dark patio devoted to an adolescent ritual: the nightly rape of an idiot beggar woman (la Opa), a sort of polluted earth goddess (mother of outcasts) whose counterpart, in the dreams of the insulted and injured, is the heroic market woman, doña Felipa, who leads the peasant revolt.

A thoughtful boy; like his father, absorbed in memories; attuned to the voices of small magic objects that concentrate his inner world: stones, flowers, insects, and that symbol at once of art—in the sense in which *Deep Rivers* is a portrait of the artist as a young man—and the powers of nature momentarily restored to harmony: the *zumbayllu* (an onomatopoeic fusion of Spanish and Quechua, sound and light) or spinning top, with its open-eyed dance to the music (and animistic language) of trees, rivers and precipices.

Then, in Lima, years of survival; studies, work, a period in jail—student politics—where he met "the best and the worst" of the country; a Marxist phase; a thesis on the Peruvian language problem (when Spanish still "seemed a clumsy and alien language to me"); marriage; literary successes, after great efforts and depressions ("In May 1944 I succumbed to a mental ailment I'd had since childhood and spent nearly five years without being able to write"); dozens, perhaps hundreds of anthropological articles (in search of remembered landscapes); prizes, honors, editorial positions, public office, university chairs; a life "perhaps without personal ambition," devoted to a country with "ten thousand years of history" and "all the climates of the world," but, to the end, deeply divided against itself.

As he was: "not an acculturized man," but a dancer of dissonance: the mestizo, torn between the two irreconcilable halves of his nature: the homeless Indian and the rootless white man. In other terms: "the poet's soul and his language." Or: the spirit of the land and the foreignness of the city ("the fox above and the fox below"). And, in time, the inner voice (and vision) so painfully attained over the years, and changing literary styles and fashions.

And so, in April 1966, a first suicide attempt, somehow redeemed by "the life-giving gayness" of "a buxom young native prostitute" who reestablished his "vital tone." A "somewhat mutilated, intermittent life," after that—his "love of reading" is gone: "In all these years I've read only a few books"—but still strong enough for him to be able to "translate the substance of things into words."

Until, once again (in May 1968, according to the diaries he kept and published as parts of his last novel), "I feel incapable of fighting well, of working well," and "living this way is worse than death."

There is a message, in these diaries, to the Cuban utopians who think suffering can be eliminated by fiat; and another to the members of the "Boom" by whom he feels rejected (an outcast again). And, always, the obsession with childhood memories: a village bluebottle boring into the velvety yellow heart of a mountain flower: "the ugly, slow pain I feel in the back of my neck." A daydream, too, of rolling in the village dust with the stray pigs and dogs, under the roar of the high waterfalls that are "the image of the world for those of us who sing in Quechua." On May 17, a fable of destitution about a pregnant mestizo woman (another Opa), wild as a mountain vine (the *salvajina*), who clings to him one night (a mother-mistress to the child of sorrow) and the next morning is "off to have an orphan."

And then (apart from some letters to friends and colleagues; hopeful trips to Cuba and Chile), the silence of the dancer ("Sometimes," he said, "the world keeps a silence that only one perceives"), on December 2, 1969, after four days of agony.

Chronology:

José María Arguedas

WILLIAM L. SIEMENS

1911 José María Arguedas Altamirano born January 18 in Andahuaylas, Peru. His mother is from a distinguished family; his father is a lawyer of some importance. "My father was an *Apradista*, and when Leguía assumed power they applied to him the law of the Ratification of Judges. Then he dedicated himself to the exercise of his profession from town to town."

1914 His mother dies; José María lives with his grandmother.

1917 His father remarries and José María moves to Puquio to live with his stepmother. "I am the handiwork of my stepmother.... Since she held me in as much contempt and hatred as she did the Indians, she decided that I was to live with them in the kitchen, to eat and sleep there.... They treated me just as if I were one of their own." He is deeply influenced by their thinking: "I can't believe that a river is not a man as alive as I myself am." "Two things have been very firmly established in my character since I learned to speak: the tenderness and limitless love of the Indians ... and the hatred they feel toward those who ... make them suffer." There was in Puquio "a formidable Indian community with large land holdings, who never allowed the masters to abuse them.... In Puquio I felt the uncontainable, the infinite strength of the Indian communities."

1918 "Another modeler as effective as [my stepmother], and a bit more brutal, my stepbrother," slams a plate of food in José María's face for an imagined offense and tells him, "You're not worth what you eat." The boy spends hours face down in a cornfield, praying that God will let him die.

1919 Visits to Cuzco with his father. "During this period I came to know eight provinces, sometimes traveling great distances. Once I went from Nazca to Cuzco on horseback (about 700 kilometers)." "I learned to speak Spanish with a certain fluency only after the age of eight; until then I spoke only Quechua." Enters fourth grade in a religious school in Abancay.

1921 Runs away with his brother Arístides to Hacienda Viseca to live with his uncle.

1924 Travels with his father. "In every town we heard music and sang and danced with the Indians, whom my father always sought out, although ... he spoke ill of them."

1926 First year of secondary school as resident student at Colegio San Luis Gonzaga in Ica, "where they treated me as a mountaineer, and roughly."

1928 Travels with father to Huancayo, where he enters his third year of secondary school. He is known for his pensive, solitary air. His first literary efforts appear in the student journal, *Antorcha* (Torch) as articles, such as "The Dehumanization of Art" and "Present and Past of the Indian." "I began to write when I read the first narratives about the Indians; writers that I respect described them in such a false way.... No, I must write [the situation] as it is, because I have enjoyed it, I have suffered within it."

1929 Enters merchants' school in Lima. Frequently travels to Yauyo to visit his father. Eventually comes to spend more time there than in Lima.

1931 Returns to Lima to enter the University of San Marcos. Lives with Arístides, from whom he is inseparable. Establishes himself permanently in Lima. Studies letters. "I was never treated like a mountaineer at San Marcos."

1932 Father dies and brothers lose financial support. José María obtains a position in the postal department through the influence of a friend of his father.

1933 Studies singing.

1935 *Agua* (Water) is published: three short stories in their second version, since Arguedas has rejected the first, "mixing a little of the Quechua syntax into the Spanish, in a really infernal battle with language," desiring to "communicate in what was almost a foreign tongue the substance of our spirit." The book wins second prize in an international competition sponsored by the *Revista Americana* of Buenos Aires.

1936 Discovers the work of Marxist theorist, José Carlos Mariátegui. Together with Alberto Tauro, Augusto Tamayo Vargas, José Alvarado Sánchez and Emilio Champion, founds *Palabra*. "It was at this time that I read at one sitting, seated in the university patio, Vallejo's *Tungsten*."

1937 Completes his major in literature. A visit to the San Marcos campus by Mussolini envoy General Camarotta provokes a student protest. Arguedas is arrested and spends eight months in the Sexto prison. Loses his position in the postal service. The Sexto was "as good to me as my stepmother, exactly as generous as she was. There I met the best of Peru and the worst of Peru."

1939 Prepares a thesis, "The Mestizo Popular Song: Its Poetic Value and Possibilities," for his degree in the humanities. Never presents it. For the doctorate he submits "The Problem of Language in Peru and the Poetry of the Mountain and Coastal Regions." Becomes professor of Spanish and Geography at Mateo Pumaccahua boys' school in Sicuani, Cuzco. Marries Celia Bustamante Vernal.

1940 Travels to Mexico to represent Peruvian educators at the Inter-American Indian Conference in Pátzcuaro. Spends two years in Mexico.

1941 *Yawar Fiesta* is published. "In . . . *Yawar Fiesta* I described the power of the indigenous people." Promoted to a position in Ministry of Education "to aid in the reform of secondary education programs."

1944 "In May . . . a psychological ailment contracted in my childhood grew to a crisis stage and I was neutralized for writing for almost five years."

1947 Graduated from the Institute of Ethnology at San Marcos.

1948 Appointed Chief of the Section of Folklore and Fine Arts of the Ministry of Education. Moves to the Colegio Mariano Melgar.

1949 Loses his position at the Colegio Mariano Melgar; he is suspected of being a communist.

1953 Appointed head of the Institute of Ethnological Studies in the Museum of Culture. He is secretary of the Inter-American Committee on Folklore, which is based in Peru, and edits its official organ, *Folklore Americano*. The government of dictator Odría appoints him Director of Cultural Affairs; he declines.

1954 Publishes *Diamantes y pedernales* (Diamonds and Flints), which includes the stories of *Agua* plus two new stories and an introductory note explaining his difficulties (and progress) in rendering the Quechuan world in Spanish.

1955 Receives a prize from *El Nacional* of Mexico for his story, "Death of the Brothers Arango."

1958 *Deep Rivers* is published. "The thesis was this: these people revolt for a reason of an entirely magical nature. Are they not going to do so, then, when they struggle for something that affects them much more directly, such as their own lives. . . ?" As a result of the book's appearance, "I came to have some prestige in Lima." Receives the Javier Prado Prize for the Enhancement of Culture for his thesis in Ethnology, "Evolution of the Indigenous Communities." Travels to Europe to study in Spain and France. Becomes professor of ethnology at San Marcos.

1959 Receives the Ricardo Palma Prize for the Enhancement of Culture for *Deep Rivers*.

1960 Named Secretary of the International Folklore Committee. Attends the Third American Book Festival in Buenos Aires.

1961 *El Sexto* is published. Arguedas travels to Guatemala to study popular art.

1962 Attends the First Colloquium of Iberoamerican and German writers, organized by the journal *Humboldt*, in Berlin. Again receives the Ricardo Palma Prize, for *El Sexto*. Publishes his poem "A nuestro padre creador, Túpac Amaru. Himno-canción" (Hymn to Our Father and Creator Túpac Amaru), in a bilingual edition (Spanish/

Quechua), with an introductory note on the literary potential of Quechua; and the story "The Agony of Rasu-Ñiti."

1963 Appointed Director of the Casa de la Cultura of Peru. His view is, "The country... should become modernized without losing its ancient roots." Receives his doctorate in ethnology; his thesis is "Communities in Spain and Peru." Becomes full professor at the University of San Marcos.

1964 *Todas las sangres* (All Bloods) is published. "I meant to write a novel in which I would show all these hierarchies [of Peru] with everything they contain by way of promise and all they contain that drags them down." "Which is better for man, how does man progress more, by way of individual competition, the incentive of being more powerful than anyone else, or by way of the fraternal cooperation of all men, which is what the Indians practice?" *Cultura y pueblo* appears under his editorship. Later he is responsible for the *Revista Peruana de Cultura*, before resigning his position in the Casa de la Cultura. Travels to Mexico to be present at the inauguration of several cultural sites. Takes a position as Director of the Museum of Natural History. Edits the first issue of *Historia y cultura*.

1965 Separates from Celia Bustamante. Later marries Sybila Arredondo (date unclear). Participates in a Colloquium of Latin American Writers in Genoa and in the Primer Encuentro de Escritores Peruanos in Arequipa. Makes appearances at major universities of the United States. Travels to Chile and France. Publishes *El sueño del pongo* (The Pongo's Dream), a "Quechuan story," bilingual edition, in booklet form.

1966 Appointed full time professor at La Molina Agrarian University, where he has taught part time since 1962. Travels to Chile. Attends the 37th International Conference of Americanists in Argentina. Visits Uruguay. First attempts suicide. "A pharmacist refused to sell me three seconal pills; he said that with three I might go to sleep and never wake up; and I took 37." "Fortunately the pills... did not kill me." "I live to write, and believe it is necessary to live... to interpret chaos and order." Keeps a suicide diary (later incorporated into his last novel).

1967 Attends the Second Latin American Writers' Conference in Chile and a meeting of anthropologists in Vienna.

Publishes *Amor mundo y todos los cuentos* (World Love and Complete Stories). "Amor Mundo" was written "not for publication" but "on doctor's orders."

1968 Heads the Department of Sociology at La Molina. Travels to Cuba to serve on the selection committee for the Casa de las Américas Prize. "When socialism like that of Cuba arrives here, the trees and pathways which signify the good land and paradise will multiply." Receives the Garcilaso de la Vega Prize. Travels to Chile twice. May 10: "Now I am again at the gates of suicide, because once again I feel incapable of struggling well, of working well." "Death has been molding me since I was a child."

1969 Publishes new edition of *The Pongo's Dream* in *El sueño del pongo. Canciones quechuas* (which includes a recording of Arguedas reading from the texts). Travels to Chile three times. On August 29 he writes, "In Chile I obtained a 22-calibre revolver. I have tried it. It works. It's all right. It won't be easy to choose the day, to do it." On that day he writes of *El zorro de arriba y el zorro de abajo* (The Fox Above and the Fox Below), "It has been written in a series of frightful experiences, in a real struggle—halfway triumphant—against death. I am not going to survive the book. Since I am certain that my faculties and weapons as a creator, professor, student and instigator have become weakened to the point of near exhaustion and all that remain are those that would relegate me to the condition of a passive and impotent spectator of the formidable struggle that mankind is entering into in Peru and everywhere else, it would not be possible for me to tolerate that destiny. Either as an actor, as I have been since I entered secondary school forty-three years ago, or nothing." Fires a shot into his head on November 28 and dies on December 2.

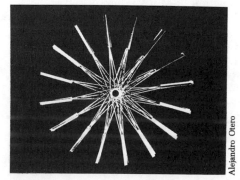

Alejandro Otero, *Light Catcher* (Model) 1972

1971 *El zorro de arriba y el zorro de abajo* is published.

1972 Bound edition of *Temblar/Katatay* (Quake), a bilingual poem previously published (1966) in a magazine.

1974 Editorial Losada (Buenos Aires) publishes Arguedas' *Relatos Completos* (Complete Stories) and plans an edition of his complete works. 🦃

Main sources: E. Mildred Merino de Zela, "Vida y obra de José María Arguedas," *Revista peruana de cultura*, 13-14 (Dec. 1970), pp. 127-78; Gladys Marín, *La experiencia americana de José María Arguedas*, Buenos Aires, Ed. Fernando García Cambeiro, 1973, pp. 14-17: the "Diaries" in *El zorro de arriba y el zorro de abajo*, Buenos Aires, Losada, 1971; Arguedas' opening remarks, *Primer encuentro de escritores peruanos (Arequipa 1965)*, Lima, Casa de la Cultura del Perú, 1969, pp. 36-43.

WILLIAM L. SIEMENS teaches Spanish American and Golden Age literatures at West Virginia University.

Between Quechua and Spanish

JOSE MARIA ARGUEDAS

Translated by Luis Harss

Vallejo marks the beginning of the distinction, in Peru, between the poetry of the coast and that of the highlands. Because with Vallejo begins the tremendous struggle of the Andean man who feels the conflict between his inner world and his use of the Spanish language. The violent change that occurs between *The Black Heralds* and *Trilce* is primarily the effect of that problem. As José Bergamín observed, the obscurities in *Trilce* are a consequence of the struggle between the poet's soul and his language. Although Bergamín is not aware of the deeper cause of this conflict, we know what it is. And the conflict also explains the backwardness of our poetry inspired by mestizo themes.

Quechua is the legitimate expression of the man of this land, the man born of this landscape and under these skies. In Quechua one touches depths that speak of the soul and the light of this land as a sense of beauty and a place of residence.

But came another people with another language which expressed another race and another landscape. And it was in this language that the people from our part of the country wrote bad literature for so many years. On the coast the fusion between man and this language was accomplished over a period of four centuries. And it happened fast because the Yunga language was culturally less resistant than Quechua; because the coastal landscape has less of an influence on man than the Andean world and its men are less attached to the land; and because the advance of Spain and the West was more violent and sustained along the coast. After four centuries, [José María] Eguren and [Emilio Adolfo] Westphalen speak Spanish, as a Frenchman speaks French and a Spaniard his own tongue.

In us, the people of the highlands, the language conflict, as a conscious problem, explicit in our literature from Vallejo to the last Andean poet, began a few years ago. It was the same conflict felt—though more crudely—by [the 16th-century chronicler and poet] Huamán Poma de Ayala. If we speak pure Spanish, we say nothing of our landscape or inner world; because the mestizo has not yet mastered Spanish as his own language and Quechua is still his legitimate means of expression. But if we write in Quechua the result is a narrow literature condemned to neglect.

And allow me here to refer to my own problem, which is probably typical. When I started to write about the life of my people, I was painfully aware of the inadequacy of trying to do it in Spanish, a language incapable of expressing the skies and rains of my land, let alone our attachment to the soil, to the trees of our valleys, not to mention the urgency of our human hates and loves. Because having inwardly chosen my Indian nature, as a definition of race and landscape, I could only touch the depth of my thirst and joy in Quechua. Which explains my style in *Agua*, of which a reviewer dubiously and somewhat contemptuously suggested that it was neither Quechua nor Spanish but a mixture of both. And he was right; but it was the only language in which I could convey to others the soul of my people and my land. A mixture, too, and even more so, was the style of Huamán Poma de Ayala; but if anyone wants to have a feeling for the life of the Indian population in colonial days, he is the person to turn to.

The mixture has a reason: Andean man has not achieved a balance between his need for total self-expression and the inevitability of the Spanish language. And there is now, in the mestizo, a sort of desperate yearning to master that language.

One cannot, on the evidence of the bad and borrowed literature written in the highlands until recently in Spanish, decide conclusively that Spanish is not the appropriate language for the mestizo. Until the early years of this century, our only literature was written by people uprooted from the land, with no feeling for our landscape and totally isolated from the concerns and the soul of our people. And that explains the self-defeating poverty of their literature.

But now that the man rooted in this land feels the need to express himself and to do it in a language he does not command, he finds himself in a painful dilemma: the Spanish learned with great effort in school, college or the university is not fully equipped to express his soul or the landscape of the world where he grew up; and the Quechua he still feels to be his genuine language, in which he can give full voice to his concerns and fulfill his deepest need to express his people and his land, is an untimely language without universal value.

This is the root of the mestizo's current urge to master Spanish. But when he has achieved his purpose and is able to speak and write in Spanish with the same fluency that he now has in Quechua, that Spanish will no longer be today's Spanish, with its almost total lack of Quechua influence, but a Spanish in which there is much of the genius, perhaps even the intimate syntax, of Quechua. Because Quechua, as the legitimate expression of the man of this land, born of this landscape and under these skies, is an essential part of the mestizo's genius and his being.

This urge to master Spanish will put the mestizo into full possession of the language. And its effect on the Spanish language will be due to the fact that he will never cease adapting Spanish to his deeper need for self-expression, in other words, translating into it every particle of his being, under the command of his Indian self.

And why is it only now that mestizo literature has run into this problem of expressing itself in Spanish?

During most of the republican period the mestizo was kept in the same state of inferiority and silence that he was in during the colony. Therefore neither colonial nor early republican literature produced any work of real value as an expression of the Andean people and their landscape. This I have already mentioned above. But the mestizo increased in numbers and culture and came to constitute a social and spiritual majority in the Peruvian Andes. And the West was not able to dominate this mestizo

because of his deep Indian roots. And he struggled, and is still struggling, to establish his own cultural identity.

As the mestizo assimilated the spiritual climate of the Andean people, the inner struggle between the Spanish and the Indian, which began with the first mestizo, took shape in him. The Indian element already predominates in the psychology of the Peruvian mestizo, because of the overpowering presence of this Andean world: the land, the air, the light, and this great Indian people which still makes up sixty per cent of Peruvian humanity. And that is why—because the mestizo spirit is already more Indian than Spanish—pure Spanish can never be his legitimate means of expression.

The human and social reality I have been describing had to find expression in literature. Increasingly, the literature composed in the Peruvian Andes is mestizo in spirit. And in all that literature you can feel the mestizo's anguished yearning for a legitimate means of expression. And this anguished yearning is to blame for that literature's failure, so far, to achieve any lasting value. And whatever has been achieved has been through the influence of Quechua on the Spanish language.

We are witnessing the agony of Spanish as a spiritual climate and a pure and untouched language. I can see it and feel it every day in my Spanish class in the Mateo Pumaccahua school in Canchis. My mestizo students, who have assumed their Indian identity, strain the Spanish language, and in the intimate patterns and broken syntax of the Spanish they speak and write I recognize the genius of Quechua.

Sicuani, Perú, 1939

From *La Prensa*, Buenos Aires, 1939

The Word and the World in Arguedas

SARA CASTRO-KLAREN

Translated by Mary H. Lusky

José María Arguedas establishes a world with the primary intention of naming it, and thereby making it known. The most significant peculiarity of the world created by Arguedas is a fundamental schism. For Arguedas (particularly before the writing of *Todas las sangres* [1963]) this schism appears as an irremediable, silent fact and also as a rift whose basic meaning will be located in a moral context. The world is divided, in a Manichean way, between forces of good and evil. In turn, Arguedas' Manicheanism suggest the following alignment, although not always in as schematic a way as I shall here align it:

Good	Evil
Rural mountains	Urban coast
Servants	Masters
Quechua	Spanish
Childhood	Adulthood
Memory	The present
The authentic	The falsified
Purity	Sin/corruption
The boy Ernesto/	The Old Man/Priest/Master
Pantacha, Rosendo	Prostitutes (Their sign
Wives/virgins	changes in
	Los Zorros)
	Sex

With the world divided in this way, especially in Arguedas' first texts, we find the writer assigning a positive value to one language and a negative value to another. Speaking of Vallejo as a writer whose work articulates Peru's cultural problematic, Arguedas postulates in the author of *Trilce* a "conflict between his inner world and Spanish as his language."[1] Arguedas asserts that "the obscure style of *Trilce* is a consequence of *the struggle* between the poet's soul and the [Spanish] language. Although Bergamín is not aware of

the most deeply rooted cause of this conflict, *we know it.*" Arguedas develops and refines his thesis still further, adding that:

Quechua is the legitimate expressive medium of the man of this land, of man as a creature of this landscape and this light; with Quechua one can talk in a deeply felt way, one can describe and tell forth the soul of this light and this country, as beauty and as residence.... (My emphasis.)

In view of his interpretation of the linguistic problem in *Trilce*, how ought one to formulate a general theory of language for Arguedas, himself a bilingual writer? The problem comes into sharper focus if we recall that he is the originator and principal propounder of the thesis that his first stories are born of and embody the "implacable struggle between Quechua and Spanish," a struggle which, expressed indirectly, he perceives in the work of the monolingual Vallejo.

Moreover the majority of his critics, with the exception of Peter Gold and William Rowe, allowing ourselves to be swayed by Arguedas himself, have accepted the notion that the value of his work resides, in part, in the creation of his now famous "Indian Spanish" which, in its varied range of expressiveness, would be the supposed syncretic result of that "hellish struggle" between the two linguistic sources from which his work springs.

It seems to me that, having gone thus far with Arguedas, we find ourselves with two theses which to a certain extent seem contradictory. First: there exists a mutually excluding opposition and antagonism between Quechua and Spanish as the language capable of expressing Andean—let us not, for the moment, say Peruvian—reality. Second: Arguedas' work, with the creation of Indian Spanish, does achieve a syncretization. That is, it either goes beyond or falls short of the required mutual exclusivity of the struggle enunciated in the first thesis. Thus we find ourselves facing a troublesome problem, one which needs elucidating.

a) In the first place, if Indian Spanish is a syncretization, one must ask *what* it syncretizes, since it does not constitute a natural hybrid language. In this regard, what must first be established is that, despite all the "subtle disorderings"[2] that Spanish suffers in the mouths of Quechua-speakers, be they monolingual or bilingual, the language of Arguedas' texts remains Spanish. And this is not merely because the lexicon is Spanish but because the deep-structure that continues to function, that is, to signify, belongs to the generative possibilities of Spanish and not of another language.[3] However, one cannot fail to note that in Arguedas' linguistic practice a substratum is operative, influencing or determining the kind of "subtle disorderings" that he calls into play, and this substratum, naturally, is Quechua.[4] Nevertheless, the *language system* remains Spanish. William Rowe argues quite convincingly that "no matter how much Arguedas' Spanish is modified, it cannot but be judged to be Spanish."[5] And he adds, contradicting those who contend that with his Indian Spanish Arguedas manages to "portray" the thought of Quechua-speakers, that

the bond between syntax and modes of thought belongs uniquely to each individual language and culture. Therefore, the transference of structures from one language to another does not guarantee that the original modes of thought are transferred as well.[6]

Thus we see, from the outset, that Arguedas' work is irrevocably located, is embodied, in Spanish, and what he as the writer of *that* language achieves is to activate, infuse with life or, as he himself would say, *charge* the word and the structual systems of Spanish with a new energy or creative sensitivity that constitutes in itself an original or vision of the world. Arguedas' syncretization, then, is not linguistic but cultural.

We must therefore conclude that Indian Spanish, despite its original expressive force, can neither serve as Arguedas' resolution of the posited struggle between Quechua and Spanish nor can it be considered Arguedas' chief creative accomplishment.[7] He himself, many years after *Agua* (1935) and the prologue to *Diamantes y pedernales* (1954), states in 1970 that *Agua* constitutes a new style in Spanish and explains that "new *styles* ... generally appear because there is a new world to reveal. And *it took me a long time to master* Spanish well enough so that it would serve me as a truly *legitimate* expressive instrument."[8] (my emphasis). Thus we see that Arguedas himself recognizes (1970) that he is an innovative writer of Spanish, perhaps owing to the "spirit" of Quechua, but not a syncretizer or writer of Quechua systems in Spanish.

b) Returning to Arguedas' Manichean posture, ought we then to conclude that Spanish won out in that "implacable struggle"? And what of Arguedas? Has he lost or betrayed Quechua as "legitimate expression" (for "legitimate" read "authentic of Andean man")? I believe that simply to posit a struggle between Spanish and Quechua, as Arguedas does in his assessment of Vallejo, would lead us to mistaken conclusions. The struggle is a real one for the Arguedas of the *Agua* period, and, in another guise, it will be so again for the Arguedas of *El zorro de arriba y el zorro de abajo*

(1971). Its moral significance remains intense but in this struggle it is not so much two different languages that compete as two systems of perception, that is, two sensibilities. On the one hand we have the system of affective education of Quechua as an *oral* linguistic system and realm, and on the other hand we have the *literary* system of Spanish. One must not forget that Arguedas' most difficult and decisive encounters with Spanish are associated almost exclusively with the written word, with his readings in secondary school, and later as a poor provincial youth at the University of Lima. It is worth mentioning, in this context, that in *Los ríos profundos* (1958) no one pays attention to the literary-minded Valle, and this is especially true when he compares the lived experience of the boarding school with the reality of the books he is reading. One must also keep in mind that Arguedas never became a voracious reader. "In all these years I have read only a few books,"[9] he says in 1971. Thus it is hardly surprising that Regina McDonald, in her paper (Modern Language Association, 1976) on *A nuestro padrecreador, Tupac Amaru* (1962), should note that "the verbs *to speak, to shout, to listen,* are constantly referred to, which reveals a culture in which language is oral."

The battle Arguedas perceives raging in himself as a bilingual individual and as a novice writer is intensely Manichean in the years when he has not yet mastered Spanish, a tongue which thus seems doubly strange, presenting itself to him as "that other language," and also seeming always to be lurking, ready to "falsify things." Arguedas' bilingualism, at this particular juncture, plays the decisive role in his attitude toward and relative appreciation of both languages; impulsive, nearly blinded by rebelliousness, Arguedas fails to appreciate the importance of the double leap he has attempted in deciding to write in Spanish. He has propelled himself from his abode in an oral linguistic matrix, with no tradition of written language, into another linguistic realm, a world that for him, given his circumstances, exists almost exclusively through the written word and which, as should be only logical, presents itself as enigma, enemy and threat.[10]

The innocent coincidence between world and word that Arguedas had taken for granted within Quechua is disrupted because of the *strangeness of the word*—the written word—in Spanish. Thus at first it strikes him as a "false, made-up language." However, thirty years of contending with "that other language" will make him feel that Spanish is malleable and ductile in expressing the penetrating, *individual subjectivity* (Emphasis added.) of *Amor mundo* (1967) and *Los ríos profundos*.

18

The estrangement between man and language, particularly clear and intense for the writer of our time, an alienation of which Vallejo was fully aware, befalls Arguedas at the same time that he is attempting to acquire and subdue "that other language," and therefore the rift between words and reality, or words and the perception of things, is seen by Arguedas solely in terms of the problematic of "that other language," that is, the tongue he is striving to master and mold.

The adult Arguedas misinterprets his insightful perception of the gap between the world and the word, perceiving instead a struggle between Quechua and Spanish. If apparently a struggle between Quechua and Spanish does exist, it is because Arguedas posits, and feels, Quechua as a referent fused with things and out of joint with the word in Spanish. His first language having been part of a highly emotive—and abruptly truncated—childhood, Arguedas preserves Quechua in a sort of bell jar where the objects of memory meld in an inseparable union with their name in Quechua. It is in this way that Spanish initially comes to figure in the "evil" column. It is part of "the other" whose presence vitiates the purity of the Andean world. Confronting written language as the essence of otherness sharpens, in Arguedas, an awareness of his own severing of ties with words and childhood. Writing offers him a world that is enigma, and this awareness of the oppositions world-self, writing-writer, world-word is what Arguedas, confusing cause with effect, calls the "implacable struggle."

If his contact with writing makes him feel alienated, his contacts with Quechua, often renewed, help him to maintain affectively the oral tongue as a sort of paradise and refuge. When he writes in Spanish, Arguedas neither betrays "good" nor abandons his Andean culture. On the contrary, as on other occasions, he accepts the historical subjugation of his own reality to the world of the masters. Accepting this fact as a sort of existential challenge, he sets out to conquer *written Spanish* in order to express, through its richness and tradition, as a yet unpublished Quechua referent.

Arguedas makes no attempt to cross over to the other side of the Manichean split with which he perceives the world. Quite the reverse. Realizing that the struggle is inevitable, he makes of it, of his own artistic activity, a mediating zone where he goes about creating his own space. The good, the pure are, for Arguedas, those who, beseiged by evil, contend with "the other" and change the sign of reality. Writing, like music, can be a purifying, redeeming activity.

However, unlike music, which is always good, writing more closely resembles sex, and is thus attended by the terror of sin with which sex imbues him. On certain occasions, sex becomes the only form of human contact through which he can escape from depression. In 1944, for example, "the encounter with a fat Zamba woman, a young prostitute, restored to me what doctors call vital tone." The pure invade the zone of evil and, by struggling with it, lay hold of its force and transfigure it; they alter its sign, producing a reversal of values.

Furthermore, in *Los Zorros*, in which the world of the novel is not the *sierra* and therefore Quechua is not confused with the true referent of the word, or used as a crystalizing filter through which reality is revealed, we see that Arguedas begins to lose his previous confidence in the word as existential vehicle. Despairing of being able to imagine a world for Chimbote, the author of the Diaries yearns for the moment when he can roll in the dirt with the mountain dogs and pigs, hear their delicious grunts, scratch their hardened hides. Toward 1967, the world of the logos—written or oral, Hispanic or Quechua—is still a contested zone, but by now its meaning has ceased to be clear. What Arguedas exalts and calls the *bond* between himself and things[11] has been broken or can no longer be sharply discerned. The word once again seems to him inadequate, this time because it is inauthentic, false. Language fails to coincide with, or correspond to the world. Quechua is no longer a safe abode. As a result he is transfixed with nostalgia *for* and *of* the beasts that existed prior to the logos, prior to the split between man and the world, and prior, too, to the moment in which "the word like a god or demon confronts man not as a creation of his own, but as something existent and significant in its own right, as an objective reality."[12]

Probing deeper, we see that in *Los Zorros* the characters that engage Arguedas' interest, and who are most fully developed (Bazalar, Maxe, Don Esteban), are bilingual (except for Moncada). They are people who struggle daily with a chaotic world that presents itself in a language they have not mastered, a language which is, for them, both fetter and fraternal bond. There is little difference between gringos and Indians; both groups are marginal, and speak Spanish badly. In the speeches of the gringos, especially Maxe, the linguistic substratum is not English but Quechua. With *Los Zorros* Arguedas attempts once more to conquer for writing the language of an oral culture, a collectivity that has unanimously apprenticed itself to another tongue. This collectivity is not only still engaged in fashioning a style, an activity that would take place on an individual level, but also in forging a language capable of embodying a bilingual, bicultural experience. Here Arguedas positions himself at the same juncture, on the same battleground, on which he had been a passionate combatant when he began his career as a writer. Once more the word corresponds neither to the reality of the world nor to the internal reality of the self. Of all the characters, Maxe has the sharpest awareness of this misalignment: "these are the *lame* ("cojas") *words*. I should say, Don Cecilio, begging your pardon, the only fucking ("cojudas") *words* I remember to express experiences that Spanish or English naturally cannot express well, I think, because *we no longer feel their joy or their pain*," (Emphasis added.)

c) With Maxe's words, Arguedas seems to have come full circle, for they are, almost literally, the words he had used to describe the purpose and problematic of his task as a writer: "I have to write things *just as they are, because I have felt their joy and their pain.*"[13] (Emphasis mine.) Here we reach a statement of the third problem implicit in the struggle: that of authenticity vis-a-vis the falsification of reality, which in turn poses the problem of language, referent and reality. Arguedas implies a serialization of referents whose immediacy and thus value *as* reality varies according to reasons of several sorts. He begins his struggle with literature by forestalling, resisting the tendency of the written language to retreat into its own world, the world, let us say, of literature as a cultural institution. Such a tendency, if not countered, would of necessity allow the literary structures in force in the writer's time to become the determining referent of his writing. At all cost, Arguedas wishes to keep literature from becoming the closest referent of his text. In an adamic sense, he seeks to establish a link between words and things that will prove so immediate and direct as to be scarcely perceptible. Better still, it should disappear altogether, so that it could be said that he "writes things just as they are." By accepting the word within a written tradition, Arguedas risks interposing between words and things a series of diluting and falsifying filters. It would thus seem safer to invade the text with the *oral logos* of Quechua which, precisely because it is oral (temporal and not spatial), makes each word a unique act, an act without precedents, and therefore capable of the authenticity that only a spontaneous act can possess.

Nevertheless, the only factor that truly guarantees authenticity is the *"I have felt their joy, I have felt their pain."* (Emphasis mine.) In other words, the perception of total identity, of the indivisibility of words and things, is possible if and only if the *affective self* exists and

guarantees that coincidence. For Arguedas, words are not objectively transparent and inhabitable by things; rather, words have meaning only when a subjectivity, and not the things themselves, establishes an invisible, indestructible bond between words and the world they name. In this regard, Arguedas says: "When that bond is intensified, I can transmit to words the substance of things." And Cassirer, discussing the origins of language, states: "Speech is rooted not in the prosaic, but in the poetic aspect of life so that its ultimate basis must be sought...in the primitive power of subjective feeling." Thus, for Arguedas, the referent that confers reality—authenticity—on words is neither the world nor language as a system, but the self. It is the individual subjectivity that charges the word with relations, and, by virtue of *feeling*, language sustains it as significant, and as existence itself. The poet is he who, by feeling things and *intervening* between the world and the word, by naming things, infuses them with a vitality consonant with that of their own being.

Octavio Paz, expressing the fragile, somber sentiment of our modernity, concludes in *El mono gramatico* (Barcelona, 1974) that "language is the consequence (or the cause) of our exile from paradise; it signifies the distance between us and things." "The poet is not the namer of things, but he who dissolves their names, he who discovers that things have no name and that the names by which we call them are not theirs. The critique of paradise is language." Nothing could be more opposite to Paz's pessimism, then, than the vigor and desire for existential affirmation expressed by Arguedas, who fixes in the affective self the faculty of naming things and, by naming them, of transfusing them with existence.

For Arguedas, the great Manichean, words are not, in the end, the critique of paradise; rather, they create, like sin in sexual love, the zone of potential mediation wherein two implacable historical worlds are reconciled. The possibility of existence finally comes to terms with the possibility of redemption, or recovery of paradise. But, toward 1966 Arguedas finds himself once again in a dead-locked struggle with writing. *El zorro de arriba y el zorro de abajo* entails the resurgence of two separate worlds, devoid of mediation. The affective self, that ancient bridge between two passive poles (the world and the word), discovers that things rebel and arrogate to themselves that unattainable reality of which Paz speaks. It finds, also, that words are no longer empty, that they can even conspire among themselves to make their own meaning. Estranged from the world of things, astonished by the gulf that has grown between his word and the world, Arguedas decides that writing no longer affords him a mediating zone, a place of refuge and redemption.

Before the final estrangement of *Los Zorros*, Arguedas, in *Deep Rivers*, for example, had been master of the ancient ties to the impassioned, "authentic" word, of the affective ties which had ensured the identity of language with reality. Command over the affective bond between the word and the world had ensured for him and his reader, a total identity between the word and reality, so much so that when asked about the ontological nature of reality he answered that it was "reality/reality." Thus, Arguedas, unlike Paz, had not allowed himself to learn that the critique of paradise is the reflexive language of fallen man, because he had made of writing a zone of encounter, of struggle and, in the end, of the necessary reconciliation attendant on the forging of a new identity.

[1] José María Arguedas, "Entre el quechua y el castellano," *La Prensa*, Buenos Aires, Sept. 20, 1939.
[2] José María Arguedas, "La novela y la expresión literaria," *Bohemia*, Havana (1974), p. 49.
[3] See: "Indigenista Fiction of José María Arguedas," *Bulletin of Hispanic Studies*, No. 50 (1973), pp. 56-70.
[4] See: Alberto Escobar, ed., *El reto del multilingüismo en el Perú*, Estudios Peruanos, Lima, 1972, pp. 123-42.
[5] William Rowe, "Mito, lenguaje e ideología en *Los ríos profundos*," *Textual*, No. 7 (1973), p. 5.
[6] William Rowe, *Textual*, p. 15.
[7] In this regard it is also pertinent to remark that the "Indian Spanish" used by Arguedas' characters is not his own invention *ex nihilo*, but on the contrary, constitutes a sort of lingua franca among the Quechua-speakers whose grasp of Spanish is not yet perfect. See: Pedro Luis Gonzalez, "Fisonomía lingüística de la obra narrativa de José María Arguedas," *Lengua y Ciencias*, Arequipa, No. 12 (1972), pp. 41-52.
[8] José María Arguedas, "La literatura peruana," *Bohemia*, p. 50.
[9] José María Arguedas, *El zorro de arriba y el zorro de abajo*, Buenos Aires, 1971, p. 11.
[10] See: Antonio Cornejo, *Los universos narrativos de José María Arguedas*, Buenos Aires, 1973.
[11] "For him (Ernesto), representation, rather than serving as the ideal measure of reality, is reality. Things, for Ernesto, have no meaning beyond their being, and therefore they do not signify, they are." J.C. Curutchet, "José María Arguedas: peruano universal," *Cuadernos Hispanoamericanos*, No. 228 (1968), p. 754.
[12] Ernst Cassirer, *Language and Myth*, New York, Dover, 1953, p. 36.
[13] And years later he repeats that "it was indispensable to make an effort to discover Andean man exactly as he was, and exactly as I had come to know him by living so closely with him." "La literatura peruana," *Bohemia*, p. 49.

SARA CASTRO-KLAREN is the author of *El mundo mágico de José María Arguedas* (Lima, 1973) and teaches Latin American and Comparative Literature at Dartmouth College.

Zumbayllu: The Spinning Top

JOSE MARIA ARGUEDAS

Translated by
Frances Horning Barraclough

The Quechua ending *yllu* is onomatopoeic. *Yllu*, in one form, means the music of tiny wings in flight, music created by the movement of light objects. This term is similar to another broader one—*illa*. *Illa* is the name used for a certain kind of light, also for monsters with birth defects caused by moonbeams. *Illa* is a two-headed child or a headless calf, or a giant pinnacle, all black and shining, with a surface crossed by a wide streak of white rock, of opaque light. An ear of corn with rows of kernels that cross or form whorls is also *illa*; *illas* are the mythical bulls that live at the bottom of solitary lakes, of highland ponds ringed with cattail reeds, where black ducks dwell. All *illas* bring good or bad luck, always to the nth degree. To touch an *illa*, and to either die or be resurrected, is possible. The term *illa* has a phonetic relationship and, to a certain extent, shares a common meaning with the suffix *yllu*.

Tankayllu is the name of the inoffensive humming insect that flies through the fields sipping nectar from the flowers. The *tankayllu* appears in April, but may be seen in irrigated fields during other months of the year. Its wings whir at a mad pace to lift its heavy body with its ponderous abdomen. Children chase and try to catch it. The dark, elongated body ends in a sort of stinger, which is not only harmless, but sweet. Children hunt it to sip the honey with which the false stinger is anointed. The *tankayllu* is not easy to catch because it flies high over the bushes, looking for flowers. It is a strange, dark, tobacco color, and has a bright striped abdomen; and because its wings make such a loud noise, much too strong for such a tiny figure, the Indians believe that the *tankayllu* has something more inside its body than just its own life. Why does it have honey on the end of its abdomen? Why do its weak little wings fan the air until they stir it up and make it change direction? How is it that whoever sees the *tankayllu* go by feels a gust of air on his face? It cannot possibly get so much vitality from such a tiny body. It fans the air, buzzing like a big creature; its velvety body disappears, rising straight upward in the light. No, it is not an evil being; children who taste its honey feel for the rest of their lives the brush of its comforting warmth on their hearts, protecting them from hatred and melancholy. But the Indians do not consider the *tankayllu* to be a godly creature, like all the ordinary insects; they fear it may be a reprobate. The missionaries must have once preached against it and other privileged beings. In the Ayacucho towns there was once a scissors-dancer who has since become legendary. He danced in the town squares for important fiestas and performed diabolical feats on the eves of saints' days—swallowing bits of steel, running needles and hooks through his body, and walking about the churchyards with three iron bars in his teeth. That dancer was called Tankayllu. His suit was made of condor skins decorated with mirrors.

Pinkuyllu is the name of the giant flute that the southern Indians play at the community celebrations. The *pinkuyllu* is never played for home fiestas. It is a heroic instrument, not made of ordinary reed or cane, nor even of *mámak*, an extraordinarily thick jungle reed which is twice as long as bamboo. The hollow of the *mámak* is dark and deep. In areas where there is no *huaranhuay* wood, the Indians do make smaller flutes of *mámak*, but they do not dare to use the name *pinkuyllu* for these instruments. They simply call them *mámak* to distinguish them from ordinary flutes. *Mámak* means the mother, the source, the creator—it is a magic name. But there is no natural reed that can be used as material for the *pinkuyllu*. Man must make his own, fashioning a deeper, heavier *mámak*, unlike anything that grows, even in the jungle. A great bent tube. He removes the hearts from *huaranhuay* poles and then bends them in the sun, binding them together with bull sinews. The light that enters the hole at the smaller end of the hollow tube can be seen only indirectly, as a half-light flowing through the curve, a soft glow, like that on the horizon just after sunset.

The *pinkuyllu* maker cuts the instrument's finger holes, seeming to leave too much space between them. The first two holes should be covered with the thumb and either the index or the ring finger, the player opening the left hand as widely as possible; the other three holes are for the index, ring, and little fingers of the right hand, with the players' fingers spread quite

widely apart. Indians with short arms cannot play the *pinkuyllu*. The instrument is so long that the average man who tries to use one has to stretch his neck and put his head back as if he were looking directly upward at the zenith. Troupes of musicians play them, with drum accompaniment, in town squares, in the fields, or in the corrals and courtyards, but never inside the houses.

Only the *wak'rapuku* has a deeper, more powerful voice than the *pinkuyllu*. But in areas where there are *wak'rapukus*, the *pinkuyllu* is unknown. Man uses both of them to express similar emotions. The *wak'rapuku* is a trumpet made of bull's horn, of the thickest, most crooked of horns, and is fitted with a silver or brass mouthpiece. Its damp, twisting tunnel is darker and more impenetrable than the *pinkuyllu*'s and, similarly, it can be played only by a chosen few.

Only heroic songs and dances are played on the *pinkuyllu* and the *wak'rapuku*. Drunken Indians work themselves into a frenzy singing the ancient war dances; and while some sing and play, others whip themselves blindly, to bleed and weep afterwards in the shadow of the lofty mountains, near the abysses, or before the cold lakes and the steppe.

During religious festivals the *pinkuyllu* and the *wak'rapuku* are never heard. Could the missionaries have forbidden the Indians to play these strange, deep-voiced instruments inside or in front of the churches, or alongside the images carried in Catholic processions? The *pinkuyllu* and the *wak'rapuku* are played at communal ceremonies such as the installation of new officials, during the savage fights between young men at carnival time, at the cattle branding, and at bullfights. The voice of the *pinkuyllu* or of the *wak'rapuku* dazzles and exalts the Indians, unleashing their strength; while listening to it, they defy death. They confront the wild bulls, singing and cursing; they build long roads or tunnel through the rock; they dance unceasingly, heedless of the change of light or the passage of time. The *pinkuyllu* and the *wak'rapuku* set the pace, stimulating and sustaining them; no probe, music, or element can penetrate deeper into the human heart.

Alejandro Otero, *Lunar Fire*
(Model) 1972

The suffix *yllu* signifies the diffusion of this kind of music and *illa* is the diffusion of non-solar light. *Killa* is the moon, and *illapa* the ray. *Illariy* names the dawn light which streams out over the edge of the world just before the sun appears. *Illa* is not the term for fixed light, like the resplendent, supernatural light of the sun. It represents a lesser light—a radiance, the lightning flash, the rays of the sun, all light that vibrates. Those kinds of light, only semi-divine, which the old men of Peru still believe to be intimately related to the blood and to all kinds of shining matter.

1951

From *Deep Rivers*, translated by Frances Horning Barraclough, Univ. of Texas Press, 1978.

On Translating *Deep Rivers*

Frances Horning Barraclough

A problem I had in translating José María Arguedas' novel, *Los ríos profundos*, was that of avoiding interruptions. One day I had to stop work to take a man who had been shot in the heart to the hospital.

It was also a struggle trying to keep from freezing while I sat working in a cold house in Santiago, Chile. I got around this by pausing to carry heavy chunks of wood up the stairs to the fireplace and by wearing three layers of wool clothing topped by a thick woolen poncho and, on particularly cold days when there was snow outside, a Patagonian sheep-herder's cap with a slit for eyes and mouth. Thus attired I rested my left foot on a tea kettle full of hot water and my left-hand on a small copper tea pot. With Spanish, English, Quechua-Spanish and at times Italian and German dictionaries spread out all about me, and a typewriter at hand, I would begin work, to the accompaniment of the smoking chimney and sometimes of voices from the road below calling "*Gringuita, dame pan duro,*" (Little *gringa*, give me some stale bread"), the voices of the poor boys sent up the mountain by their mothers to gather firewood. I was also accompanied by the small ghost of my dead son, who persisted in going 'round and 'round the house carrying a snowman in his arms. It was to exorcise this ghost that I wrote.

For me the work was not difficult—it was a great pleasure, "a surcease from pain." Actually, much of the first draft was written while I waited in various dentists' offices in Santiago. Dental work, in Chile, is interminable.

Sometimes, as I worked at home, I could hear machine gun fire from the target range at the Chilean Army base across the road, or, in the last years of the Allende period, from the firing range of the police at their "rest house" a block to the north. Also, in 1973 I'd sometimes hear bombs going off in the military reservation—the types of bombs soon afterward set off by the right to cause confusion which could be blamed on the "revolutionary leftists," disquieting sounds that would have been even more disturbing had I understood their true portent for the future.

Despite interruptions and distractions I worked on, a bit at a time, turning words over and over in my mind to observe them from every angle, piecing them together in a sort of mosaic reproduction of the original. I asked my friends the meanings of some words. Carlin Baraona, an American who had lived in Chile and Peru for twenty years, helped me, as did the Peruvian sociologist, José Sabogal Weisse.

I had the benefit of the Italian and German versions of *Deep Rivers*, which had already been published when I began on the English translation. Sometimes I did not agree with their interpretations, but they helped on some decisions as to when to put in additional explanatory footnotes.

As for the Quechua words and syntax in the novel, these were not so difficult to understand for a person who had lived in Chile for fourteen years as they might have been for people familiar with the kind of Spanish spoken in more northern parts of Latin America. Some Quechua words such as *taita* (father) and *guagua* (baby) are used in everyday speech in Chile. After all, the northern half of the country had been a part of the Inca Empire for 100 years before the Spaniards arrived. Also the Spaniards brought with them *yana* servants and women from the area which Arguedas was later to describe, and the conquerors used Quechua terms for local things, especially common household items and foods that were non-existent in Spain. I also had the help of Peruvian friends in the Cornell anthropology department.

To me the most difficult problem was to make the dialogue plausible. As I had lived for almost twenty years in Latin America, I felt my

English was unfashionable. I feared I might be the only translator alive engaged in transforming Quechuaized Spanish into Pennsylvania Dutch English. Martin Wolf made many useful editorial suggestions, especially for the conversation of the school boys, as did Claire Eisenhart.

There was the additional problem of what to do with the dialogue of characters who spoke Spanish with a Quechua accent. Now and then I changed the usual word order, or at times omitted certain words, particularly if the text explicitly stated the people were speaking broken Spanish, but for the most part I simply tried to translate the speech as literally as possible, believing that the things the people in the novel spoke about were unusual enough to give a connotation of strangeness to their words. It was, for me, impossible to invent a Quechua-English dialect. Even though it was not possible to convey all the nuances of Arguedas' writing in English, I persisted in translating *Los ríos profundos* in the belief that English speakers deserved a chance to become acquainted with him and to experience the reality of life in Peru as it still exists today, even though the novel describes a period of about fifty years ago. I followed the rule of leaving the Quechua words the author had used in the original in Quechua, and explaining them in footnotes or in the glossary.

Specific Problems

How to translate the many diminutive suffixes used (the *ito's* in Spanish) without having "little" repeated too often was a puzzle. This was only solved at the galley stage when I realized that the *cha* ending in Quechua has several meanings. In the case of the expert harpist, Oblitas, whom Arguedas calls "*Papacha*," the author himself added the footnote: "This may be translated 'Great Father'; it is a term of respect." But in addition to meaning "great, honored," *cha* can also mean "little," as well as expressing the speaker's affection. In this case the characters were translating Quechua literally (and incorrectly) into Spanish. They somehow believed (I think) that the suffix *ito* meant great and honored. For example, when the Indians called their master *patroncito* they did not mean to say "little boss" but rather "great, honored master."

When the small Indian school boy, Palacitos, called the school bully "*hermanito*," he did not mean "little brother" or "buddy," as I thought at first, but rather "respected brother." All of the *papacito's* and *padrecito's* used by the boys when addressing the priests who conducted their boarding school implied respect

rather than unwonted familiarity. I finally explained these suffixes in a strategic footnote and in the glossary. Their use is a real example of Arguedas' characters speaking Quechuaized Spanish. (It may be that the woodboys in Chile were doing the same thing when they called me *gringuita*, instead of merely *gringa*.)

The word *señor* also gave some difficulty. Anthropologists writing about the early colonial period have translated it as "lord" in the sense of *seigneur*, the lord of the manor. In the times and places Arguedas describes, it is used by the Indians and by other lower-class people when referring to the landowners, as if they were calling them something like "lords and masters". In fact the landowners themselves speak about each other as "the *señores*". It seemed wrong to merely use the word *señor* in the English translation, as the word means only "sir" or "mister" to most people familiar with spoken Spanish in this country. In the end I resolved this difficulty by using *señor* and explaining it in a footnote the first time it was used in a significant fashion, when the boy, Ernesto, meets his uncle and treats him as a large landholder would be addressed by an Indian servant. He respectfully calls him *señor*, instead of uncle, to prove he does not wish to show him any affection or family feeling.

In the novel there are several Quechua songs with the author's rather free Spanish translation beside them. I first translated Arguedas' Spanish version into English. Then, with the help of a Quechua dictionary and of Peruvian friends, I arrived at a word-for-word English version of the original Quechua. Curiously enough, the Quechua was sometimes closer to English syntax than the Spanish had been. The final result was a mixture of the two in which I attempted to imitate, in some cases, the onomatopoeia of the Quechua.

One Spanish phrase I found quite moving was "*Y yo había habitado hasta entonces en pampas de maizales maternales e iluminadas.*" On page 61 of the English version this was translated as "And until then I had always lived in valleys bright with fields of maternal maize." It would have been more beautiful, but not so literal, to have said simply "in valleys bright with maternal maize."

Arguedas was preoccupied with the qualities of light, as can be seen in his many references to different types of illumined, bright, shining, glossy materials. The translator of Arguedas finds there are many decisions to make, Thesaurus in hand, as to which of the many English words for shining and light are most appropriate. This is surely a reflection of an Andean way of thinking, as, according to the author himself, the Indian language has many terms for different types of light. In chapter six of *Deep Rivers*, after a discussion of various kinds of Indian flutes, Arguedas explains: "The suffix *yllu* signifies the diffusion of this kind of music and *illa* is the diffusion of non-solar light. *Killa* is the moon, and *illapa* the ray. *Illariy* names the dawn light which streams out over the edge of the world just before the sun appears. *Illa* is not the term for fixed light, like the resplendent, supernatural light of the sun. It represents a lesser light—a radiance, the lightning flash, the rays of the sun, all light that vibrates. Those kinds of light, only semi-divine, which the old men of Peru still believe to be intimately related to the blood and to all kinds of shining matter."

The problem is not that the foregoing is so difficult to understand, but that this Andean way of looking at things permeates Arguedas' writing and challenges the translator to find adequate ways of transmuting it into English.

For example, the following sentence from chapter one puzzled me on first reading: "*La calle era lúcida, no rígida.*" It describes a Cuzco street lined on both sides with the ancient stone walls of Inca buildings. How could a street be "lucid, not rigid"? I finally realized that, to Arguedas, the street was not rigid because it was vibrating with light. So I translated the sentence as "The street was luminous, not rigid."

The book is full of such Andean ideas and Quechua word uses, which an American finds unfamiliar but does not recognize as being of Indian origin. A Peruvian who has grown up in Lima or elsewhere on the coast finds the book almost equally strange.

Arguedas' personalization of inanimate objects may be another reflection of his Andean view of life. For instance, on page 12 of the English version, when speaking of the same Cuzco street previously mentioned, he says "This street was like the walls carved out by the rivers, between which passes no one but the waters, tranquil or turbulent." The English translation does not do justice to the Spanish version, which seems to say that no one but the waters *walks* between these walls:

"*Como esa calle hay paredes que labraron los ríos, y por donde nadie mas que el agua camina, tranquila o violenta.*"

Another passage where Arguedas' description of the light sets the mood is taken from page 60 of *Deep Rivers*.

"*Había aún luz a esa hora, el crepúsculo iluminaba los tejados; el cielo amarillo, meloso, parecía arder. Y no teníamos a donde ir. Las paredes, el suelo, las puertas, nuestros vestidos, el cielo a esa hora, tan raro, sin profundidad, como un duro techo de luz dorada; todo parecía contaminado, perdido o iracundo.*"

"There was still light at that hour; the setting sun illumined the rooftops. The sky, yellow as honey, seemed to be aflame. And we had nowhere to go. The walls, the ground, the doors, our clothes, the sky at that hour—so strange and shallow, like a hard roof of golden light—all seemed contaminated, lost, or full of anger."

My children and I left Chile on the first plane out, two weeks after the *coup d'etat* of 1973. To me, then, it seemed as if the sky had turned to lead and was coming down on us. The day we left we rode through the silent city at 7 a.m., seeing clumps of soldiers with machine guns on all the downtown corners, and trucksfull of military personnel about their work of rounding-up and slaughtering or imprisoning former friends and Allende supporters. The airport was officially closed, but it was full of armed soldiers. Our plane was a small, two-propeller craft belonging to the copper company, and was to carry an American high school swimming team, some newspapermen and other strays.

I was frightened, after many nights of listening to automatic weapons fire and seeing flares being dropped from helicopters onto the slums. My daughter had been shot at from a sideless helicopter in which six soldiers sat, machine-gunning the self-construction housing project below our house. They were shooting at poor people who were really anti-Allende and in favor of the military takeover. These people, many of whom were friends of ours, had been given their house lots by the Christian Democratic government in the pre-Allende period, and were grateful. That is, the soldiers were shooting their own supporters.

The last place we passed through at the airport was the room where they searched people's suitcases for subversive literature and weapons. In addition to the manuscript of *Deep Rivers*, I carried the notes and research material for a book my husband was preparing on the Chilean land reform—a pile of papers full of references the military might easily find "subversive". I told my seven and nine-year old children to try to be good and to look cute near the customs man, so as to distract his attention from the contents of the four suitcases we were able to take out with us.

The baggage inspector opened one suitcase and started looking through the papers. His expression changed to one of fixed attention as he happened to open the folders to a picture of the head of the MAPU (the Christian Left party), who only two weeks ago had been Minister of Agriculture and who was now in hiding. The next pamphlet he saw had been written by the former head of the Land Reform agency, a man who was also on the "wanted" list.

"Are those your kids?" he asked me. When I meekly answered "Yes," he slammed the suitcase shut, strapped it up, and, without searching further, ordered us to board the plane.

A Chilean exile told me recently that he and other political prisoners were being interrogated and tortured in the Cerillos airport on the same day we left from there.

I felt extremely lucky to leave Chile with the manuscript of the Arguedas translation—to escape without its being confiscated, as were such books as *Thoreau, Concord Rebel* and *The Green Revolution* (on increasing wheat and rice production), which were taken by the soldiers when they raided our house in Santiago a week later.

FRANCES HORNING BARRACLOUGH, whose English version of *Deep Rivers* won the Columbia University Translation Center Award for 1978, teaches at Ithaca College.

From *Deep Rivers*, translated by Frances Horning Barraclough, Univ. of Texas Press, 1978.

A Comparative Note on Arguedas' Vitalism:

The Inca Wall:

ALAN CHEUSE

The stones of the Inca wall were larger and stranger than I had imagined; they seemed to be bubbling up beneath the whitewashed second story, which had no windows on the side facing the narrow street. Then I remembered the Quechua songs which continually repeat one pathetic phrase: yawar mayu, "bloody river"; yawar unu, "bloody water"; puk'tik yawar k'ocha, "boiling bloody lake"; yawar wek'e, "bloody tears." Couldn't one say yawar rumi, "bloody stone," or puk'tik yawar rumi, "boiling bloody stone"? The wall was stationary, but all its lines were seething and its surface was as changeable as that of the flooding summer rivers which have similar crests near the center, where the current flows the swiftest and is the most terrifying. The Indians call these muddy rivers yawar mayu because when the sun shines on them they seem to glisten like blood. They also call the most violent tempo of the war dances, the moment when the dancers are fighting, yawar mayu.

This striking passage appears in the first scene of the opening chapter of José María Arguedas' *Deep Rivers* published in Buenos Aires in 1958. It announces at once the complex symbolic scheme of an important modern novel that only with its recent translation by Frances Barraclough has become known to readers in the English-speaking world. The very nature of that imagery points toward the difficult emotional and physical maturation that lies ahead for Ernesto, the adolescent narrator. The language, with its opaque phrases from the Quechua and its seething forceful imagery, dramatizes the dual life led by the young Peruvian criollo who becomes immersed in an education that bridges the abyss between Spanish and indigenous cultures. To paraphrase the poet Ogden Nash, the novel treats the difficulties of growing up in *two* worlds the hero never made.

Arguedas' novel then speaks to the question of adolescent education, an old interrogation. From the Telemachus section of the *Odyssey* to *Portrait of the Artist as a Young Man*, stories arising from the situation of educating an innocent give the narrator the opportunity to instruct the most jaded member of the audience in how to view the world with fresh eyes. Arguedas begins with this motif. But he upsets the modernist's expectation that once he has seen himself in the context of his surroundings the hero will reject the verities of national life and language for the free and cosmopolitan view of the ex-patriated artist. Ernesto educates himself *back into* the society which most of his young fellow bourgeois in the cities, and many in the country, find themselves in the process of rejecting. The values of Joyce's Ireland are reversed: imagine the Joycean hero turning his back on European values and immersing himself in his native culture to the point of transforming the English language by means of Gaelic syntax, ameliorating Flaubertian irony with peasant wisdom, and interpreting European history in terms of Irish mythology. That is to say, he would take seriously everything that the suave Yeats pretended he was practicing.

At the heart of Arguedas' novel lies this question which is truly modern in nature and international in character. The investigation of its binary linguistic structure is better left to readers with appropriate skills. But the drama of change and transformation of character and culture that grows out of this dual syntactical linguistic base—Spanish modified by Quechuan grammar—may be understood and enjoyed quite apart from any knowledge of the linguistic situation. All the problems of adolescence are present here, and thus all the fictional possibilities for richness of feeling and image attendant upon the conscious awareness of that transitional phase of life—doubled. The passage in which Ernesto describes the Inca wall in Cuzco, where he goes on a trip with his itinerant lawyer father prior to the older man's installing him in the provincial school where most of the action of the novel occurs, suggests a double life of the usually inanimate things of this world. The wall is a wall but it becomes transformed, as Ernesto regards it, into a river, the stones seeming to bubble up beneath the whitewashed second story of the house. Its lines "seethe" and its surface is "as changeable as that of the flooding summer rivers which have similar crests near the center...."

Ernesto's indigenous education makes it possible for him to understand as metaphoric truth what another observer might take to be mere optical illusion engendered by the hot morning sun. He recalls the Quechua phrases referring to water that gives the appearance of blood—"when the sun shines on them they seem to glisten like blood". He recollects as well that the same phrase applied to the violent motion of the river—"yawar mayu"—explains the tempo of the violent war dance. Given this use of the term usually employed to describe water, it seems plausible to Ernesto to apply it to apparently solid stone walls—"yawar rumi" in which the adjective yawar retains the presence of the noun—"mayu", river, or "unu" water—when applied to the description of the inanimate wall.

Thus even as the novel opens his education in the double-vision of Latin American culture is virtually complete. All that he must do is write about it, the last but absolutely necessary lesson in understanding which all story-tellers from Odysseus to Proust's Marcel have discovered. Naturally he doesn't understand this until some time beyond the completion of the narration, although he has by the novel's end crossed over the bridge, both literally and figuratively, from boyhood to young manhood. The genre itself is a bridge, between reader and writer, other and self, past and present generations. In the case of Arguedas, it performs yet another function, serving as a mediating element between the disparate segments of Peruvian culture.

But no novel could successfully direct us inward toward the hidden life of the Indians of Peru's austere mountain ranges without also directing us outward toward the greater world. In other words, the genre by its very nature makes the hidden known and exposes the links, usually analogical, between the mysterious and the given. Thus as I have tried to suggest, the action of Deep Rivers is on one level classic. However, its nature as a piece of con-temporary writing by a member of an underdeveloped society confounds or struggles against the classical elements within it, and lends it an attractive and distinctive tone and texture.

This latter aspect links the novel with the fiction of other emerging artist groups around the world, particularly those in Africa and the North American southwest. Two writers who are contemporaries of the late Arguedas are Amos Tuotola, Nigerian novelist, and Guayanese novelist Wilson Harris. Both have written important novels in which we find similar presentations of the seemingly inanimate landscape, and objects invested with vital, possibly magical force. Tuotola's The Palm-Wine Drunkard, published in 1954, was one of the first serious, modern African novels to reach North American readers. Its action takes place in the bush where the dry facts of West African animism take on a plausible life.

In the best of Harris' so-called Guayana Quartet—the novel called The Palace of the Peacock (1960)—the world of northeast Latin America, where English still has a preserve among the former slaves, contemporary shopkeepers and professionals of the country that was once British Guiana, reality becomes a charged field of language, a vortex of time and images, in which scenes and characters merge with the land and the land takes on an elemental character itself.

In North America, there are a few good novelists with clear affinities with Arguedas' syncretic style. It would take a much more intense and a broader scrutiny than I have space for in these pages to look at the traces of this style in the work of European-oriented novelists such as Bernard Malamud and Ralph Ellison, whose fiction has moments of pure native American wildness and rewarding leaps of irrational faith in presences such as inform Arguedas' Inca wall. A writer such as Ishmael Reed who proclaims a "neo-HooDoo" esthetic liberates American objects from their supposedly fixed and permanent places, but his work smacks too much of self-conscious surrealism of the French school.

Native American and Chicano novelists Leslie Silko and Ron Arias, whose novels Ceremony and The Road to Tamazunchale, respectively, have been, despite their great rewards, almost totally ignored in the press and critical journals, stand closer to the spirit of Arguedas. Ceremony, with its allusions to the storytelling tradition of the Southwest Indian tribes, presents a peculiar hybrid in which native American and European narrative styles mingle freely and fruitfully. Arias' fiction borrows from some first-generation North American writers such as Malamud but in such a way as to enhance its own roots in the magical fantasies of Mexican-American folklore. Both writers share a keen and sensitive awareness of the vitality that lurks in the supposedly inanimate world, a view that divides the indigenous mind from the rationalism of the European oriented writer.

And reader. I don't think I'm setting up a strawman when I suggest that lurking in the education of most of North Americans is a voice that shouts down the positive qualities of animation in Arguedas' Inca wall as cartoon and fantasy pure and simple. Did we give up the beliefs of our grandfathers' in banshees and dybbuks only to confess that we now believe in corn-spirits and seething, boiling stones? Yes and no. Another voice calls out to us, quoting Hamlet, that there are more things in heaven and earth than are dreamed of in Horatio's philosophy. We listen to both and notice the chorus they form. And go back to the invaluable analysis of Balzac's "atmospheric realism" that Erich Auerbach gives us in *Mimesis* in which he points out how the novelist's linguistic strategy shows us, for example, in the opening scene of *Le Pére Goriot* a room full of objects seething with life, "a particular milieu, felt as a total concept of a demonic-organic nature and presented entirely by suggestive and sensory means."

In this light, we might consider the possibility of regarding realism, the main literary mode of the modern novel, as another form of tribalism. The Inca wall, rather than closing off Arguedas' view of reality from the main stream of contemporary fiction, may in fact mark off a boundary common with our own. 🐾

ALAN CHEUSE has written extensively on Latin American subjects. His article on Alejo Carpentier appeared in the Fall 76 issue of REVIEW.

Arguedas'
Todas las sangres

WILLIAM ROWE

In a recent article that responds to the spread of dictatorships throughout Latin America, Eduardo Galeano writes: "All memory is subversive, because it is different, as is any project for a future." *Todas las sangres* (All Bloods) was written in the early 1960s, a time of liberalization in Peru. Until the prospects awakened at that time had shown themselves finally to be exhausted, it seemed important to point to the political contradictions and confusions in the novel. Now that reactionary dictatorships predominate in Latin America, and the radical phase of military rule in Peru is over, it is the utopian-critical aspect of *Todas las sangres* that speaks most strongly.

There are two main actions in the novel: that of Bruno, feudal landowner threatened by the rapid advances of capitalist society, who symbolically destroys both worlds, the old and the new; and that of Rendón Willka, leader of the Indians, who, passionately committed to a revolution which is both a turning upside down of the world and a return and rebirth of the past, is willing to die for what he believes in. Both are left, by history, with no place to stand in: and in that sense trace the options of Arguedas's life and books. Bruno is located at the terminal point of the old, traditional society, the ceremonies of innocence now lost. When he goes to commit his two murders, which genders the destruction both of the old society and the new, others notice that there is a "river of blood" in his eyes. The term Arguedas uses is *yawar mayu*, defined in the novel as "extreme grief, ... the first head of floodwaters in a river, the moment in [folk] dances when the men fight," and as containing "from the first human tear to the last." The *yawar mayu* is a surge of passion, breaking the boundaries that hitherto have contained it. The confining limits are described by Arguedas in several articles and interviews published around the time of *Todas las sangres*, as those which had kept the different forces of Peruvian society locked in static and sterile confrontation, but which were now, in "these times of convulsion," being shaken to the foundations. The major pattern of the last two novels is that of a confluence of forces that overflow the banks of the old forms. It is presaged in the ending of *Los ríos profundos*, where the Indian serfs invade the town. But there the rivers are contained within their inherited bounds: the metaphor is of continuity and survival, the overcoming of obstacle and interruption, the onward flow against contrary forces as generating beauty and knowledge. The book testifies to Arguedas' struggle for the continuity of his own life. *Todas las sangres*, on the other hand, is located at the point of breakage, where the disintegration of traditional constraints opens up the greatest possibilities for the birth of a new historical order. *El zorro* (The Fox) represents a move beyond that: disintegration does not become reintegration, the new is problematic, no forms, including those of language, will hold as they did before. The two metaphors that exemplify its structure are *hervor* (boiling or seething) and *huayco* (avalanche). Arguedas gives the word *hervores* to the short compositional units which, as the writing moved on, he came to use instead of chapters. *Huayco* is the Andean word for an avalanche and as Emilio Westphalen points out, it translated that sense of the precariousness of Arguedas's own life which permeates *El zorro*.

When he wrote the First Diary of *El zorro*, Arguedas had recently re-read *Todas las sangres* in order to correct the text for a new edition. He says of it: "There, in that novel, the Andean *yawar mayu* conquers, and conquers well. It is my own victory." But is the victory, finally, Bruno's, or Rendón's? Arguedas said that they both contained parts of himself. Bruno's character is destructive and demonic, incapable of carrying the violence of the opposites it is torn between. But the overall pattern is not tragic: there is no sanctification of current limits as final limits. Given Arguedas' life, and the history of Peru, the tragic option would seem a likely one: what resources did he draw upon in his refusal of a tragic and/or nostalgic stance?

The main resource was his own childhood, "a childhood bearing the stamp of millenia." In later life, he looked back on the experience of having lived among the Indians of an *ayllu* (peasant community) as crucial: they made "my heart like theirs", and "they instilled into me the unrepayable tenderness in which I live." The qualities he habitually attributed to the other culture were *amargura* and *escepticismo* (bitterness and scepticism). When he went to the *ayllu* as a child, it was to escape from one of the worst creations of our own culture: the family, through its destructive relationships, as transmitter of social violence. The *ayllu* gave him the experience of a supportive environment, where community could be felt as mutual tenderness. *Todas las sangres* was the last novel which could be nourished primarily by childhood: with *El zorro*, childhood would no longer hold as the shaping principle.

Rendón's project is a new society based on the *ayllu*, in opposition to the competitive, individualistic (and sceptical) world of capitalism. Bruno's action is a kind of Last Judgment: the end of the class he comes from and of the historical world inhabited by it. Rendón's action is not so much the opposite of Bruno's as complementary to it: the dismemberment of the old structure makes possible the birth of a new one: the *ayllu* generalized as the universal form of the new society. The authorities can only see Rendón as a leader in an individualistic sense, making him part of *their* structure. An Indian woman is told she will be shot if she doesn't reveal where Rendón Willka has got "his people": "Rendón Willka? His people? He's got no people of his own. We're *comuneros*; we're in the whole hacienda, we're everywhere."

The *yawar mayu* is Bruno's emblem, not Rendón's. Rendón is the wise builder, a creator of order, and an embodiment of the principle frequently reiterated by the Indians: "let there be no anger"; i.e., there should be harmony, everything taking its due place in the human and natural orders. The breaking of boundaries is only one part of the process occurring in the novel: there is also a sense of integration and wholeness, made possible by the removal of old divisions. The moments of synthesis tend to interrupt dramatic development in order to amplify and comment on it. When don Andrés, the feudal patriarch whose death opens the novel, distributes his belongings to the Indians and *mestizos*, in a reversal of traditional hierarchies, the scene suddenly takes on a mysterious but also wider presence: "Some red and black butterflies were flying from the garden towards the street; they moved their silent wings in the peace of the world." "World" becomes something possessed and experienced: a human space. The felt totality embraces the whole of existence, creating an opposite to social antagonism and separation. The *mestizo* Gregorio, because of his inherited status, is the object of antagonism from both sides, Indians and landowning class: the violence of the social divisions amidst which he lives makes his position virtually untenable (his death is in some sense an act of suicide), but emerging out of those tensions a new wholeness is glimpsed:

"Gregorio's fixed eye ... seemed to have received the silence of all the things of the world which the loving starlight exalts, bringing, especially to the attentive heart, the total image of the world in which we're living." The new space, which replaces the old, is one of love. There are similar moments of synthesis, of the overcoming of division, in *Los ríos profundos*, but they do not carry the same social and historical charge. No such synthesis is possible in *El zorro*, which witnesses a new division and fragmentation: the world there is "the human labyrinth."

Rendón and the *comuneros* refuse the postconquest sensibility of "cosmic solitude,"[1] which speaks out of the destruction of the preColumbian universe, and instead reclaim the old autonomous Quechua world. The word Arguedas gives that world is, instead of *solitude*, *alegría*, i.e., joy. It is there in the *wanka*, or work-song, which the *comuneros* are singing when the armed men of the state come to reestablish the regime of private property:

La golondrina agita sus alas
pero no tanto como tú,
mozo, hombre.
El pez, aguja de plata, cruza el agua
en el lago y en el río,
pero no tanto como tú,
mozo, hombre.

The swallow beats its wings
but not so much as you,
boy, man.
The fish, silver needle, crosses the water
of lake and river,
but not so much as you,
boy, man.

When the *vecinos* (lesser landowners) lose their land because of its expropriation by a capitalist mining company, they burn their church: but, as Rendón sees it, this binds them even more to their God, creating more *anger*. What Rendón wants is fraternity without God: "For the *comunero* there will be no God, just man ... Joy comes from seeing in every *comunero* a brother who has an equal right to sing, to dance, to eat, to work." Bruno, profoundly shaken by the symbolic self-destruction of the *vecinos*, finds, in Rendón's eyes, the token of an alternative world: "he found in the eyes of the *comunero* a kind of reflection of the peace and the sweetness of the sky, and of the gentle, silent water in the springs ... up in the heights ... The sand plays, as though moved by the hidden hand of the immense protecting snow-peaks, in the water ... It plays, it transmits joy, illumination; it portrays the soul without its shadows and every grain is a world of delight." The sense of joy, peace and harmony is an outstanding feature of the special

presence which Rendón projects, and is also closely connected with the natural world of the Andean highlands. Emanating from it there is a great stillness which surrounds events, especially the most dramatic ones: the silence permits the human drama to radiate its meanings.

In Arguedas' work, to be connected with nature is to be connected with other men; being part of nature means being part of other people, of a larger body. The community which is based in the *ayllu* is disalienated: its currency of social relation is use-value, not exchangevalue. Work is *for* the community, not *for* money, that false universal. And work creates genuine identity, instead of feeding the power of others: on both occasions when they are raided by the police, the *comuneros* are working, and even their dead work, before resting at night.

Rendón's plans do not spring solely from rational or conscious politics: to an important extent, they rely on myth and magicalreligious belief (given his atheistic stance, this is an ambiguity in him, but a fertile, rather than a weakening one). Inkarrí, in the contemporary millenarian myth (recorded by, among others, Arguedas himself) has, like the historical hero Túpac Amaru, been dismembered by the Spanish; but on the Day of Judgment his body will come together, underground. His body is also the collective body of the (Indian) community: to remember becomes to re-member, the commune, what we've lost and cannot forget. As Ernesto Cardenal puts it in his poem *Oráculo sobre Managua*: "All the great unconscious/ is communist." In fact the Inkarrí myth, with its motif of the hero going underground, is a kind of model of unconscious memory as that which current reality forbids, but myth can speak of.

The issue of *Todas las sangres* is actual social cohesion and cooperation over against competitive and atomized society. Peter Marin takes, as fundamental image of cohesion, the harvest, and writes of Levin laboring with the peasants in *Anna Karenina*: "It is an image of ecstatic relation which is as much an expression of Eros as is the emblem of two lovers tangled in embrace."[2] Just as the harvest song sung by the men and women in Rendón's *ayllu* is a celebration of sexuality: "the young men and girls went out into the fields ... The girls became women; they enjoyed the world; they drank it, transmitting to the earth the fire of their young bodies." The same sense of joyful and guilt-free sexuality in the culture of the Indians can be found in the autobiographical story "El ayla" (The Ayla), which was published shortly after *Todas las sangres*. Eros is recognized and fostered as collective reality, and is not cut off from the general fund of basic tenderness. Which is at opposite poles from the repressive Spanish inheritance, splitting off the erotic into the type of idealized sensuality which tortures Bruno as it does the autobiographical protagonists of *Los ríos profundos* and *Amor mundo* (Love World, the collection to which "El ayla" belongs). The Spanish influence, as Arguedas sees it in the Diary of *El zorro*, is demonic: sexual turmoil enacting social violence. Bruno's tortured sexuality makes him a *condenado* (damned man), but, significantly, his increasing closeness to the Indians brings about a change and he finds peace with the *mestizo* woman he marries.

Arguedas's art is profoundly concerned with personal and social transformation, and of his novels *Todas las sangres* is the one where this is most fundamentally so. In ways that recall the episode of the *chicheras'* uprising in *Los ríos profundos*, the Paraybamba *comuneros*, the *vecinos* of San Pedro, and the *colonos* (serfs) in the surrounding haciendas all go through a metamorphic process. At these moments, Arguedas's prose changes its rhythms and becomes more highly charged. Also, they are the moments at which sustained drama is achieved: there is none of the informative filling-in or the explanatory monologues that sometimes weaken other parts of the novel. In the epigraph, Arguedas refers to his own "resurrection". All of his writing, from *Agua* onwards, comes out of a concern with creating a space for himself in the world. In *Todas las sangres* the breaking of old boundaries leads to new belonging; it was the "severed link with reality," as he puts it on the first page of *El zorro*, which had repeatedly prevented him from writing. The First Diary reveals the extent to which this was for him a sexual issue: as I have suggested, the sense of community in *Todas las sangres* is also a dimension of eros, the world of others creating, in Peter Marin's words, "a body as truly one's own as the flesh." In works like "La agonía de Rasu Ñiti" (Rasu Ñiti's Agony) and the poem composed in Quechua, *A Nuestro Padre Creador Túpac Amaru* (To Our Father and Creator Tupac Amaru), which were written while *Todas las sangres* was in progress, the subject is the collective rebirth of the Quechua nation and its culture. The dancer in "La agonía" is, as Antonio Cornejo Polar writes, the symbol "of a whole people, the Quechua people who have endured centuries of oppression and who will nevertheless restore themselves and triumph."[3] "Agonía" is also the name of the music played at the death of the dancer, and is what the Quechua violinist Máximo Damián Huamani played at Arguedas's funeral.[4]

The issue of the peasant commune as solution to historical problems is one of the most difficult aspects of the novel. For instance, the *ayllu* did not prevent the Inca tyranny of the past, nor does it seem to offer any actual solution to the problems of dependent capitalism. On the other hand, there is the context to be considered: that of Latin-America as an area where, owing to uneven and combined development, history folds over on itself, breaking sequences, reviving lost causes, exposing unfinished revolutions which have been won in name and appearance only. The major modern novels articulate, in different ways, this special sense of history. *Todas las sangres* specifically explores the simultaneity and confrontation of the modern and the primitive, and shows the latter transforming itself into a critical alternative, the autonomous *ayllu* being both a recuperation of the past and a projected model for the future. With the break up and termination of a whole historical period, the very basis of social living gets called into question: the peasant commune supplies the exemplary image of an alternative which functions not by compulsion but through mutual aid. As Kropotkin points out, it is a form which was "anterior to serfdom, and even servile submission was powerless to break it."[5] Moreover, Rendón's programme is not a return to the past but the past read by the present, potentiated by the present: for instance he does not reject technology but welcomes it. One must beware of the danger of political cliché and/or anachronism in taking the *ayllu* as a socialist structure: it can only be seen as such insofar as modern historical developments allow us to generalize and universalize, in the same sense in which Marx writes of the soil in primitive agricultural societies as man's "natural workshop." In this sense the *ayllu* is a "commune".

Mauro Rodriguez

Alejandro Otero, *Solar Mirror I*
(Study) 1973

In the Primer Encuentro de Narradores Peruanos (First Congress of Peruvian Novelists), which was held in 1965, Arguedas spoke of his preoccupation in *Todas las sangres*: "Peru, in fact the whole world, is at this moment involved in the conflict between two tendencies: What is best for man, how does man progress most, through individual competition, the incentive to be oneself more powerful than all the others, or through the fraternal cooperation of all men, which is what the Indians practice?" Rendón in the novel is for fraternity and against God, reminding us of Peru's unfinished bourgeois revolution. In any direct sense the idea of the *ayllu* does not solve the problems of capitalism in a dependent country. On the other hand, though, it is a utopia which powerfully expresses human needs and, in that sense, an answer to the nightmare of the history of Peru. ▓

[1] See Arguedas, "La soledad cósmica en la poesía quechua," *Idea* (Lima), Nos. 48-49 (July-Dec. 1961), pp. 1-2; and my article "*Todas las sangres*: lo mágico y lo social en las canciones folklóricas," *Proceso* (Huancayo), March 1975.
[2] Peter Marin, "The New Narcissism," *Harpers*, Oct. 1975, p. 56.
[3] Antonio Cornejo Polar, *Los universos narrativos de José María Arguedas*, Bs As, 1973, p. 184.
[4] See Máximo Damián Huamani, "With Tears, Not Words," in this issue.
[5] Peter Kropotkin, *Mutual Aid*, London, 1972, p. 118.

WILLIAM ROWE recently published a book on Arguedas (Lima, 1979). He teaches at University of London, King's College.

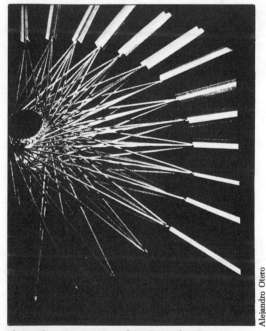

Alejandro Otero, *Another Ring for Saturn* (Model)

On Arguedas' Poetry

ANTONIO CORNEJO POLAR

Translated by Margaret Sayers Peden

The poetry of José María Arguedas is not widely known, although with remarkable unanimity critics have noted in his narrative prose the qualities characteristically found in poetry. This is the case, for example, in "Warma kuyay" (1935), *Deep Rivers* (1958), and "The Agony of Rasu-Niti" (1962), to name only a few exemplary works that are milestones within a vast and flowing evolution of singular coherence. But Arguedas' poetry, the works that consciously assumed the explicit criteria of a genre and consequently were defined by its specific internal requirements, his poetic poetry, if such a term is suitable, has passed almost unnoticed.

There are reasons for this. Arguedas' poems were published in numerous South American journals, and some came to light only recently, following the author's death.[1] In addition, compared to the volume of his narrative, and compared to the vigor, subtlety, and complexity of that narrative, Arguedas' few poems were eclipsed and diminished, a phenomenon that happened in inverse order to the stories of Cesar Vallejo, which when compared to the overriding importance of his poetry were brushed aside rather condescendingly. The basic explanation, however, is to be found on a different plane: that of language. All of Arguedas' poems were originally written in Quechua, and although in the majority of cases one has the Spanish versions written by Arguedas himself,[2] in reading them in Spanish one encounters the limitations of translation, always major in the case of poetry.

These limitations—which are a symbol of Peru's divided and plural culture which is, in turn, the result of a dual reality—will be discussed in the following pages whose specific object is to consider the Spanish versions of the poetry of Arguedas.

THE POETIC QUALITIES OF QUECHUA

José María Arguedas had a "realistic" concept of language. For him, "words are the names of things or of thoughts or of reflections that originate in things,"[3] and the highest quality of language, the blazing peak of creativity, is achieved only in those privileged moments when man can "transmit to words the matter of things," when he can make them vibrate with "all the weight of suffering, of conscience, of sacred lust, of manliness, of...human ash... and stone, and water, and the violent fermentation that leads to birth and song."[4] For this to be possible, for language to be fully realized, man must bind himself closely to the roots of the world; he must be an "unconditional" part of the universe, "in order to be able to interpret chaos and order."[5]

Guided by these assumptions, which constitute the basis of his literary art, Arguedas reflected upon the essence of Quechua and Spanish. It was a meditation that became a part of what he himself called "the heroic and beautiful *via crucis* of the bilingual artist."[6] As a native speaker of Quechua ("I learned to speak Spanish with some facility when I was eight, until that time I spoke only Quechua"[7]) José María Arguedas, from the earliest stages of his career, defended the richness of his native tongue. In 1938 he stated that "Quechua is a language that is sufficiently rich for man's subtlest expressions," and he made a point that although obvious, continued to have important repercussions both for his own creative work and for the development of certain aspects of indigenist literature:

Those of us who speak this language know that Kechwa is superior to Spanish in the expression of some of the sentiments that are most characteristic of the Indian heart: tenderness, affection, and love of nature.[8]

In 1949 Arguedas went even further. He maintained that Quechua "contains almost in its substance" the beauty of the Andean world, and that though Spanish was a language with "limitless riches," only if it were made more poetic could it equal the strength of ordinary Quechua, whose "diffuse and penetrating virtue" thus became inimitable.[9]. Finally, in 1962, in the note that accompanies the *haylli-taki* of Tupac Amaru, Arguedas said:

This haylli-taki that I am venturing to publish was originally written in the Quechua with which I am best acquainted, my mother tongue, Chanka, and then translated into Spanish. An uncontrollable impulse compelled me to write it. As the theme was developing, my conviction that for expressing many crises of the spirit, and above all of the soul, Que-chua is a more powerful language than Spanish constantly increased, inspiring and inflaming me. Quechua words, with their incomparable density and liveliness, contain the matter of man and of nature, and the profound bond that fortunately still exists between one and the other.[10]

Consequently, if language attains its poetic quality to the degree that it reaches the roots of the "matter" of man and the work, and if Quechua consistently attains this virtue, and realizes it in an "incomparable" manner, then— for Arguedas—Quechua becomes a kind of poetically-privileged language. From this perspective it is natural that Arguedas made use of this language for his poetry. The superiority he believes he finds in Quechua is most observable when Arguedas begins to write in Spanish and makes the supreme effort to transfer to a new linguistic system the overwhelming richness of meaning he finds in the most ordinary Quechua word. One may recall his very beautiful commentary on the grammatical voices *yllu* and *illa*,[11] or, on a different level, his translation of the word *kachaniraqmi*, used "when an individual wishes to express that in spite of everything, he *is*, that he exists, that he contains still the possibilities of restoration and growth."[12]

But the preference for Quechua of Arguedas the poet, in contrast to Arguedas the narrator who chooses Spanish as a "means of legitimate expression of the Peruvian world of the Andes,"[13] has a second significance. If in his fiction José María Arguedas struggles with the dual obligation of being faithful to his Indian world and intelligible to his Western readers, in his poetry he chooses the former; that is, he decides to submerge himself in the universe of the Indian, to be its authentic voice, and to find in it his legitimate audience: "This *haylli-taki* is written in a Quechua that is totally comprehensible to all the inhabitants of the great area of *runasimi*," he wrote in reference to his "Tupac Amaru Kamp Taytanchisman."[14] Playing with the subtle distinction sketched by José Carlos Mariátegui, it could be said that José María Arguedas' prose is *indigenist*, but that, most simply stated, his poetry is *indigenous*.

HYMN/POEM: AGAINST DESTRUCTION AND DEATH

Much of Arguedas' poetry is based on the identification of the voice of the poet with the voice of the Quechua people. This union is evident in the first fragments of "Tupac Amaru Kampa Taytanchisman/To Our Father Creator Tupac Amaru":

Here am I, fortified by your blood, not yet dead,
still crying out.
I am crying out, I am your people.

Similarly, in almost all of Arguedas' poems, the functions of the singular and plural voices are interwoven and blended. Both voices correspond to a collective speaker who thus speaks at a level beyond the personal. This device allows the poem to house its meaning in a multiple and age-old experience that is at times mythic, at times historic, and which creates a distinctively solemn and ceremonial tone.

Modulated by this collective voice, and with great variety, Arguedas' poems express the historic moments that have most deeply affected the Quechua people (the Spanish conquest, the rebellion of Tupac Amaru, the problem of acculturation, the hope-giving beacon of the experiences of Cuba and Vietnam) and they reaffirm his obstinate faith in the final triumph of the people. This explains the hymn-like quality of Arguedas' poetry. In some poems he poses an enormous opposition between what has been and what is, between the past and the present, and their relation to what is imagined for the future. All these works allude to the age-old exploitation of the Indian and to the Indian's tragic contemporary situation, and at the same time each insists upon the futility of oppression: in the long run, beyond blood and tears, a people, this same badly-wounded people, will arise triumphant. Addressing Tupac Amaru, commemorating his sacrifice, Arguedas sings:

The dawn comes.
They tell me that in other lands
men who were beaten, men who suffered,
*   now are eagles,*
now are condors with soaring and far-ranging flight.
Wait with calm.
We shall go beyond everything that you wished
*   and dreamed.*
We shall hate more than you hated;
We shall love more than you loved, with the love
of the enraptured
*   dove, of the lark.*
Wait with calm, with your hatred and your
fierce
limitless love; what you could
*   not do,*
we shall do.

At other times, perhaps more common in Arguedas' poetry, the opposition does not develop in time, but rather upon the very axis of chronology. Triumph not only is something that will come, it is also the daily practice of tenacious resistance to oppression and abuse.

They have corrupted our very brothers, they have
turned their hearts against us, and using them,
armed with arms the very devil of devils could not
invent or manufacture, they kill us. Even so, there is
a great light in our lives! We are shining!

In his prose, particularly in *Yawar fiesta* (1941) and in *All Bloods* (1964), José María Arguedas invents representative universes that put to the test the strength of the Quechua people. In his poetry, within a context in which the fire of conviction is internal and not related to men of the outside world, that strength is expressed directly as a reality that exists because of its own vigor, a reality that does not need to be demonstrated in order to be accepted as fact. Merely to state it is sufficient. Such strength is ultimately expressed when repeatedly the collective voice reciting the poems insists that death has been defeated: "We no longer fear death," one reads in the hymn/song to Tupac Amaru.

Abolishing the boundaries of death is a basic theme in Arguedas' writing. In his prose it culminates in "The Agony of Rasu-Ñiti," and also, from a different perspective, in *All Bloods;* for example, in the final speech of Demetrio Rendón Willka, and his scorn for "*la muertecita.*"[16] It is not surprising, then, that the theme also appears in Arguedas' poetry. In both prose and poetry this ability to transcend death is linked with other elements of the world-concept native to Quechua man; expecially with his deeply-rooted ties to nature, from which he draws the ability to transform himself without dying, to generate life from death itself, in a kind of permanent and tenacious "flowing":

From the movement of the rivers and the stones, from
the dance of the trees and the mountains, from their
movement, we drink powerful blood, stronger, al-
ways stronger.

But the theme is also related to the living presence of a coherent tradition. The continuing protection offered by the Indian heroes who became unconquerable gods through the magical memory of the people (as happened with Tupac Amaru, who was converted into the "Serpent God") represents one of the means through which an individual can assume as his own, radically his own, the historical evolution of his people. If in the past mythic figures arose for whom death had no meaning, and if one believes that in the future he will encounter a continuously-expanding way of being that will infiltrate even the world of the oppressors, then the mockery of death becomes considerably more than a metaphor: it is the concrete result of the identification between a man and his people, and between individual history and the history of a society and its particular culture.

In fact, in "To Our Father Creator Tupac Amaru," as well as in "Challenge to the Learned Doctors," Arguedas casts his lot with the social and cultural triumph of the Quechua people. He believes that the whole nation eventually will be impregnated with the values of the Andean peoples, and that even Lima, "the enormous village of the señores," will be influenced by the virtues of the men who slowly descend from the high sierras to begin to occupy it:

We are millions. Here. Now. We are united. We have congregated, village by village, man by man, and we are pressing down on this enormous city that despised and scorned us as if we were the dung of horses. We must change it into a village of men who chant the hymns of the four regions of our world, into a happy city where every man can labor, a huge village free of hate, clean as the snow of the mountain gods where the pestilence of evil shall never reach.

This certainty allows Arguedas to propose an egalitarian dialogue between his own world, confident of itself, and the Westernized world; between the Quechua world and—as he said on a different occasion—"the generous side of the oppressors."[17] With energy and tenderness he addresses himself to the men of that "other world" so that they may understand the ancient and lasting values of the Quechua culture; so they may respect them and make them their own. He exclaims: "Do not flee from me, Doctor, come close! Look at me carefully. Recognize me." Within this context he emphasizes the need for authentic integration ("We breathe the same air"), and he repeats the certainty that constitutes the true nucleus of all his poems, his confidence in the inconquerable strength of the men who speak through the voice of the poet. Even if that integration should fail, the Indian will nevertheless survive. He repeats: "We are the children of the father of all the rivers, of the father of all the mountains".

The paradigms of Cuba and Vietnam, where the oppressed eventually became the victors, where the men who manufactured the machines of war could not prevail against the seething rage of the humble, are instructive. The poems about Cuba and Vietnam reaffirm the general themes of the poetry of José María Arguedas, but also underscore his growth towards universality. This history of a Quechua man is the history of the Quechua people, and the history of the people is at the same time the history of all peoples who struggle for liberation. ✒

[1] José María Arguedas: *Temblar/Matatay* (Lima: Instituto Nacional de Cultura, 1972). In fact, only this very recent, and regrettably incomplete, edition of Arguedas' poems exists to offer an idea of this aspect of his work. It contains a few poems not published during the author's lifetime: "Qué Guayasamín," and "To Cuba." All quotations are taken from this edition.

[2] The only Spanish translations lacking are "To Cuba," and "Qué Guayasamín" (in the latter case the Spanish version was never completed).

[3] *Primer Encuentro de Narradores Peruanos* (Lima: Casa de la Cultura del Perú, 1969), p. 140.

[4] José María Arguedas. *El zorro de arriba y el zorro de abajo*, p. 15.

[5] *El zorro...*, p. 26.

[6] José María Arguedas. "La novela y el problema de la expresión literaria en el Perú." The definitive version was published as a prologue to *Yawar Fiesta* (Santiago [Chile]: Universitaria, 1968), p. 16.

[7] *Primer Encuentro...*, p. 41.

[8] José María Arguedas. *Canto kechwa. Con un ensayo sobre la capacidad de creación artística del pueblo indio y mestizo* (Lima: Cia. de Impresiones y Publicidad, 1938), p. 16.

[9] José María Arguedas. *Canciones y cuentos del pueblo quechua* (Lima: Huascarán, 1949), p. 13.

[10] *Temblar...*, p. 67.

[11] See pp. __, this issue.

[12] *Temblar...*, p. 68.

[13] "La novela y el problema...," p. 17 This choice is not permanent, but serves to differentiate the directions followed by Arguedas as poet and as narrator.

[14] *Temblar...*, p. 68.

[15] José Carlos Mariátegui: *Siete ensayos de interpretación de la realidad peruana*, 8th ed. (Lima: Amauta, 1963), p. 292.

[16] José María Arguedas. *Todas las sangres*, p. 470. [Trans. note: The diminutive form of *muerte* (death) expresses contempt or indifference.]

[17] José María Arguedas. "No soy un aculturado" (an address delivered upon the receipt of the Inca Garcilaso de la Vega Prize, October 1968); published as an epilogue to *El zorro*, p. 297.

[18] The poem "Al pueblo excelso de Vietnam," not included in *Temblar...*, was printed in mimeograph by the Federación de Estudiantes de la Universidad Agraria. It has appeared since in numerous reviews, for example, in *Oiga*, 8, No. 353 (1969). Similarly, *Temblar...* does not include poems Arguedas incorporated into his stories, some of which were published independently by the author: "Haraui," *Haraui*, 1, No. 3 (1964). With slight variations, this is the song, "Oye Gertrudis," found in *Todas las sangres* (p. 423).

ANTONIO CORNEJO POLAR is a Peruvian critic and the author of *Los universos narrativos de José María Arguedas* (Buenos Aires, 1973).

"As a Child You See Things We Older People Cannot See"[1]

CECILIA BUSTAMANTE

Translated by Christopher Maurer

"When I was fourteen years old, I was reclaimed by 'white' society. My mother died when I was three.... After an adolescence of travels through diverse, beautiful human and geographical regions, I was able to enroll in the University of San Marcos, in Lima. My father died just after I entered San Marcos. After becoming a teacher in the School of Mateo Pumacahua in Sicuani, in 1939, I married...."
—Interview with Tomás Escadajillo

My father had travelled to northern Peru to seek his fortune. He returned to Lima in 1939 with several children and little fortune. We children were eager to meet the grandparents, uncles, aunts and cousins whose names and images our father had kept alive in strange stories. In the lantern light of the remote hacienda of Parihuanas, he had told of our grandparents—and *their* parents and grandparents—who lived all over Peru and Chile. He had told of those who were closer to him—his brothers and sisters and Alicia and Celia Bustamante, whom I imagined extraordinary women. When we spoke of them his voice was full of admiration and love.

When we arrived in Lima after three days of sea travel from Paita to Callao, we saw our grandparents, our family, our little cousins. I felt, and would always feel, great admiration for Alicia and Celia, so unlike other people. They were bound by some hidden source of strength, some animating passion, that made them singular and beautiful. Later I learned that one source of this strength was their political ideas, which favored the natives of Peru. Travelling constantly through the towns of the coast and the mountains, they were beginning to acquire a collection of folk art that would later become famous. They had a fierce love for Peru, especially for everything native.

It was natural for José María Arguedas to join them. Someone had taken him to the Peña Pancho Fierro, a sort of club that Alicia had founded, where artists and intellectuals met for twenty years, forming the vanguard of Peruvian cultural life. José María and Celia fell in love, and were married in 1939.

José María, Celia and Alicia were an affectionate threesome, united in their actions and ideals. For more than a quarter of a century their house was a haven for folk artists who came to the big city from the heights of the Andes. The arrangement was vitally important for all of them, and they searched most deeply and produced the most while they were working together. José wrote, Alicia painted the world that José described, and Celia gave her wholehearted support, especially to the writer from the mountains who now had to make his way in the class-conscious, shallow milieu of society in Lima. My aunts knew this atmosphere very well. They were always defying it and shocking my grandparents, who secretly approved of them. They made their relatives censure them in the tone of aristocrats who had come down in the world.

I can still remember a few fleeting images of that wedding day. My grandparents' house at 333 on the Calle Mariquitas (where my family, the Bustamante Moscosos, also lived) was more crowded than usual. My grandmother, Josefina Vernal y Luza, had been blind for several years. Celia was her youngest child and her favorite. My grandmother wanted to know what was happening around her, how Celia was dressed, and what time it was, for her daughter was to leave right after the ceremony.

I had learned to read very early, and because I was very close to my grandmother I had become her "reader and companion." Hungry for conversation, she used to tell me long, confidential stories of her life as a schoolgirl, her memories and desires, moments in a life that had ceased to exist. She spoke as one does to a child who will soon forget what he hears.

It seemed that Celia was about to marry a writer who spoke Quechua, who even *wrote* Quechua, mixing it with Spanish in his stories. An intelligent boy who had found a teaching post in a distant town, called Sicuani, near Cuzco. He would take my Aunt Celita there, once they were married. A shame they had no money. In her darkness, my grandmother let a few tears fall.

"He calls me 'Josefina, the little old blind lady'. How I wish I could see him. A good boy. A writer. A shame they are going to work so hard and be so far away, but that's what artists are like."

Something else was troubling her:

"José isn't going to be here. They are getting married by proxy, understand?"

"No, Grandma."

"That means someone will stand in for the bridegroom. And they won't even go to the church. They don't believe in things like that."

She sighed, dried her tears with her little handkerchief (it smelled of lime!), and hid it in one of her sleeves.

Aunt and writer went off to the mountain village. From time to time letters and photos would arrive. Plenty of sun, fields, wheat, music: the very essence of what they liked. Emilio Adolfo Westphalen went to visit them there. I can remember a photograph of him with Celia and José, arm and arm, wearing swimsuits, smiling in the sunshine. I suppose it was Emilio Adolfo who represented José that day, surrounded by half-closed suitcases, close relatives and a handful of friends. Celita looked hurried and very pretty in a white, two-piece suit, woven by hand. Alicia grew emotional and fussy, putting things in order. They were about to separate, doubtless for the first time.

Later we received a visit from "the two of them" (as my grandmother used to say). It was then that I met José María, a very simple, modest, sweet man. He reminded me of the friends I used to have in the mountains where we grew up. He had a childish air about him that made you want to play, to tell stories. I saw that he was quite fond of asking questions: he wanted to know our stories, what we had learned, heard, eaten, played; what the Indians used to talk about in the villages we knew. The taste of those conversations came back to me years later when I opened *Songs and Tales of the Quechua People*, a collection of traditions, myths and legends he had gathered with a group of researchers from the school where I studied. When they returned, Celia and José moved into my grandparents' house. They were working hard now; every day there was less of an opportunity to play with him. For me his room was a strange place, part workshop and part living-quarters. Filled with Peruvian and Mexican folk art, saddlebags, Indian caps and flutes, blankets, charangos, guitars, papers, a noisy old typewriter my aunt was always pecking at. José wrote in longhand. One of his hands was maimed. I heard my grandmother say that he had had a very bad stepmother who mistreated him as a child. I imagined that probably explained his crooked fingers, and felt sorry.

José María often talked with my grandmother in the half-light of the dining room. I watched them through a glass door on a winter afternoon in Lima that made me feel something like fear. From my little rush-covered chair I saw how close they were, at the head of the table, as though he were complaining to her of the things they had done to him as a child. Grandmother shook her head, asked him questions, touched his hand. He talked quite often with "the little old lady" (as he used to say).

When he was working we weren't supposed to enter his room. Sometimes they would call us to meet some friend or relative, but only for a moment. It was there that I first saw Alliocha, the son of their friends the Ortiz Rescanieres. He was a favorite of theirs, a restless, very intelligent boy. José María would refer to him almost as a son in his letter of resignation from the Universidad Agraria. Alejandro Ortiz, his "disciple." One afternoon we received a visit from a tall, thin boy with a big nose, his hands in the pockets of his trench coat, a hurried air and friendly smile: this was Sebastián Salazar Bondy, who had arrived from Buenos Aires. He too entered the group of friends of the Peña. Nor can I forget how his bullfighter friends once visited him, wanting to watch a religious procession from our balcony and throw flowers to "Our Lord of the Miracles" as the incense rose from below. Once it was Manolete, another time Dominguín and some other gentlemen.

They had a little house on the beach at Supe, two or three hours from Lima. It was a lovely port then, without factories. They would invite their friends from the Peña there, and later tell my grandmother about that summer's romances and other goings-on. I only visited the place once, when it was not yet finished— roofless rooms, a courtyard facing the sea, flowerpots, shells incrusted in the walls of the bathroom, *indigenista* paintings on the dining-room walls. They went there summer after summer, with painters, poets and musicians. One night in 1973 Celita died in an accident on the road to the port. Alicia had died in 1967, and José María in 1969.

During their last years together, José María's illness was worsening and Alicia had fallen incurably ill. They separated in 1963 after a long, frustrating struggle, in a country that is unkind to its creators.

"Celia, her sister Alicia and their friends opened the doors of Lima to me, made my new life there easier and more profound. Speaking with my father, studying books, I acquired a better understanding of the Spanish half of the world. Then too, with Celia and

Alicia we began breaking down the barrier that sep-
arates Lima and the coast: the mentality of the om-
nipotent creoles, colonists representing an indefin-
able mixture of Spain, France, and the U.S., and the
colonists of those colonists."
From the letter to Gonzalo Losada, Dec. 5, 1969.

One afternoon my grandmother said that
José was finishing another book, that we were
to be on our best behavior, keep out of his
room, and not touch any papers.

"He is going to publish a new book. Your
Aunt Alicia has made him two sketches;
vignettes, I should have said."

Yes, I already knew. I had seen Alicia at her
easel. I liked to watch her paint, but annoyed
her by asking questions. One of my questions
irritated her so much that she hit me on the
head with her palette. I stormed out of the
room, and from resentment I never described
her paintings and sketches to grandmother. I
used to read her the reviews of Alicia's shows,
and whatever was published about José María.
I didn't understand a thing (once in a while I
caught a word or a name), but my grandmother
enjoyed it greatly and practically burst with
pride.

"Read that again. What does it say? 'Excep-
tional'? 'Authentic'?"

A little later *Yawar Fiesta* appeared. The day
the package of books came from the printer, his
room was packed with friends, my other uncles
and aunts, my cousins—a real madhouse. My
grandmother called me that afternoon after tea.
She had decided not to listen to the radio
today.

"Come here, Yola, read me José's book," she
said from the head of the enormous table. "And
tell me what the drawings are like."

She handed me a copy. It was not a large
book and I described it to her in minute detail,
printer's marks and all. My grandmother had
lived in Europe from the time she was a girl,
and had returned to Peru when she was
twenty-six, to marry Don Carlos Bustamante
Gandarillas. She spoke five languages, but preferred German and knew by heart poems of
Goethe and Schiller. As I read *Yawar Fiesta* to
her we stopped at the Quechua words.

"Sounds like German," she said. "Do you
think people will like so much Quechua in a
book?"

"What am I? I am a civilized man who, in my
heart of hearts, am still a native of Peru. Na-
tive, not Indian. That is the way I have walked
the streets of Paris and of Rome, Berlin and
Buenos Aires."

After dinner at the big table, with my grandparents, three uncles, the seven grandchildren
and my parents, Celia and José would sometimes choose one or two of us to accompany
them to the Plaza de Armas to mail their letters.
I used to enjoy that walk, and remember them
taking us by the hand out into the darkness and
drizzle of Lima. Lima had not yet been invaded
and depersonalized. It still had character—old
family houses, entranceways, window grates
with flowerpots, colonial balconies like lacy
boxes tracing the light within. José and Celia
would talk about the latest meeting of the Peña,
their work, their projects. Although I didn't
understand their conversations, I felt those two
possessed some sort of secret that made them
different, special, and admirable. On other
evenings, he would play with us at *perinola,* a
sort of toy top with inscriptions. We played for
kernels of corn or beans. José would speak to us
in Quechua, making us remember what we had
learned on our vacations in Huariaca, the mining town where my father was now working.
He used to find our mispronunciations hilari-
ous, and he taught us some expressions that
proved to be curse words when we said them to
our Quechua-speaking friends—the sort of
things one hears from Indians when they are
euphorically drunk.

They went to Mexico, too, and talked a lot
about that; they were good friends of Moisés
Sáenz, and my aunt Alicia kept a photo of him
beside the easel in her room. They talked of
how folk art had been destroyed by tourism,
and how the Indians were being abused. When
they began to work they were far, far away, in
a world I could not see, a world which allowed
them to live just as they really *were.*

And I remember them most as happy, creative, passionate beings, still young. Everything
around them seemed beautiful—their clothes,
their things, the arrangement of the furniture,
their souvenirs, their plants, the cats that José
could not do without. I remember them. I remember José thrumming the strings of his *cha-*
rango on a leisurely, happy afternoon, softly
singing the *huaynos* that I knew, or loudly
singing "Wifalalá! Wifalaláaa!"

From time to time he danced. José was like
one more child in the house. Everyone admired
him, because they respected intelligence.
When my sister Nora was born, my mother
asked him to hold her at the baptismal font.
José liked being a godfather.

"Since 1943, many Peruvian doctors have ex-
amined me...and even before that, I would
suffer from insomnia and depression...."

During the last years of his life I saw little of

José María. Sometimes he visited me at *La Crónica*, the daily newspaper where I was working, and asked me to show him my poems. He was different now—nervous, tense. He traveled much, had become famous; they had moved a couple of times to escape the noises that used to disturb José: the barking of dogs, cat fights, the noise of the neighbors and the streets. Something was collapsing. Celia perished in that chaos. They separated in 1964. She did not often accompany him on his travels. He used to go to Chile a lot. My large, conservative family could not understand why José left Celia.

The last time I saw him, he was in the gallery where his new wife was working. He introduced me to Sybila. She was young, with a profound but lively expression, and her eyes seemed veiled in warmth. I was surprised: she looked like Celia. José María left no children. Some books, the same as my aunts. A few paintings, a collection of folk art. Somebody said to me one day, "It seems as though he never existed." But as the years go by it is as though he was singing more strongly— singing, with Oblita, the master harpist in *Deep Rivers*,

I am still alive,
the falcon will tell you of me,
the star will tell you of me,
I will come back soon,
soon I will return.

---

[1] Quoted from *Deep Rivers*, p. 11.

CECILIA BUSTAMANTE won Peru's National Poetry Prize (1955) and is currently in charge of coordinating exchange programs with U.S. for Peru's National Institute of Culture.

Arguedas' Last Novel

JULIO ORTEGA

Translated by William L. Siemens

El zorro de arriba y el zorro de abajo (The Fox Above and The Fox Below, Buenos Aires, 1971), José María Arguedas' posthumous novel, is a complex and extraordinary document. One must ask at the outset how to take this passionate book. The first page, dated May 10, 1968, announces the author's determination to commit suicide; Arguedas had already attempted to kill himself in 1966, and he does not wish to fail this time. He is writing under doctor's orders, "because people never tire of telling me that if I manage to keep on writing I will recover my sanity." But at the same time his decision to kill himself seems to be without appeal. These two motions—to kill himself and to save himself—are strikingly combined in a single impulse: with unconcealed fervor ("This preoccupation of mine is wondrously disquieting"), Arguedas writes while foundering in that strange paradoxical region in which a page both hastens and retards the final act.

The book consists of three diaries and a "Last Diary?," in which, in effect, the author achieves the final balance and decides on his death. Between these diaries there has grown, with agonizing difficulty, a novel that is to remain unfinished. There are no fictional relations between these diaries and the novel as such; the relationship is more an internal one. Arguedas writes his diaries when the depression or the profound uneasiness he is suffering prevent his going on with the novel. The first of them opens with his decision to kill himself, but it is evident that the act is being postponed by the novel that has imposed itself upon the writer and which, as a consequence of this fervent exorcism, is beginning to take form. The "Second Diary" (February 1969) seems to indicate that the author has deferred his suicide because, in fact, he has in hand a novel, one that is growing despite his enormous difficulties; it is curious that Arguedas should say here that the desire for suicide originated in his exhaustion, but in part also in his fear of the difficulties of writing a novel about the port of Chimbote, an industrialized city, which he suddenly believes he does not know well enough. At the end of this diary two lines announce that the author has managed to take up his work again.

The "Third Diary" (May 1969) states that "suffocation" is detaining his work of fiction; nevertheless, his uneasiness does not demand suicide here either, but rather the recourse of travel: Arguedas writes these pages, and the novel itself, between Chimbote, Lima, Arequipa and Chile. But once again, a postscript announces that the author is finding it possible to resume the work of fiction. Still, the "Last Diary?" (August 1969) puts an end to this process: "I have struggled against death, or believe I have struggled against death, face to face, in writing this faltering, complaining tale." Suicide reappears, ineluctable now. An epilogue, added by the editor, collects the final letters and messages, which reveal the meticulousness—sober and devoid of all pathos—with which Arguedas attempted to order the facts before shooting himself on November 28, 1969.

Perhaps it is not coincidental that the "Last Diary?" should carry these questions, because in fact the novel was being composed in the midst of a fight with death, as its postponement, but perhaps also as its exorcism. Perhaps Arguedas knew that salvation was no longer possible, but his having attempted it, in a passionate struggle, endowed his novel with a fervent if desolate character. The book can be read in this way, as an agonized attempt to play one last game. An unsettling reading, to be sure, since the novel is obviously truncated and, even more importantly, a pitiful failure. It has noteworthy moments—scenes and dialogues of great dramatic intensity, in addition to the vertigo with which he manages at times to communicate the hell of a port whose life revolves around perversity and annihilation—but the quality of the work steadily declines and the text loses its form. How, then, evaluate literarily a book which by its very imperfection transcends literature? That very lack of fulfillment is another level, and not only of the fiction, but of the documentary aspect of this book. Because, in the final analysis, the book reveals to us Arguedas' faith in the act of writing: perhaps he felt that writing could in some manner accomplish his salvation. To save oneself by words: this gamble, dark and tortured, presides over these pages. A complex wager, nevertheless, now ballasted by the malaise that was undermining the creative power of this man; thus, salvation by means of words could only be the reverse side of a salvation by death.

There is a moment when words forsake him: he writes the last diary questioning whether it is in reality the last because—as he himself understands—the fact of being in the process of writing even about his own failure, the very act of being in the process of using language, retrieves him in the continuity of a writing that in some manner exceeds and prolongs him, as if his life were being sustained in that final possibility of following a phrase through. But now the plot of salvation and death could have no other outcome: the novel itself is, at bottom, a metaphor of the internal uneasiness that was overwhelming him; not only on the surface of its incompleteness, but above all in the image of deterioration that he proposes for a city where worlds parallel to his (characters from the Peruvian Sierra, victims of rootlessness) are destroyed in the distortion and perversity of the industrial city.

Thus one might say that the wager on saving himself by means of words is in reality the final preparation for taking death upon himself. From the perspective of his suicide ("this theme, the only one whose essence I live and feel"), after the "First Diary," the book surrenders to him for the length of two chapters that establish several characters and their setting. The "Second Diary" reveals the tremendous difficulty of writing about the city and its chaos, and in the confession of this burning impotence Arguedas finally says that his fear of the theme was another factor in his suicide—as strange (but perhaps symptomatic) statement that would indicate precisely that for a moment he is living the work as a postponement because words avert the outcome. But here the central paradox of this work is revealed to us: it is the diaries, in directly taking upon themselves his uneasiness and failure, that avert suicide, because they constitute the fall and the transition, the recovery each time of the work which had stopped. And it is upon the resumption of the work that suicide seems to return, no longer as a theme, but arising from the metaphor of deterioration and in the lonely frustration of writing. From this springs the relationship of necessity between the diaries and the novel: on the simplest level they are the confessions of a man writing a novel with a sense of bold helplessness; on another level the work demands to be stopped, interrupted, so that its frustration may take on a sense of incompletion, because the work leads towards the tragic conclusion while the diaries recover the energy of postponement within that same helplessness. At the end, the diaries forsake the author and he forsakes the work. The last confessions also tell how the plots, the lives of the characters would have continued if the author had gone on with the work. But this not only is no longer possible, but no longer seems necessary. The questionings, the doubt, in the final diary suggest that the author perhaps still hoped to find new strangth at last. But why go on? If the work had concluded like any other novel we would then find ourselves before a fraud or before a simple psychological process, and not in the presence of a tragic text.

In fact, not even the last diary (because of the question mark) is the last; the work and the diaries thus remain incomplete and the book founders (like the reading) in the solitude of unfulfillment. Nevertheless a writer—even in losing this battle—has gained the resonance of his own tragic destiny. At the end all that remains is for him to kill himself in order not to deny himself; he dies paying off all the accounts, trusting in the destiny of his country and its peoples, trusting in his own work, denying to himself only the uneasiness that has undermined it.

In the "Third Diary" Arguedas finds himself lacking the energy to go on and says, "Perhaps it is because I have entered the most intricate part of the lives I seek to tell about, in which my own involvement, instead of working itself out, threatens to get out of hand or cloud over."

Thus in the text are found the two great difficulties inherent in this adventure: the complex existence (even more complex for Arguedas) of the people of the industrial city, as well as his own personal situation. The novel, that is to say, and the diaries. His life would have to penetrate other lives; there would have to exist a functioning continuity between confession and fiction, or, perhaps better, between the fragmented autobiography and the expository chronicle. It is interesting to observe that to the worsening situation he is living at this time (and which his sudden trips reveal as well as do his confessions), Arguedas is to oppose the almost naïve will to coherence of the narrative: not only have the characters been chosen as types, but it is clear as well that the very situation of the industrial port (the image of a semi-modernized, capitalistic Peru, which Arguedas rejects) appears explained or schematized, as if the author wished to expound for himself a complete and coherent understanding of this social hell, which attracts him with its human chaos and repels him with its dehumanized origin and present state. Capitalist mechanics have converted the port into an enormous urban sprawl into which people from the entire country are pouring, attracted by the illusion—ludicrous to be sure—of industrial progress: that social vertigo fascinates the author and he wants to tell the story of certain peoples, understand the destiny of certain

characters who have taken the road he himself followed: from the mountains to the coast, from the traditional communal society to the class-oriented urban society, although the former does not fail to suffer also from depredation, as well as injustice. In that exchange a metaphor of uneasiness is established: the port is fundamentally perverse; it has been turned upside down by industrial exploitation, and thus the infernal metaphor is the new context of that inhabitant who has lost a potential place of residence. Already in his previous novel, *Todas las sangres*, capitalist industry (in this case mining) was destroying communal life and announcing the distortion of a nation forced into dependency.

But the mere attempt to explain that painful situation to himself in a coherent manner is, to be sure, insufficient for the author's perspective; the work demands to be more than a chronicle, although the chronicle is the initial impulse that permits this work. Since its inception Arguedas has acted out of that impulse: to make known a hitherto unknown world was a point of departure for fiction. Therefore it is revealing that he warns, in the last quotation, that his search for expression, his labor with the literary work, "instead of working itself out, threatens to get out of hand or cloud over." It clouds over because his own uneasiness has for him a dark zone which in some manner is liberated by fiction as it takes upon itself that uneasiness in a broader process, now involving the various "countries" that make up Peru, because the work seldom if ever achieves the vertigo of poetry translating these relationships. It is for this reason that the uneasiness threatens to "get out of hand." This statement is essential to the composition of the work because it alludes to its central impulse; in fact, from its hellish perspective, the work demands of the author another language, another discourse, a writing that should stand ready to serve the fever of its urgent and compulsive dilemmas.

It is for this reason that alongside the intended coherence of the story the work imposes a delirious discourse: the dialogues soon drift towards a frenzied vertigo where speech seeks to capture that unattainable reality within the living chaos of the industrial city, that infernal labyrinth so resistant to reason. It is a discourse of this sort, about to break loose, about to lose its bearings, that appears as the central impulse of the work, as its appeal and also as its best poetic possibility. A discourse burned by agony, impelled by the necessity of totalizing a speech that embraces that variegated and discordant reality of the city. In the diaries, too, that discourse began with the fervor of suicide, with the arbitrariness of summary judgments, with the necessity of reasoning unconventionally and freely about the author's vital situation, following the discontinuous flow of facts, memory or ideas of hope and redemption. That heated discourse also takes upon itself the situation of the writer who develops from his early regionalism a well delineated perspective; not without ingenuousness, Arguedas feels the necessity of stating precisely his vision of literature, thus running the risk of oversimplifying the evident complexity of his writer's world. That complexity makes him a contemporary of the Inca Garcilaso, César Vallejo and us at the same time, because his work develops within the context of a Latin American debate that concerns us in the question we ask about ourselves.

The delirious discourse is thus at the center of the work in progress. This impulse towards vertigo also reveals how the author wished to violate a principle of fiction, to amplify it by questioning it, thereby putting pressure upon rational discourse, not only delineating that social chaos but also desiring that poetry say of its own accord what the narrated chronicle can no longer say. To say more—perhaps to say it all. It is possible that with his discourse the author was searching for a total understanding, one that would be critical, social, poetic and in some measure prophetic.

The dialogues submit to delirium, and sometimes conclude in a sort of dance of characters, complete with songs and new voices. One of the characters, Tarta, is called "the poet," "the intellectual," but is, revealingly, a stutterer. More important is Moncada, a madman, who "preaches" in the streets and marketplaces, bearing a large cross. Arguedas takes pains to make this character, who is drawn from the life situation of the Chimbote countryside, stand out. The speech of a madman allows him to confront the work and the city by way of a discourse which, while it is delirious, is also critical, out of a sort of holy wrath, as a total accusation which is at the same time an internal rending. That discourse finds its echo in Esteban de la Cruz, ex-miner, now terminally ill; the dialogue of both characters exacerbates the vision of the industrial city, provides the keynote of the drama of those lives wrecked by the penury of the nation. De la Cruz says, "When drunkard speak truth, true truth, about justice her foundation God, then authority cop, injuneer, etcetera, say, 'You drunk, you drunk, you under arrest, dammit.' An' they arrest you, they beat you. Fucked up. Word of drunk, even if it's true truth, very heart and body of the Lord, no good...." This marginal speech, this

language of the madman, the drunkard, the man condemned to death, opens up the exacerbation of the discourse in a total protest, in an agonized appeal; in Moncada's preaching that appeal becomes accusatory, the delirium of a sorely wounded discourse. It is no coincidence that at the conclusion of the novel a character reads from the Bible a flaming paragraph from the pen of St. Paul.

The fox above and the fox below are characters drawn from the mythology of Huarochirí; in the novel one represents the mountain region and the other the coast. At one point they engage in a conversation about the novel, and they also intervene in the fiction behind the faces of certain characters. But this mythic plane is never developed; it appears only as the possibility of what is perhaps a choral dialogue, of another suprarational discourse, between the two zones of a divided Peru.

Novel, document, text about the work that makes and unmakes us, this book by José María Arguedas is, at its deepest level, an unusual testimony concerning the tragic destiny of a man who lived the beauty and discord of a cruel country. On the last page he wrote, "In me you will bid farewell to a time for Peru whose roots will forever suck juices from the earth to nourish those who live in our nation, in which any man not chained and brutalized by selfishness may be a citizen, and a happy one, of all nations." All of Arguedas' books speak to us of the happiness and the desolation with which he lived that country; his work unveils for us a world torn between utopia and despair, fed by the dream of redemption by the exercise of criticism. Even though this novel is not, as such, on a par with his previous books, as a document it possesses a value of a different order, and its peculiar intensity and character confer upon it a heightened and deepened life. In Latin American prose fiction the voice of Arguedas is our "consciousness of misfortune," but also the dream of another time. ▼

JULIO ORTEGA is a Peruvian poet, novelist and essayist. "Arguedas' Last Novel" is from Ortega's *La imaginación crítica* (Lima, 1975).

The Agony of Rasu-Ñiti

JOSE MARIA ARGUEDAS

Translated by
Angela Cadillo-Alfaro de Ayres
and Ruth Flanders Francis

He was lying on a bed of sheepskins on the ground. A cowhide hung from one of the roof beams. Bright sunlight entered by the room's only window near the ridge of the roof and fell on the cowhide which shaded one side of the dancer's bed. The rest of the room was uniformly in shadow—not quite in darkness, for it was possible to distinguish clay pots, sacks of potatoes, piles of carded wool, and guinea pigs a bit scared but coming out from their hiding places and exploring quietly. The room was wider than most Indian dwellings.

There was a place for grain storage, a sort of attic, in one corner of the room, and a ladder of *lambras* wood for climbing up to it. Enough sunlight entered to show a few black ants going up the *lambras* bark that still had a sweet smell.

"My heart is ready. I know the signs. I can hear the Saño waterfall. I am ready!" said the dancer, Rasu-Ñiti.

He got up and was able to reach the leather-covered trunk in which he kept his dancing clothes and his steel scissors. He put a glove on his right hand and began to play the scissors.

The birds that were preening peacefully in the *molle* tree in the small enclosed yard were startled.

The dancer's wife and his two daughters who were shelling corn in the corridor stopped to listen.

"Mother, did you hear that? Is it my father or is the song coming from within the mountain?" asked the older daughter.

"It's your father!" said the woman, because the short strokes of the scissors sounded louder.

The three women ran to the door of the room. Rasu-Ñiti was getting dressed. Yes. He was putting on his jacket ornamented with mirrors.

"Husband! Are you bidding us farewell?" the wife asked, respectfully, from the doorway. Trembling, the two daughters looked at him.

"I feel it in my heart, woman. Call Lurucha and Don Pascual! Send the girls for them!"

The two girls ran out, and the woman moved close to her husband.

"Good. Wamani [mountain god that appears in the form of a condor] is speaking!" he said. "You can't hear him. He's talking right to my heart. Let me lean on you. I'm going to put on my pants. Where is the sun? It must be well beyond the center of the sky."

"It is. It's coming in. There it is!"

In the fiery sunlight on the room's floor some black flies were crawling.

"The *chiririnka* [blue fly] won't come until a little before death. When it comes we won't hear it no matter how loud it buzzes, because I'll be dancing."

He put on his velvet pants, leaning on the ladder and on his wife's shoulders. He put on his slippers, his sash, and his hat. The sash was adorned with threads of gold. On the broad brim of his hat, among patterned ribbons, gleamed star-shaped mirrors. Ribbons of different colors hung from the hat down the dancer's back.

The wife stooped before him. She embraced his feet. He was already decked out in all his insignia! A white handkerchief covered part of his forehead. The blue silk of his jacket, the mirrors, the cloth of his pants, blazed in the narrow sunbeam that glowed in the dim light of the hut that was the home of the Indian Pedro Huancayre, the great dancer Rasu-Ñiti, whose presence was awaited, almost feared, as the highlight of the fiestas in hundreds of towns.

"Do you see Wamani above my head?" the dancer asked his wife.

She raised her head. "Yes," she said. "He is not moving."

"What color is he?"

"Gray. The white spot on his back is shining."

"That's right. I am going to bid farewell. Go take down the corn from the corridor. Go."

The wife obeyed. In the corridor, from the roofbeams, hung clusters of corn of several colors. Neither the snow nor the white earth of the roads, nor the sand of the river, nor the happy flight of the flocks of doves at the harvest, nor the joy of a playful calf had the appearance, the luxuriance, the glory of those clusters. The woman took them down, swiftly but ceremoniously.

The commotion of the people who were coming to the dancer's house was heard not far away.

The two daughters arrived. One of them had

stumbled in the field and had a bloody toe. They cleared the corridor and then went to see their father.

He already had the red scarf in his left hand. His face, framed by the white scarf, stood out clearly as if apart from his body because his colorful and shining costume and large hat fused to enclose and spotlight it. His face was not pale but olive-colored, harsh, and almost expressionless. Only his eyes seemed sunken, in a world of their own, between the colors of his costume and the rigidity of his muscles.

"Do you see Wamani on your father's head?" the mother asked the older daughter.

The three of them watched quietly.

"Do you see him?"

"No," said the older daughter.

"You are still not strong enough to see him. He is peacefully seated on your father's head, listening to all the skies. Death lets him hear everything—what you have endured, what you have danced, what more you will suffer."

"Does he hear the galloping of the master's horse?"

"Yes, he does," answered the dancer, although the girl had spoken in a very low voice. "Yes, he hears! And knows what that horse's hooves have killed. The filth that has splashed on you. And also the power of our god who will swallow that horse's eyes. Not the master's eyes. Without his horse, he is only ram's dung!"

He began to play his steel scissors. In the semi-darkness of the room the pure sound of the steel was intense.

"Wamani is signaling me. They are coming!"

"Do you hear that, daughter? The scissors are not being handled by your father's fingers. Wamani makes them play. Your father is only obeying."

The steel blades are not tightly joined. With his fingers through the handle loops, he clicks the blades and makes them play. With this instrument in his hands, each dancer can produce a subtle music like the murmur of water, or even of fire; it depends on the rhythm, on the orchestra and on the spirit that protects each dancer.

They dance alone or in competition. The great skill that they display and the fervor of their blood during the figures of the dance depend on who is poised on each head and in his heart while he dances or raises and hurls digging bars with his teeth, pierces his flesh with awls or walks on a tight rope stretched from the top of a tree to the town tower.

I saw the great father Untu, dressed in black and red, covered with mirrors, dancing on a moving rope in the sky, playing his scissors.

The song of the steel was louder than the voices of the violin and the harp which were being played near me. It was at dawn. Father Untu seemed black in the uncertain delicate light; his figure swayed against the shadow of the great mountain. The voice of the scissors overpowered us, coming from the sky to the world, to the eyes and hearts of the thousands of Indians and mestizos who watched him advance from the immense eucalyptus to the tower. His journey lasted maybe a hundred years. He reached the window of the tower when the sun lighted the calcimine and the white, hewn stone of the arches. He danced a moment near the bells. Then he dropped out of sight. The song of the scissors came from within the tower; the dancer must have been groping down the steps of the gloomy tunnel. The world will never sing again in that way, compressed and resplendent on two blades of steel. I remember that the doves and other birds which slept in the tall eucalyptus sang while father Untu balanced in the air. The little birds sang jubilantly, but heard close to the steel's voice and the dancer's figures, their trills were like a barely perceptible filigree, as when man reigns and the beautiful universe seems only to adorn its master and nourish him.

The dancer's genius depends on who lives within him: the spirit of a mountain (Wamani), of a precipice whose silence is transparent, of a cave from which golden bulls and condemned souls come out on litters of fire. Or the cascade of a river that falls from the heights of a mountain range, or perhaps only a bird, or a flying insect that knows the meaning of abysses, trees, ants and the secret of night; some of those cursed or strange birds, *hakakllos*, *chuseks*, or the black red-winged San Jorge insects that devour tarantulas.

Rasu-Ñiti was the son of a great Wamani, a mountain with eternal snow. By then, he had sent him his spirit, a gray condor whose white back was shining.

Lurucha, the dancer's harpist, arrived playing and Don Pascual, the violinist, followed him. But Lurucha always directed the duet. With his steel fingernail he made the strings of wire and gut explode, or wail blood, during the sad steps of the dances.

Behind the musicians marched a young man, Atok'sayku [the one who tires the fox], Rasu-Ñiti's disciple. He too was in costume, but he was not playing his scissors. He walked with his head lowered. A dancer who cries? Yes, but he cried inside himself. Everyone noticed it.

Rasu-Ñiti lived in a village of no more than twenty families. The large towns were a few leagues away. Following the musicians came a little group of people.

"Do you see Wamani, Lurucha?" asked the dancer from his room.

"Yes, I see him. It's true. Your hour has come."

"Atok'sayku! Do you see him?"

The young man stood on the doorsill and gazed at the dancer's head.

"I only feel his wings. I don't see him well, father."

"Is he flapping his wings?"

"Yes, master."

"All right, young Atok'sayku."

"I already feel the knife in my heart. Play!" Rasu-Ñiti said to the harpist.

Lurucha played the *jaykuy* (introduction), and right away changed to the *sisi nina* (fire ant), another step of the dance.

Rasu-Ñiti danced, swaying a little. The small audience entered the room. The musician and his disciple stood rigid against the ray of sunlight. Rasu-Ñiti took the floor where the strip of sunshine was dimmest. His legs were burning. He danced the *jaykuy* without fervor, almost tranquilly; at the *sisi nina* his feet came alive.

"Wamani is flapping hard!" said Atok-'sayku, looking at the dancer's head.

Now he was dancing vigorously. The shadow of the room began to expand as from a gust of wind; the dancer was being reborn. But his face, framed by the white scarf, was expressionless, severe, although with his left hand he waved the red scarf as if it were a piece of struggling flesh. His hat with all its mirrors swayed; nothing else showed better the rhythm of the dance. Lurucha held his face close to his harp. Where was that music descending or springing from? It was not only from the strings and the wood.

"Now! I'm coming! I'm almost there!" the dancer said in a loud voice, but the last syllable came out in tatters, as if from a parrot's beak.

One of his legs became paralyzed.

"Wamani is there! Calm down!" exclaimed the dancer's wife, because she noticed that her younger daughter was trembling.

The harpist changed the dance to the tune of *waqtay* (the battle). Rasu-Ñiti raised his scissors higher and played them in the direction of the ascending ray of sunlight. He remained nailed to the spot, but with his face even stiffer and more sunken, he was able to turn on his good leg. Then his eyes, which before had seemed not to focus on anything, lost their vagueness and fixed almost jubilantly on his older daughter.

"The god is growing. He will kill the horse!" he said.

His mouth was already dry. His tongue moved as if rolling in dust.

"Lurucha! Master! Son! Wamani tells me that you are of white corn, your music comes from my heart, from my head."

And he fell to the floor. Seated, he didn't stop playing his scissors. Now his other leg was paralyzed.

With his left hand he waved the red scarf like a chicha seller's banner in the windy months.

Lurucha, who did not seem to be watching the dancer, began to play the *yawar mayu* (river of blood), the final step in all Indian dances.

The small audience remained quiet. Not a sound was heard in the yard or in the fields farther away. Did the chickens and guinea pigs know what was happening, what that farewell meant?

The dancer's older daughter went slowly out to the corridor. In her arms, she brought one of the large clusters of corn ears of different colors. She placed it on the floor. One guinea pig was brave enough to venture out of its hole. It was a male with wavy hair; with its very red eyes it looked at the men for an instant and then jumped into another opening. It whistled before going in.

Rasu-Ñiti saw the little animal. Why was he impelled to continue, like the dragging along of a turbid river, the slow rhythm of the *yawar mayu* that Lurucha and Don Pascual were playing? Lurucha slowed the devilish rhythm of this step of the dance. It was the *yawar mayu*, but slow, very deep; yes, like those immense rivers loaded with the first rains; rivers in the proximity of the jungle that also flow slowly, under the burdening sun. In them all the dust and mud, the dead animals and trees can be seen dragged along without stopping. And those rivers move between low mountains, dark with trees, not like the highland rivers that rush leaping in the bright light. No forest darkens them, and the rocks of the precipices give them silence.

Rasu-Ñiti followed this dense rhythm with his head and scissors. But the arm which waved the scarf began to bend; it was dying. It fell, out of control, until it touched the ground.

Then Rasu-Ñiti lay on his back.

"Wamani is flapping his wings on his forehead," said Atok'sayku.

"No one else can see him," said the wife to herself. "I no longer see him."

Lurucha revived the rhythm of the *yawar mayu*. It seemed that mourning bells were ringing. The harpist did not take great pains in striking the wire strings with his metal fingernail; he played the longest and heaviest ones, the strings of gut. Then the song of the violin could be heard more clearly.

The younger daughter was seized by the desire to sing something. She was excited, but like the others, solemn in her attitude. She wanted to sing because she saw that her father's fingers, which were still playing the scissors, were becoming exhausted and were also going to get stiff. And the ray of sunlight had retreated almost to the roof. The father played the scissors, rolling them a little in the deep shadow that was on the floor.

Atok'sayku moved a very short distance away from the musicians. The dancer's wife took a half step forward in the line she and her daughters formed. The other Indians were silent and remained almost rigid. What was going to happen now? They had not been told to go outside.

"Wamani is now over his heart!" exclaimed Atok'sayku, watching.

Rasu-Ñiti dropped the scissors. But he continued moving his head and eyes.

The harpist changed the rhythm, played the *illapa vivon* (the edge of the thunderbolt). All of it on the wire strings, in a cascading rhythm. The violin could not follow it. Don Pascual, with his bow and violin hanging in his hands, adopted the serious attitude of the small audience.

Rasu-Ñiti moved his eyes; the cornea, the white part, seemed to be most alive, the brightest. No one was frightened. The younger daughter was still seized by the desire to sing as she used to do close to the river, in the fragrance of the broom flowers that grow on both banks. But now her desire to sing, although equally violent, was different. But just as violent!

The *illapa vivon* lasted a long, long time. Lurucha constantly changed the melody, but not the rhythm. And now he looked at the dancer. The dancing flame that came from the wire strings of his harp followed the movement of the dancer's increasingly straying eyes, like a shadow. Because Lurucha was of white corn, according to the message of Wamani. The eye of the dying dancer, the harp and the hands of the musician functioned together. The music stopped the black ants that were now marching in line on the window frame, against the sunlight. Sometimes the world keeps a silence that only one can perceive. This time it was the harp that had accompanied the great dancer all his life, in hundreds of towns, under thousands of arches and awnings.

Rasu-Ñiti closed his eyes. His body looked immense. The hat with its mirrors shone on him.

Atok'sayku jumped next to the corpse and immediately raised himself, dancing, playing the sparkling scissors. His feet flew. Everybody was watching him. Lurucha played the *lucero kanchi* (shining of the star) from *wallpa*

wak'ay (the rooster's crow) with which the dancers' contests began at midnight.

"Wamani is here! On my head! In my heart, fluttering his wings!" said the new dancer.

No one moved.

It was he, father Rasu-Ñiti, reborn, with the tendons of a young animal and the fire of Wamani, the flow of centuries being renewed.

Lurucha invented the most intricate, the most solemn and fiery rhythms. Atok'sayku followed them; his legs, his arms, his scarf, his mirrors, his hat were all raised as they should be. And no one flew like that young dancer, born to dance.

"Very good!" said Lurucha. "Very good! Wamani is pleased. There he is on your head, the white of his back shining like the midday sun on the snow-capped mountain."

"I don't see him!" said Rasu-Ñiti's wife.

"We shall bury father Rasu-Ñiti tomorrow at sunset."

"He's not dead!" exclaimed the younger daughter, laughing. "Not dead! It is he who is dancing!"

Lurucha gazed intently at the girl. He approached her, almost staggering, as if he had drunk a large amount of *cañazo*.

"A condor needs a dove! A dove needs a condor! The dancer does not die!" he said.

"No one sheds tears for the dancer. Wamani is Wamani."

Alejandro Otero, Models
(Display) M.I.T.

Suicide Diary

JOSE MARIA ARGUEDAS

Translated by Luis Harss

May 10, 1968

... Last night I decided to hang myself in Obrajillo, in Canta, or in San Miguel, in case I couldn't find a gun. It won't be pleasant for those who find me, but I've been assured hanging produces a quick death. In Obrajillo and San Miguel I'll be able to spend a few days scratching the backs of the stray pigs, chatting with the dogs and even rolling in the dust with some of those curs that accept my company to the end. I've often played with the village dogs, as one of them. It was a way of feeling alive. Yes: less than a fortnight ago I managed to scratch a pig on the back of the head, in San Miguel de Obrajillo. It was a big one and pretended to shy away, but the pleasure made it stop; it started to grunt happily, and then (how hard it is to find the right words!) slowly rolled over and lay there with its eyes closed, moaning gently. The high waterfall that comes tumbling down from the unreachable peak of the rocks sang in that moan, in the pig's hard bristles, which softened; and the sun that warmed the rocks, my chest, the leaves of each bush and tree, warmed and transfigured everything, including the sharp and energetic face of my wife, came alive, better than anywhere else, in the sweet drowsiness of the pig's language. The waterfalls of Peru, like the one in San Miguel, tumbling into the deep, hundreds of meters of almost vertical fall, watering terraces with flowering crops, will be in my eyes when I die. They are the image of the world for those of us who sing in Quechua, who could spend an eternity listening to them, in their plunge down those rugged mountains capriciously broken into valleys as deep as death and never prouder in life: jagged strips of land where man has farmed, has built orchards with his brains and fingers and planted trees that stretch transparently to the sky, from the depths of precipices. Useful trees, as savagely alive as that teeming abyss from which men rise as beautiful, powerful worms, somewhat underrated by the skillful murderers who govern us today....

May 15

...Each of us, knowingly, sips his poison now and then; and at this moment I feel its effects. In my memory, the sun over the highflung village of San Miguel de Obrajillo has again taken on a particular yellow color, like that of a certain flower in the shape of a baby's slipper, a flower that grows or prefers to grow not in the fields but on man-made stone walls, in all the mountain villages of Peru. It's a velvety flower that dusts the bodies of the jet black bluebottles, the *huayronqos*, with a yellow dust that makes them seem blacker and steelier than when they're among the white lilies. Because here, in this flower, the huge *huayronqo* lingers, buzzes and thrashes around and sinks in. The surface of the flower is velvety, that of the bluebottle slick, almost bluish black, like the mane of a jet-black colt. I don't know if it's because of the shape and color of the flower or the half-deadly, devouring way in which it swallows up the bluebottle as it picks it way with anxious limbs, sucking up the yellow dust; I don't know if that's why the people in my village call the flower *ayaq sapatillan* (dead man's slipper), and it represents the corpse, and they strew it on the coffin and on the floor alongside the body. My remembering the *huayronqo* and those flowers and the sun of San Miguel de Obrajillo at dusk, with such force, is a bad symptom. I was hopefully approaching life again, until yesterday. Today I don't feel near death, as I was May 11. To say so, in a way, would be to show or affirm the opposite. Now, at this moment, the color yellow, which is not only a bad sign but the very substance of death, the dusty yellow of that bluebottle which people kill so thoughtlessly in my village, is ingrained in my memory, in the ugly, slow pain I feel in the back of my neck. Will I have to stop writing? Goodbye, for a few days, a few hours!...

May 16

The effects of the poison continue. It's as if my eyes were clouded over with the yellow dust that clings to the *huayronqo's* black body, the ,weight of that flying insect burrowing into the dust with its mineral head, its legs with almost microscopic hairs stretching out slowly but avidly from the wide body in its brilliant black armor, like a hunger gradually satisfied, throbbing with effort at each anxious thrust, triumphant in the explosion of life from a body that when crushed sounds like an egg-shell, a brittle web of dry membranes. No wonder the Quechuan villagers consider the *huayronqo* the soul of the dead man lingering in the dusty pollen deep in the velvety bag of the flower that represents the corpse. And the flight of the *huayronqo* is strange, something between a fly and a hummingbird. I saw one only forty-five days ago, in San Miguel de Obrajillo. Like the helicopter and the hummingbird, and the preying sparrow hawk, it can hover in midair. The *huayronqo* has an enormous body, almost as bright as a hummingbird. And in San Miguel it flies higher than in any other of the hundreds of towns where I kept constant track of it. It's almost as nimble as the hummingbird and as sudden and unpredictable. But it's an insect! In San Miguel de Obrajillo it rises ten, maybe twenty meters overhead. It's a fly and at that distance, holding itself up with the peculiar motion of its dark wings, it seems to be at such a great distance that the eye strains to focus on it, to absorb into our life the intense meaning of its dangling legs, often with their yellow dust, and its body, not unlike that of a turtle. And suddenly it's off, like a streak of lightning, but not so fast that the eye of the observer can't follow it. An entrancing sight, this armored bluebottle, for those of us who know what it is. At this moment I feel it in my forehead, slowly spreading its graveyard dust, aggravating my sickness. But no thoughts of suicide any more! To the contrary, there's a certain hardness in the globes of my eyes, a throb and ache, as in a malignant dream of death no longer willed, but feared.... 🐦

Excerpted from "First Diary," *El zorro de arriba y el zorro de abajo.*

Child of Sorrow

JOSE MARIA ARGUEDAS

Translated by Luis Harss

She had come from Ukuhuay, a hot village. They said she was a *chichera.* The trees of the narrow valley leading down to the little houses of Ukuhuay were overgrown with flowering parasites and "salvajina". The "salvajina" seems inert: its long leaves, dangling like heavy threads, take root in the bark of the trees growing along the mountain gorges; they

are light gray and don't rustle except in a strong wind, because of their dense vegetable weight. The "salvajina" hangs over precipices ringing with the song of birds, especially traveling parrots; *ima sapra* is its Quechua name in Ukuhuay. The *ima sapra* stands out because of its color and shape; the trees reach for the sky and the *ima sapra* for the rocks and water. When the wind blows, the *ima sapra* sways heavily or shakes in fright, transmitting its fear to the animals. The shade is sweet in that burning valley. The red-crested ducks swim longingly in the backwaters, as in pools of tears, according to the songs of the region. Fidela came climbing out of the depths of the valley; she stopped in the mountain village, on her way, she said, to Huamanga. She was pregnant and aiming for that distant city, without help or provisions. She spent three days in Lambra; she was a mestiza and could expect no charity. The mistress of the house where I was a servant offered her a sack of jerky, roast corn and hard cheese, and a mangy blanket. She gave her both these things in the flagstone patio, in the blazing sun. A few loose strands of hair crossed her face, to the corner of her mouth, which was wet with spit. She was whitish and dirty, frightened and determined. That night, in the kitchen, the cook and the houseboy were chatting in the dark; I was listening from the big kneading pan that I used as a bed. The woman slept on some animal skins, next to the hearth, far from the pan. I felt her sliding toward me like a snake; she put a hand on the edge of the pan. In the sun of the patio, she had stared at me; I was the lady's calf: as dirty as the mestiza, and white. I felt Fidela's hand raising the woolen shawl that covered me. The houseboy and doña Fabiana, the cook, were arguing. Fidela drew closer to me; she must have been halfway inside the pan. And her hand began to move down my belly. Her rough fingers seemed burning hot [....] I was short of air, I thought I was going to stifle in her hot breath. My whole body yearned for her. She got in under the shawl—as children we never undressed in that cold weather—and lay at my side. She had raised her skirt; I touched her body with my hands. Through the skin of my hands, frozen raw as they were, I felt her throat tighten, as my body weighed on her and I commended myself to God, with Quechua prayers ....

[The next morning] Fidela climbed the steep slope with her sack on her back. The other servants and I accompanied her as far as the Terrace of Departure, which all the Spanish-Indian towns used to have in those days. She cried when she said goodbye. She still had a snatch of hair in her wet mouth. The whole contrasting sky, with its gathering high clouds, as well as the twitching of the little *qopayso* herb, was in that arch that crossed her face, drawing spit from the corner of her lip, especially when she started to cry. I was behind doña Fabiana, clinging to her skirt. Again the unknown traveler stared at me, then knelt before the cook and kissed the hem of her skirt. Then she started climbing the steep and broken slope. We watched her slowly fade in the distance. She crossed behind the thornbush hedge that guarded a pasture belonging to the mistress of the town and started up the jagged slope. "Off to have an orphan, an outcast; who knows where," said doña Fabiana. She was already far up; too far to return.

Excerpted from "First Diary," *El zorro de arriba y el zorro de abajo.* Omitted passages are digressions that lead away from the story as the diarist's mind wanders. [Translator's note]

With Tears, Not Words

MAXIMO DAMIAN HUAMANI

Translated by Luis Harss

I am Máximo Damián Huamani, the one he mentioned [in his last diary], asking me to play the violin at his funeral. So I was there, playing *Agony*, which is such a sad song, because it's the death of the dancer. A song he liked so much when he was alive.

I saw him Tuesday, the second. At the Plaza San Martín, we met to talk over a Quechua book he was working on. Just last June I'd come to Huarmillacta, Parinocochas, a town without men, only women. He wanted to know about that, wanted to know everything about it.

I came to Lima from my village, San Diego de Ishua, and I went straight to him, before going to the museum. I wanted to be on television; he saw the dancers and heard my violin and arranged to have us appear on the educational channel.

On the 23rd of November he was in Balconcillo, on Esmeraldas Street; we were all gathered there, all the villagers of San Diego, for the feast of St. Isidore the Great [patron saint of farmers]. With a Cuban he came, a friend of his, and a Frenchman, and another writer, he said he was, Alejandro Ortiz. And there don José María danced the *huayno Karamusa* which is very gay, full of joy. There he saw the Ayacuchan dancers of my village dance on the violin, on the harp, without breaking them, on feet light as silk.

How to know he was saying goodbye, to us and the music. He used to come have lunch at my house in Pueblo Libre, used to just drop in, never minding the alley flies, the dirt, the poverty, what did he care about such things. He ate a lot, all sorts of village food, piles of *patasquita* [corn stew with pork], or *tinke*, which is a mixture of beans, peas and cheese, that was what he liked best of all. He was a kind man and I've cried over his death, cried as we cry in my village, with real tears, not words.

With my father, too, they were great friends, my father is also a villager, he used to take him to the Bolívar to eat, who cared if the Gringos heard them talk Quechua, they talked as loud as they could so everyone could hear them. My father doesn't know about his death, but he will be heartbroken.

For years and years he used to call me, he just said, come and bring your violin, or I'll be dropping in to see you, and I'd be waiting for him, in the house of my aunt Vicenta Santiago, who has a vegetable stall in Pueblo Libre, I help her with it; he wanted to find a decent job for me, not as a servant, he said, something better, as a worker, not a houseboy, but it's difficult here, there's nothing but injustice, he said.

I'm alone, most of the time, sometimes with the villagers, when there's a feast day, but mostly alone, like an orphan, so I'd go visit him, and he never said go away, to the contrary, he said come on in and we'd have lunch, first in Pueblo Libre, then in Santa Cruz, and finally in Chaclacayo, where he wife shared his joys and sorrows. Once he was very gay, at a Karguyoc feast, he drank *chicha* with everyone, without distinctions, here's to you, here's to someone else, to the dancers, to the people who said here's to you, Doctor Arguedas; he played the harp, made up love songs, my friend Guzmán López laughed at the airs he put on, he was so kind and simple.

For six months I'll wear mourning, as we do in my village, but that won't be the end of my sorrow. I've been suffering and crying, and why not, when he was one of us.

That last day, Tuesday the second, when I saw him in the Plaza San Martín, he said I'd see him on Friday the fifth, at seven o'clock, in Pueblo Libre, in the house of my aunt, Vicenta Santiago. I waited for him with my violin, he wanted to practice Quechua, I taught him a lot of things he didn't know, he wanted to know about that town without men in Parinocochas. I was practicing scissor dances on the violin, it was eight o'clock, nine o'clock, he hadn't come. He was never late, always on time. At ten my aunt told me to put out the candle, he was always pained by the way we had to live, in such misery, he said that was the way life was for us Indians. I waited for a long time and I was sad.

As if I'd known: he didn't come because he was already fighting death, in the hospital. The next day was dark for me, I was his friend, his violinist, who knows why he did it, why he left me this way, alone in the world. 🦅

1969

In his last Diary Arguedas had requested that Huamani play the violin at his funeral. And he is one of the two persons to whom Arguedos' last book is dedicated. [Editor's note]

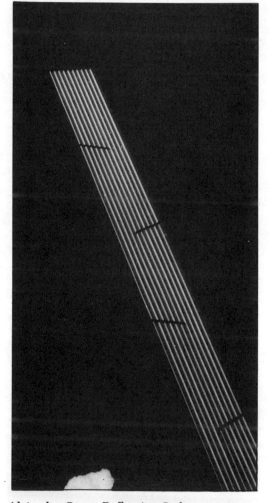

Alejandro Otero, *Reflecting Stele*
Caracas, 1958

The Pongo's Dream[1]

JOSE MARIA ARGUEDAS

Translated by Luis Harss

A little man was on his way to his master's house. As a serf he had been summoned to do his turn as unpaid *pongo* or help in the great farmhouse. He was a stunted, frightened, pathetic little man in worn clothes.

The great lord, master of the land, could not help laughing when the little man greeted him in the corridor.

"Hello! What's this, man or beast?" he asked him in front of the other servants.

Bowing humbly, the little man did not answer. He stood there frozen, with fearful eyes.

"Well, he'll do for scrubbing pots and sweeping the floor, if he isn't too weak even for that," said the master. "Get the scum out of my sight," he ordered his steward.

Kneeling, the little man kissed the master's hands and, still bent over, he followed the steward into the kitchen.

He was a shriveled little man but quite as strong as the next person. Everything he was ordered to do he did well. But there was dread in his eyes, and some of the other servants laughed at him, and others pitied him. "Orphan of orphans, born of the wind of the moon, I can feel the cold in his eyes and the sadness in his heart," the mestizo cook had said on first seeing him.

The little man spoke to no one; he worked in silence; he ate in silence. He did everything he was told to do. "Yes, little Father; yes, little Mother" was all he said.

Perhaps because of the dread in his eyes, and his rags, and perhaps also his silence, the master felt a special contempt for him. At nightfall, when the serfs gathered in the corridor to say the Hail Mary, the master made a point, each time, of torturing him in front of everybody, shaking him like a wet rag, pushing his head down till he was forced to kneel and then patting him on the cheek and saying:

"I think you're a dog. Bark!"

The little man could not bark.

"Walk on all fours then," the master said.

The little man did his best to obey.

"Sideways, like a dog," commanded the master.

The little man was good at imitating the sidelong gait of the highland dogs.

The master laughed heartily; his whole body shook.

"Heel!" he shouted when the little man had reached the far end of the corridor.

The little man made his way back, sideways and exhausted.

Meantime some of the other serfs prayed softly, as if holding their breaths and hearts for him.

"Now prick your ears, weasel[2]—that's what you are!" ordered the master. "Up on your back legs, palms joined!"

And somehow, as if he had been "weaseled" in his mother's womb, the little man managed to produce an exact imitation of the posture of one of those little animals when it sits on a rock, seemingly wrapped in silent prayer. But he could not prick his ears.

Nudging him with his boot, without really kicking him, the master would knock him over on the brick floor.

"Lord's Prayer," he would then order his Indians, who waited in line.

The little man would slowly get up, and he could not pray because he was not in his right place, nor was there any place for him.

As night fell, the serfs left the corridor and returned to their shacks.

"Off with you, dishrag," the master would then dismiss the little man.

And so it went, day after day, in front of the whole household. The little man was forced to laugh, to fake tears, and was generally made fun of, before the other servants.

But...one afternoon, at the time of the evening prayer, when everyone was gathered in the corridor and the master started to stare down the little man, this same little man suddenly spoke up quite clearly. He still looked frightened as he said:

"Master, with your permission, little Father, I want to talk to you."

The master pretended not to hear.

"What? Was it you who spoke or someone else?"

"With your permission, little Father, it's you, you're the one I want to talk to," the little man repeated.

"Well, talk...if you can," said the master.

"Father, little Father, Lord of Mine, Heart of Mine," the little man began, "last night I dreamed we'd both died, at the same time, both of us, together."

"Together, you and I? Go on, what else?" said the great master.

"Since we were both dead, my Lord, we were both naked, standing there naked before our Big Father Saint Francis."

"So then? What else? Speak up!" ordered the master, annoyed and at the same time stung by curiosity.

"Seeing us there together, both of us naked, our Great Lord Saint Francis sized us up with those eyes of his that see through things, who knows how far, sized us up, both of us, weighing our hearts, I think, yours and mine, to find out what we were and what we are. You, as a great and rich man, you met his eye, little Father."

"And you?"

"I don't know what I did, my Lord. I can't know what I'm worth."

"Fine. Go on."

"Then, afterwards, our Great Father spoke and said: 'Let the most beautiful of all the angels be brought before me. And with him a smaller angel, also the most beautiful of his kind. And let the small angel bear a cup of gold, a cup full of the purest cane honey.'"

"And then?" asked the master.

The Indian serfs listened, listened all ears to the little man, but fearfully.

"My Lord, as soon as our Great Father Saint Francis gave the order, a bright angel, tall as the sun, appeared, walking slowly, till he stood before our Great Father, and behind this bright angel came another smaller one, with the soft radiance of a flower, bearing a cup of gold."

"And then?" the master repeated.

"'Bright Angel, cover the gentleman with the honey from the cup of gold: let your hands be light as feathers on his skin,' spoke and said our Great Father. And so the Great Angel, raising the honey with his hands, carefully spread it all over your body, up and down, from your head to the tip of your toenails. And you stood there, in solitary splendor, shining in the light of Heaven, as if you were made of bright gold."

"As was right and proper," said the master. Then he asked: "And you?"

"While you were shining in Heaven, our Great Father again spoke and said: 'Let the least of all the angels in Heaven, the humblest one, come before me, bearing a gasoline can full of human excrement.'"

"And then?"

"A creaky, scaly, worthless old angel who had hardly enough strength left to hold his wings up appeared before the Great Father, his wings all splattered, dragging himself along, carrying a big can. 'And now,' our Great Father told him, 'smear the excrement you have in that can all over the body of this little man, any old way, it doesn't matter, just get on with it!' And so the old angel smeared it all over me with his knotty fingers, splattering it right and left, carelessly, the way you splatter an ordinary mud house. And I stood there, in the light of Heaven, stinking and ashamed..."

"As was right and proper," assented the master. "Go on! Or is that all?"

"No, little Father, my Lord: as we stood there again together, both of us, you and I, side by side, though looking so different, before our Great Father Saint Francis, he looked at us again, both of us, first you, then me, for a long time, with those eyes of his that seemed to see through the sky, who knows how far into the depths of things, joining night and day, past and present, and then he said: 'The angels' job is done, now lick each other! Slowly, take your time!'

"The old angel, at that very moment, regained his youth: his wings shone black and strong again. Our Father assigned him the task of seeing that His will be done." 🦎

[1] Arguedas referred to this tale as a "translation" from the Quechua, though "no doubt with quite a few touches of my own." In fact—like much of his poetry—it attempts a personal version of oral tradition. See Jorge Lafforgue's notes to *Relatos completos*, Losada, Buenos Aires, 1974, pp. 229 and 232-233. [Translator's note]

[2] The original *vicacha* (which is untranslatable) seemed too exotic for a parable and would not have permitted the wordplay that follows. My apologies to naturalists. [Translator's note]

Seeing with the Indian's Eyes

MARIO VARGAS LLOSA

Translated by Gregory Kolovakos and Ronald Christ

In 1935 José María Arguedas published a volume of short stories entitled *Agua* (Water); five years later his novel *Yawar Fiesta* appeared; in 1954 *Diamantes y Pedernales* (Diamonds and Flints) and in 1958 his major work, the novel *Los ríos profundos (Deep Rivers)* was issued in Buenos Aires. In these books, the real Indian makes his way into Peruvian literature, bringing with him the beauty and dark violence of the Andes, their crucial contradictions, their delicate poetry and their myths.

In contrast to his predecessors, Arguedas does not write about Indians from hearsay, nor is his information shaky: Arguedas knows the Indian from the inside, which is only logical since, culturally speaking, he was an Indian. Born in Andahuaylas in 1911, Arguedas lost his mother when he was still a very young boy and was forced to live in the small town of San Juan de Lucanas, where, by cruel circumstance, he had to share the life of the Indian servants. He learned to speak Quechua and his childhood was as harsh as that of any Indian. At an age when memories are branded red hot on a man's heart, he came to know in his own flesh and bone the radical injustice of which the Indian is a victim. He spent his youth among the Indians in the desolate landscape of the Andes, which he crossed and recrossed in every direction for years on end. When he arrived in Lima in 1929, Arguedas spoke Spanish with difficulty and must have suffered a great deal in order to assimilate completely the language and customs of the coastal people. After great effort, he succeeded, but without ever rejecting or forgetting his Indian childhood, to which he was always intrinsically faithful. Moreover, Arguedas' loyalty to the Andes influenced his literary career in a decisive way. When he came to Lima and read some of Peruvian literature, he suffered, in his own words, "an enormous disappointment because the most famous works of the period depicted Indians as degenerate creatures. Then," he continues, "I felt great indignation and an acute need to reveal the true, human reality of the Indian, a reality totally different from what was presented by the prevailing literature." And he began to write.

Of course, neither his vital experience in the highlands nor the sense of legitimate indignation that served as the stimulus to his career are sufficient to explain the importance of Arguedas' work. His deeply personal bond with the reality evoked in his books would have served no purpose whatsoever, literarily speaking, if Arguedas had not been a great creator, one of the purest and most original to have been born in America. These adjectives have been squandered, incorrectly applied and devalued, but in the case of Arguedas, they are irreplaceable. In lenient critical judgments, the word "purity" is often used to classify the intention behind a work: we have all come to agree with Gide that good intentions produce bad books. At other times, the word is used to designate the content of a work, as with poets who are called "pure" because they base their poetry on the perfecting of language, or with esthetes who put beauty ahead of truth. Arguedas' work is pure in the classical sense: it constitutes a simultaneous search for beauty as well as truth and, for the same reason, a battle against historical fraud and the substantial deceit signified in literature by lack of rigor, formal carelessness, rhetorical libertinism. Literature linked to life, the work's moral significance seems to be a spontaneous extension of Arguedas' own biography, because this timid, austere, touchingly modest man—often a victim himself—always concerned himself with injustice toward others. One episode in his youth is revealing: at the age of fifteen in the tiny highland village of Pampas, Arguedas witnessed scenes that horrified him. That night, by himself, he wrote his protest all over the town's streets, which he covered with graffiti and placards. Equally revealing is his having given free classes to the Indians in Sicuani. The feelings of rebellion and love that inspired these acts are the same that inform his entire work and produce its fascinating moral dimension.

Nearly all of José María Arguedas' books are dedicated to the Andes. Only his novel *El sexto* (The Sixth, 1961) takes place in Lima; and even in that brutal testimony about the prison in Lima, where Arguedas was arbitrarily incarcerated in 1937 by the dictatorship of Sánchez Cerro, the highlands also appear in pages that may constitute the most successful part of the book: the majestic parade of captive condors by an Andean village, the episode of the mountain boy raped by vagrants. In his other books, the highlands and the Indian always occupy the foreground of the narrative.

But Arguedas differs from other Peruvian writers who have taken up Andean themes, not only because of his knowledge of the *sierra*, but also because of his attitude toward the reality expressed in those themes. Arguedas does not show commiseration or charity for the Indian, nor any of those sentiments that ultimately express a *distance* between whoever is writing and whatever he writes about; rather, he reveals a prior and total identifica-

Rogelio Navanjo

tion: he speaks of the *sierra* as of himself. Therefore, although he points out vices and presents criticism, Arguedas never appears as a judge, always as an impartial witness. This attitude is reflected in the calm poise of his style, in its particular accent of sincerity. On this point, no one can be deceived: Arguedas is an objective writer, but one based in a primary, radical adherence to the Indian, an adherence born from his love for the Indian and from the fascination exercised over him by Quechua culture. Let us not forget that a large part of his intellectual labor consisted in the compilation and translation into Spanish of indigenous folklore. In *Canto quechua* (Quechua Song, 1938), *Canciones y cuentos del pueblo quechua* (*Songs and Tales of the Quechua People*, 1948), *Cuentos mágico-realistas y canciones de fiestas tradicionales en el valle del Montaro* (Stories of Magic Realism and Traditional Fiesta Songs from the Montaro Valley, 1953), Arguedas retrieved indigenous myths, legends and poems, which he beautifully translated into Spanish with a fervor and scrupulousness that reveal the depth of his spiritual identification with Andean culture.

But the essential part of his work is his own fiction. In his novels and short stories, José María Arguedas succeeds—the first to do so in Latin America—in replacing the abstract and subjective Indians created by the Modernists and Indigenists with real characters, that is, with concrete beings, portrayed objectively and situated both socially and historically. The difficulties he had to overcome in order to carry out this undertaking were enormous, and they can be measured by the failure of his predecessors. It was not enough to know the man of the Andes at close quarters and to speak his tongue; it was necessary to find a prose style suited to the reconstruction in Spanish and within Western cultural perspectives of a world whose deep roots are different and even opposed to ours. The principal obstacle, certainly, was language itself. The Indian speaks and thinks in Quechua; his knowledge of Spanish is rudimentary, sometimes nonexistent. The Indian who goes down to the coast and becomes a servant does not abandon his maternal language, but, by necessity, learns an elementary and utilitarian Spanish that lets him communicate with whites. This impoverished Spanish does not in any way represent the Indian's speech as the Indigenists seem to believe, which leads them to invent characters who talk among themselves in that bastardized, adulterated dialect of servants on the coast. Even a writer with the undeniable talent of Ciro Alegría has sometimes fallen into this trap, which is also a mystification: it is the

same as if he were to have made Algerian workers in Paris speak among themselves in the same stammering, caricaturized French that they use with French people. The answer lay in discovering a Spanish style that yielded a syntax, rhythm and even a vocabulary *equivalent* to the Indian's language. The Indigenists reduced everything to a phonetic mumbojumbo; Arguedas succeeded in bringing to Spanish-speaking readers a translation of the Indians' own language. In this way Arguedas simultaneously succeeded in recreating within Spanish the inner world of the Indian: his sensibility, his psychology, his mythology. And we all know that the emotional and spiritual qualities of a people are represented in their language.

The glaring authenticity that is so striking in Arguedas' Indians proceeds especially from the way they talk. Their language immediately defines them, distinguishes them and gives them their own three-dimensionality. We should keep in mind the *epic marketwomen* of Abancay that appear in *Deep Rivers*, the Kayau villagers in *Yawar Fiesta*, the dancer in *La agonía de Rasu Niti* (The Agony of Rasu Niti): each embodies characters of unmistakable psychology, joined to nature through a complex system of sensorial and emotive links and united among themselves by a community of interests, beliefs and attitudes. These are beings who respond to the stimuli of external reality with original actions, whose sorrows and joys are expressed in typical ways. José María Arguedas is the first writer who introduces us into the very heart of indigenous culture and reveals to us the richness and spiritual complexity of the Indian—in the vivid and direct way that only literature can. It would be very lengthy and useless to describe the formal procedures Arguedas employs; besides, I am not attempting here to analyze Arguedas' work stylistically but to indicate his position in the literary development of Peru. Nonetheless, I shall point out one such procedure: the systematic fracturing of traditional syntax, which gives way to sentences organized not in agreement with logic but, rather, in agreement with emotion and intuition. When they speak, Arguedas' Indians express sensation more than anything else and their concepts are derived from these sensations.

Let us pause for a moment at the unforgettable third chapter of *Yawar Fiesta* entitled "Wakawak'ras, Trumpets of the Earth". In Chapter One, Arguedas describes the geographical and social setting of his story: the town of Puquio rises like a hierarchical pyramid, with neighborhoods, houses and inhabitants rigorously classified according to categories of Indian villagers, mestizo merchants or white landholders. In the second chapter he traces the town's history and we witness the process that gave Puquio, originally an Indian community, its present structure as Arguedas evokes the plundering of the communal lands by the whites ruined in the closing of the mines, which forced them into ranching and cattle raising. These two chapters are like a preface to the novel—the historical and social coordinates of fear—but the novel's action begins with Chapter Three in a series of rumors and anonymous voices gathered from here and there: Indian huts, doorways of white homes, counters of mestizo stores. In the sonorous spluttering, we discover that the town is aroused by the news of a coming bullfight, in which one of the Indian communities wants to fight a beast known for its ferocity. This is a chapter without characters; the voices are anonymous, springing from all parts of Puquio. Nevertheless, there is no possible confusion in the mind of the reader, who immediately distinguishes between the speech of whites and Indians. The sentences of the latter have a special musicality, an undercurrent of gentleness that comes from their abundance of diminutives and vocatives, their breathless, whining rhythm, their poetic expressionism. In the strictest sense, this is collective, oral language, not only because of its source but also because of its structure. In Indian speech, those particularizing words, the articles, scarcely appear at all and Spanish words are sometimes phonetically deformed as well; but the basic quality of these sentences results from their unusual syntax. The reader knows that the phrases "ahí está tus ovejitas, ahí está tus vacas" and the exclamation, "¡ Dónde te van a llevar, papacito!" can only come from the Indians.

Imitating Arguedas, many Indigenists from Peru, Ecuador and Bolivia have later tried to fabricate a literature of the Indian based on a "figurative" language; and almost always, either because of imprudence or abuse, they have drowned in formalist excess, in mannerism. Certainly, the easiest thing is to flavor the figurative speech of the Indians with Quechua words and to alter the voiced sounds, to write them out in crude phonetics. What is admirable in Arguedas, however, is his having constructed an Indian language by reshaping the very structure of Spanish.

Arguedas' contributions are not only formal. Surely we should be most grateful to him for having known how to express the Indian as he is in reality: a complex being. In other words, to describe the Indian in situ, in a geographical and varying social framework within which his conduct is intelligible. Thus landscape plays such an important role in Arguedas' work and the flora, fauna, light and air of the Andes find passionate expression in him. The formation of the Indian's spirit owes a great deal to his natural environment, just as his conduct can be understood in light of his social ordinance. Arguedas' best book, Deep Rivers (and by "best" I mean the best-sustained one, the one with the most beautiful prose), is principally dedicated to the landscape of the Andes; it is a dazzling poetic testimony to the Andean world. On the other hand, his best novel (the best constructed, the one with the sharpest characters) is Yawar Fiesta, where the landscape is secondary and the human element prevails. In this novel, the Indian is portrayed from every angle: the Indian among Indians, the Indian confronting whites, mestizos. This diversity of focus is enormously instructive. These villagers who go to ask don Julio Arosemena to give them a bull to fight on the National Holiday are docile and timid: their respect for the great landowner approaches servility and frank adulation. But make no mistake. These villagers (the same ones who on their own initiative and with only their bare hands constructed a highway from Puquio to Nazca in twenty-eight days, the same ones who will defeat the Misutu by means of sheer courage) behave that way as a strategy: their servility is pretense, a means of defending themselves against the enemy. In contrast, among themselves the Indians' attitude is different: their solidarity knows no limits and their dignity governs all their domestic and work relations. These miserable Indians, who build homes for the survivors of the cane plantations along the coast, and the others, who come down from the mountains to lament the Misutus's imminent death, are exemplary spirits. And these are the same men who bend like reeds when the landowner passes by and who are obsequious and solicitous toward the whites.

Arguedas' testimony is definitive: the Indian is neither obsequious nor servile nor deceitful nor hypocritical; but his behavior, by necessity in certain circumstances, is. Those masks that he wears are really shields protecting him from further aggression and abuse. The Indian consciously shows himself that way before the man who steals his land and animals, who imprisons him and rapes his wife and daughters; but within the internal life of the community, the Indian is never humbled. There he detests lies and religiously respects the moral norms he has established for himself. When Arguedas shows the Indian in his differing situations, when he exposes the true meaning of the Indian's attitude toward the white man, when he reveals the world of dreams and ambitions concealed in the Indian's soul, he gives us all the elements necessary to judge the Indian, to understand and to approach him. This totalizing vision of a world is true literary realism.

On the other hand, besides describing the true nature of the relations between the Indian and the white man in the Andean setting, Arguedas shows the phenomena of transculturation that originate in the confrontation of the two communities, in the exchanges it gives rise to, in the Indian's assimilation and transformation of white practices and customs according to the Indian's own psychology and system of values. In order to see this more clearly, let's refer to *Yawar Fiesta* again. The novel's central episode is a bullfight, a fiesta brought to Peru by the Spaniards. But does that imported ceremony still have anything in common with the *yawar-punchay*? Almost nothing. The fiesta has been transformed into a sort of tragic, collective epic where virtuosity has been replaced by the display of pure daring, where the spectacle remains submerged in the violence. Those Indians who face the bull with their bare chests and provoke it and then defeat it with sticks of dynamite are gladiators, not bullfighters. Everything has changed: the music, the dances, the songs accompanying the festivities are Indian and it is no longer a festival but rather a terrifying ceremony that serves an entire town for the symbolic expression of its sorrow and anger. The very spirit of the spectacle has been transformed.

Arguedas does not stop there. He also reveals the opposite phenomenon: the unconscious spiritual "Indianization" of the white man in the high country. So proud of their position as whites, these brutal, racist landowners are scarcely white in reality any more: without their realizing or intuiting it, the community they are subjugating has been imperceptibly conquering, colonizing them. When the subprefect of Puquio wants to prohibit the *yawar-punchay*, the reaction of Julio Arosemena and Pancho Jiménez is symptomatic: they feel wounded, angry, personally affected. They do not consider the *yawar-punchay* savage and they scorn that man from the coast who wants to suppress one of "their" festivities.

Finally, it is necessary to point out the talent with which Arguedas has shown the collectivist spirit of the Indian. There is something surprising in his short stories and novels: the lack of individual heroes. Some characters play more important roles than others; but, in fact, the narrative action never exclusively revolves around one character who stands out from the rest. In reality, the protagonist is always collective: the villagers in *Yawar Fiesta*, the city of

Abancay in *Deep Rivers*, the larval, sub-human rabble of the common criminals in *El Sexto*. Collectivism appears in his novels and stories, simultaneously, as a characteristic of the community he evokes and as a formal device. It is one more proof of the fusion of two realities—the social and the literary—at work in the writing of Arguedas. A proof, as well, of the rigor with which Arguedas took his vocation upon himself.

MARIO VARGAS LLOSA has written numerous essays on Arguedas. "Seeing with the Indian's Eyes" dates from 1964. *Title story translated by Angelo Cadillo-Alfars de Ayres & Ruth Flanders Francis, LALR, IV, 9 (1976).

Mario Rodríguez

Alejandro Otero, *Gold and Silver Vertical Vibrant*
Caracas, 1968

Introducing José Agustín

RAYMOND L. WILLIAMS

Do Not Pass Through This Door

JOSE AGUSTIN

Translated by Don Schmidt and John Kirk

José Agustín, along with Gustavo Sainz, is the major representative of the newest and youngest in Mexico, the "onda". What these writers brought to Mexican prose was a language of a generation entertainingly disrespectful of the country's institutions, literary and other. Such an attitude is often comical, a type of humor that recalls a writer like Cabrera Infante. Agustín, like the Cuban, exploits puns, neologisms, agglutinated words and foreign languages to evoke playfully humorous effects. Both the language and the attitude are an expression of the generation's disaffection, so it's not just a matter of wittiness.

The experience of reading Agustín's fiction also recalls writers of adolescence; for example, Salinger's *The Catcher in the Rye*. The protagonist of Agustín's first novel suffers the trials of a Holden Caulfield. This first-person narrator, like the characters in his short stories, maintains an aloof posture and satirical tone as a part of, and not superior to, a very foolish world. The narrator laughs at himself as much as the people around him.

Agustín was born in Acapulco, Mexico, in 1944. He has written five novels: *La tumba* (1964), *De perfil* (1966), *Abolición de la propiedad* (1969), *Se está haciendo tarde (final en laguna)* (1973), and *El rey se acerca a su templo* (1977). His two volumes of short fiction are titled *Inventando que sueño* (1968) and *La mirada en el centro* (1977). The influence of rock music in Agustín's career is evident in his book on the subject, *La nueva música clásica* (1968).

The passage that follows is a translation from Agustín's latest novel, *Cerca del fuego*, still unpublished as of this writing. The idea for the novel apparently germinated from a newspaper account that Agustín saw describing an amnesiac experience suffered by a fellow one day while on the street. The protagonist, Lucio, has a similar experience, and cannot remember anything from the past six years, although his memory returns slowly.

RAYMOND L. WILLIAMS teaches at the University of Chicago. His *Aproximaciones a Gustavo Alvarez Gardeazábal* was published in Bogotá in 1977.

Lucio arrives home highly enthusiastic. He has managed to get out of military prison, and besides that, the day is clear, the branches of an apparently dehydrated tree are outlined against the solid blue of the sky, and they make him think that the sky and trees are one, or if not, that they have an intrinsic relationship. The house, in addition, is very beautiful. Lucio's wife—let's call her Aurora—wrote him in military prison and gave him her address, where she would wait for him.

Lucio knocks on the door, and greets it. Good morning door, he says. The door is opened and the one who answers is Aurora, who, on seeing him, hugs him forcefully, their bodies in contact, their mouths fused, their tongues in renewed familiarity.

Afterwards, Aurora takes him inside the house, which is truly immense. Lucio contemplates the different rooms with their high ceilings and enormous windows, statues in the corners, friezes for trim, carpets of delicately intricate design, large hanging lamps and mirrors that get the light that issues from all over. There are relaxed people who rest, read, chat or work. Aurora introduces Lucio to everyone she finds, and they greet him with genuine friendliness, how good that you have arrived, we were expecting you. It's true we were expecting you, Aurora confirms, but I was more than they. Only at that moment does Lucio fully comprehend, a striking awareness, (a lightening), prodigious, the blessing that there is someone who waits for him. And within himself he constructs a tiny sanctuary, and thanks destiny because it has allowed him to recover his wife and to be in this place, after all the unspeakable suffering he has been through. The only thing he can do right now to express his gratitude is to squeeze his wife's arm firmly and affectionately. Feeling it, she turns to him, leans her head close, what a delightful scent to her hair, and says: I love you.

They go through the whole house. There are two stories, with bedrooms located on the lower one and recreation and work rooms on the upper. At first Lucio thinks that the house is a museum, but then he figures out that it is more like a palace. They go up to the roof, where there are armchairs for sunbathing and terraces to view the scenery: in particular the two volcanoes which from there appear a little distant but are visible with an incomparable clarity. Aurora explains that it is on these terraces that the oldest people are in the habit of resting, and she even introduces him to many of them. The old people look at them with a little smile, and then close their eyes. Lucio feels that all of them—because of their age of course—are beyond all the agitation, the effervescence, of those he met below; and he feels a very vivid desire for time to pass right *now*, with a dizzying speed, fast forward of the tape, for him to be a gray-haired little old man who sunbathes before the volcanoes and who with a trace of a smile greets the young people who stroll about the roof and don't appreciate what that means.

Aurora takes him to the basement, which is nearly a labyrinth of dark corridors. Innumerable doors lead to tiny rooms where some people like to work in absolute isolation, and in which furniture and all kinds of things are stored, especially books, lots of books of all sizes and ages glimpsed through open doors. In the basement Lucio loses all sense of direction, because he let himself get fascinated by the books, and then by the dense, close humidity, although the air is clear, in which inevitably, even healthfully, a kind of vague apprehension develops, to what? Well, to getting lost, dummy, because one corridor leads to another and who knows where the hell the doors are that go upstairs. We're lost, Aurora, he says, feeling that his wife (if she really is his wife) is stronger now, because she is familiar with the boundaries. The boundaries, in this and in other games, determine the rules. You got yourself lost, my love, but I know how to find the way out. You really don't know where we're going? I don't have the slightest idea, he admits. What has happened is that you have gotten sidetracked, but I'm sure that if it were necessary you would find the way out, don't you think?

Aurora proposes that he try to find the door they used to come in, and Lucio begins to walk through various passageways, to go into others, to open doors, and he moves on faster and faster, with a certain fear and exasperation because he can't find the way, and because he

has gradually gotten into darker places where the silence is nearly total. Suddenly he has forgotten that he is looking for the way out, and he amuses himself by peering into almost totally darkened rooms, where metal objects can be glimpsed, and where, indeed, there is a perceptibly rarefied atmosphere, ever more humid.

I can't do it, he finally admits. Worse yet, I think I've gotten further away from the exit. The exits, she corrects, also in a soft voice. There are several, and really it's easy to find them, but you've scarcely arrived at this house, my love, while I know it well. Look, Lucio, I really like this house, but ever since I got here I have very clearly felt a great attraction to coming down to this basement, I swear you have no idea how many sensingeniational things there are here, you could spend months fascinated looking at all the nicknacks that there are in the rooms, especially the books, my love; there are incredible books, although the majority are old, and there are also manuscripts by people who lived I don't know when, and who narrated their lives and their deals and everything they thought. . . . Look, once I came down to the basement alone, all by myself, and all of a sudden, there I was lost from looking at so many things. I didn't know where the fuck I was going. Aurora, don't be gross. Why not? It's fun, well, as I was saying, I stayed very still, I mean really still, and I swear on my life that something made me walk. Just imagine, I swear it felt as if some hands were taking me by the shoulders and putting me in the right direction. I went that way without hesitating, and I found the stairway, one of the stairways, in just a little while. I tell you there are ways to get upstairs all over the place. What ticks me off, Lucio confessed, is that my sense of direction is very good. Every time I get to a strange city, I familiarize myself with the streets very easily and in two or three days I get around everywhere just as if I were at home. You, on the other hand, never know where you are. Well, now it's the reverse, lionet, Aurora commented smiling slightly. Well, let's head back now, O.K.? Don't you really know how to get out? Of course I don't, Aurora, but you do, so let's get going! Don't get nervous, my love, after all getting lost can be fun. Alright, but let's get lost some other day, O.K.?, right now I swear I feel as if I were suffocating; let's go upstairs, you haven't even showed me our room. Let's go, then, conceded Aurora the Beautiful, and Lucio figured that she was pleased because she could lead him for the first time. This calmed him, a man after all, you can certainly breathe easy now, because there was a moment when the quiet and the shadows were about to make

Our Lucio burst. Nevertheless, after they had gone on a little, and with a bit of apprehension, Lucio realized that Aurora herself wasn't so sure of the way, because she stood very still, trying to orient herself, or perhaps waiting for the Big Force to take her by the shoulders and say to her: take off that way, baby. Listen, are you sure you know which way? Yes, I know, she said with a little laugh, but at the same time I don't know.

She took him by the hand and they headed down a passageway which, in spite of the existing dimness, seemed to darken still more. Are you sure it's this way? What the hell, she exclaimed, and remained very serious. They were in an almost totally dark place: in the background the passage was interrupted by a door on which faintly glimmered a number 4 of gilded metal. What's happening? I just blew it, admitted Aurora, it's incredible!, she then added, with a nervous little laugh. What's incredible, he asked in a whisper. Listen, let's get going, he added, feeling ridiculously infantile because he couldn't stop a growing fear from getting control of him. What am I afraid of, he asked himself fleetingly—the dark: the unknown: everybody, or almost everybody, fears the unknown, daddy, don't tell me we don't. What's unbelievable is that we have gotten to this place, Lucio. Look, I have only been here once; that time Amparo, one of the owner's daughters, was with me. Well, what happened? Nothing happened, because she knows the house like nobody else. After all, it's her house, isn't it? Well then, Lucio whispered with greater impatience. Well, Amparo told me exactly the same thing I'm going to say to you; she said, and I'm also telling you/ Aurora, dammit, stop clowning around! Don't get upset, my dear, this is important, although who the hell knows why it's so important. Wai... wait a second, don't get upset. O.K., she said: Aurora, you can go through the house when you want, how you want, and you can go anywhere, everything is open to everyone, but never, never, never ever get the idea of opening this door. That is absolutely forbidden. Jees, why?, asks Lucio, feeling that the whole thing is ridiculous, emboldened because now there is something concrete to rehabilitate his strength. I asked her the same thing myself, continues Aurora, but that damned Amparo didn't explain it to me. Well, actually she said she didn't know either. Ah! I just remembered something else: she told me: when your husband comes, if it's you who shows him the basement, and if by chance you get this far, tell him that for no reason must he, more than anyone, open this door. *Really?* You're putting me on, darn you, Aurora. No, I swear I'm not. The fact is that

door cannot be opened. Don't open it, eh, my love? But why, what's in there? A tiiiiger! And he'll eat you!, she exclaimed with a (nervous) little laugh. Stop the clowning and tell me what's in there, you do know. I don't know, truly, the only thing I know is that you can't go in. *Interdit d'entrer.* Do you think it's locked?, Lucio whispers approaching the door (with prudent steps). Lucio, don't horse around! Come here! Do you think it's locked?, Lucio repeats, almost to himself. He already has his hand on the latch, when a frigid current surges up and down his spine. Lucio manages to overcome the shot of adrenalin that invites panic, he ignores the warnings—totally without humor this time—from Aurora, and he twists the knob. The knob is a protuberance around the keyhole. It moves and gives way. It's not locked, says Lucio, but before he can push the door he hears a dense, tense, heavy breathing, and although it is not very loud, something that precludes all argument makes Lucio let go of the doorknob and beat a hasty retreat to Aurora, who throws her arms around him. They both remain immobile, expectant, watching the door, until Lucio, irritated, exclaims: I'll be fucked! But he doesn't dare to return to the door (a number 4 of gilded metal) and he lets Aurora lead him toward the passageway, the passageways, and they go away from there, in (ominous) silence. Suddenly they again come upon the slightest sounds of the people who are reading books in the tiny rooms (one page follows another) of the basement.

Alejandro Otero, *Study for Civic Sculpture* (Model) 1972

Cristián Huneeus Introduces Himself

Translated by Gregory Kolovakos

Cristián Huneeus, narrator and critic. He was born in Viña del Mar, Chile, in 1937, son of a farmer from Santiago and a Buenos Aires beauty, an older brother to four women and a student of electronics, nephew of a retired colonel and of an alcoholic adventurer, grandson of a publicist and a liberal politician on his father's side and of an engineer-architect on his mother's side. His paternal grandmother was religious and authoritarian, a gentle woman who allowed him witty remarks and read the stories from illustrated magazines to him.

He lives his childhood and adolescence in the country while studying at Saint George's College. He took a year of architecture at the Catholic University and graduated with a degree in philosophy and literature from the University of Chile. With a fellowship from the British Council and the Rockefeller Foundation, he continued his studies at Corpus Christi College, Cambridge, where he received an M. Litt. with a thesis on D. H. Lawrence. When he returned from England in 1967, he taught at the University of Chile and from 1972 to 1975 he was Director of the Department of Humanistic Studies, an experimental center of research and development in philosophy, history, and literature that included such teachers, among others, as the poets Nicanor Parra and Enrique Lihn. In 1975, he left the university to devote himself to writing.

In 1976 he travelled to Australia, invited to an Australian-Latin American conference on the humanities, and for six months he was a visiting fellow in the Writing Division at Columbia University. He has been a regular contributor to *Hoy* and *Mensaje*, two magazines that have been, until recently, tolerated by the military Junta.

(*Hoy* was shut down in 1979.)

Married three times, he has a daughter from his first marriage.

His stories have appeared in anthologies and international magazines in Spanish and English. He has published three books, *Cuentos de cámara* (Chamber Stories, 1960), *Las dos caras de Jano* (The Two Faces of Janus, 1962) and *La casa de Algarrobo* (The House of Algarrobo, 1968). Scheduled for republication in 1978, these works are considered by their author as "nothing other than an experiment in prose flawed by the use of static forms and durable material, something like a work in marble set on a pedestal and belonging to an adolescence that aspired to the permanent and suspiciously prolonged itself past acceptable limits."

For several years the problem of finding a fluid form in accord with the speed of time seemed insuperable and his literary drive turned to other modes of activity: women, agriculture, business, teaching, interior decorating, university politics, nocturnal life and the consumption of whiskey.

Through the rare confluence of

1. Soledad, his present wife,
2. an unusual interest in observing plants grow,
3. theoretical discussions in humanisitic studies with Parra, Lihn, the critic Ronald Kay and the novelist Jorge Guzmán

a way out presented itself and through it *El rincón de los niños* (The Children's Corner) began to rush headlong, a text without visible end, whose protagonist seems to be change.

It could be said that *El rincón* is an investigation into the historical-social reality of Chile during the last twenty years, as an *observed* object. The emphasis falls on the inventive nature of the mechanisms of perception and on the shifting character of memory that shapes them. What is seen is seen not because it is or is not there but because it is what can and/or is wanted to be seen at the moment it is looked at. The historic-social context is created each time it is named and the habit of thinking about it as an entity unto itself and confronting itself is the severest penalty of human freedom: the full gamut from absurdity to brutality is run on the basis of this illusion.

The discourse in *El rincón* asserts its irony in the montage of linguistic planes that move from the *annoncé* toward the analysis of the *annoncé*, which is transformed into a new *annoncé*. This dynamic makes clear the process of the formulation or, in a word, the *work* of creation. The book offers itself, not as an elaborated product but rather as the elaboration of a product.

Excerpt from
El rincón de los niños

CRISTIAN HUNEEUS

Translated by Deborah Weinberger

10/24/74

From the first notes the attempt to create a universe is clear, i.e., the intention is to establish an aggregate of mutually determinant relations. On a certain level, the indetermination of the determinations is equally clear. Not so on another. To wit:

CHIRICO: 494898, Hernando de Aguirre 2072

Gloria is going around with Juan Enrique because he is famous as a man who is ambitious, successful, a sure-fire success in life. It gratifies her to be seen with him. Juan Enrique is going around with Gloria because she admires him and is a practical object who will be very useful to him: sex, interest in his things, etc.

Juan Gabriel starts going out with Valentina out of curiosity and because he finds her interesting. Valentina with him, in order to forget the dark boy and for sex.

Gloria with Manuel to try to get Juan Enrique back and because she will use him as a slave. Manuel with her, because (illegible word). Gloria is a sort of intellectual snob of the Elizabeth Hagen type. Manuel is a naive fellow; intelligent, idealistic, but naive.

Juan Enrique has what's bad in me. Valentina is like Cecilia.

Manuel is an old schoolmate of Juan Enrique's. Juan Enrique is somewhat envious of his innocence. Gloria tries to exploit this envy.

Gloria considers Valentina a phony. Valentina doesn't consider Gloria at all.

María Valentina will be called Barbara. Gloria will be called María Valentina.

Paz Francisca
Paz Francisca
H.H. Munro (Saki): Deathtrap, The
Eugene O'Neill: Before Breakfast
Anton Chekov: The Proposal
Jacinto Benavente: No Smoking

CHRONOLOGICAL DETERMINATION/INDETERMINATION: The chronicler met Paz Francisca in 1957 and indicates 1956 as the date of the writing of the text. Either he wrote the text in 1957 and dated it, incorrectly, a posteriori, or else meeting Paz Francisca made such a great impression on him that by way of recording that impression he repeated her name everywhere, including in the papers of 1956; which hypothesis is endorsed by the exclusion of Paz Francisca from the set of characters proposed in the text, reflecting a chapter evidently prior to P.F. in this story; and at the same time is refuted by a paradoxical trait of the chronicler, which is the systematic exclusion from his texts of what affects him most at the time of writing. Our narrator plots episodes which precede the story that concerns him.

In any case, I acted responsibly when I called Chirico at 494898 to ask him if it was in 1956 or 1957 that Gaspar Ruiz asked him for his phone number. But Chirico hasn't resolved anything: he told me that he's too old to waste his time remembering such crap.

10/25/74

PSYCHOLOGICAL DETERMINATION/INDETERMINATION: Gloria, ostensibly called to play, in keeping with her name, a part of majesty, splendor, and magnificence in the development of the project, is transformed at the eleventh hour into Valentina (to be more exact, into María Valentina), appellative of pale beauties. Valentina herself, after this fleeting but effective emphasis of her paleness by the anteposition of the virginal María, suddenly becomes Barbara. It's enough to confuse anybody. But one can assume some explanatory directions: Gloria on her way to heaven, i.e., access to the whole, can't control the longing to be Valentina as well: the shine, and also the opaqueness. She has in addition a third point of reference: Gloria is the same type as Elizabeth Hagen, an intellectual snob, we are told. Valentina, for her part, wants to extinguish a desire ("to forget the dark boy") and become spirit, or spirit herself away, while at the same time she wants to satisfy a desire ("for sex"): she oscillates between Valentina and Barbara, an oscillation vulnerable before the splendid observer and therefore hidden under a distant attitude. ("Gloria considers Valentina a phony. Valentina doesn't consider Gloria at all."). Again, a third point of reference: Valentina looks like one Cecilia.

Gloria, a "practical object" for Juan Enrique ("she will be very useful to him"), is herself doubly practical: Juan Enrique interests her because he is "a sure-fire success" and Manuel interests her because "she will use him as a slave." Thus, she wants to dominate but also be dominated: if it weren't for the possibility of the coexistence of both objects, she would undoubtedly not enjoy either. They are so closely tied that Gloria "tries to exploit" the relative envy Juna Enrique feels toward Manuel; she goes out with the latter "to try to get Juan Enrique back": she also wishes, by means of the secondary subjugation of Manuel, to dominate the man by whom she would like to be dominated.

Manuel, at first glance, would appear to be more of a piece than the rest. The problem is that when it is a question of specifying why he goes out with Gloria, the text offers us a blur: apparently, the text refuses to record something that does not agree with the adjectives it applies to him. We can allow for this, whatever it may be, to escape the notice of the interested party himself, since he is so naive ("He is a naive fellow; intelligent, idealistic, but naive"), but not for it to escape the notice of the text itself. There's something suspicious here. Two lines of interpretation (which could converge at some not too distant point in space): either Manuel's previously noted predisposition to slavery makes him tolerate any sort of humiliation in exchange for being accepted by the group—in which case the writer would have had to expell him entirely as unworthy—or Manuel is as capable as any of the others of experiencing a passion and breaking away from any sort of role (for example, the one according to which he ought to be idealistic and innocent), in which case our writer, seeing him get out of character, wouldn't have known what the hell to do with him. Because it is evident, from the moment in which he is accepted as blurred, that Manuel has to behave like someone put in his place.

The place of the rest is determinate/indeterminate. They are dealt fluidity and movement; Manuel's place is fixed beforehand. He has been determined: he is blurred publicly and notoriously.

11/4/74

It seems unquestionable that Manuel is an outsider. If not, let us observe that, except for him, the text doesn't bother to legitimize any character's belonging to the group. Manuel "is an old schoolmate of Juan Enrique's." This is the passport which he shows before the implicit need to cross a certain border. Manuel enters our country through Juan Enrique's influence (he must have some, since his contribution of Manuel is tolerated, perhaps even appreciated). At the same time, Manuel is not an object of sudden and ultimate enthusiasm. He is a "schoolmate," someone with whom something memorable has been shared, which explains his rescue and transplantation. And besides, an "old" schoolmate. Proven fidelity. Sterling value.

1/9/75

With respect to Juan Gabriel, as distinguished from the other characters, he is mentioned only once in the text, and deserves, for that reason alone, certain special consideration.

It is appropriate to begin by pointing out a parallel with Manuel: while Gloria goes out with the latter "to try to get Juan Enrique back," Valentina goes out with Juan Gabriel "to forget the dark boy." One and the other are second choices. Or, to say it in words that would provoke the anger, or at least the embarrassment, of both, Manuel and Juan Gabriel get the leftovers. Whether they are satisfied with them or not is something we cannot advance without the risk of being imprudent: in Manuel, as we've already said, there is a blur, foreign to his own will; in the summary mention of Juan Gabriel we have a mere intimation of traits.

(Incidentally, nothing is lost by adding that the manner of recording these secondary choices underscores the distinctions already made between Gloria and Valentina: Gloria enters into lateral combat in order to win her war; Valentina, on the other hand, already lost hers and wants to erase it from memory.)

At the same time, Juan Gabriel seems to share certain qualities with Juan Enrique. There is no prior knowledge on which to establish these definitively, but the fact that both have the same name of Juan powerfully attracts our attention. Question: what was in the mind of the writer when he separated and made them twins with a single stroke of the pen? To begin with, we know for certain that the name Juan has some special significance for him: perfect in its single syllable, its central vocalic precision, its swiftness, and its universal use, the name Juan, for the writer, is synonymous with quality (although daily evidence may frequently suggest the contrary). So, Juan Gabriel and Juan Enrique would be people of quality, and because of their quality, both would stand out together in the circle to which they belong, perhaps as its best achieved expression.

At the same time, to the extent to which they stand out, they move out of the circle. But Juan Gabriel moves out in still another sense, and this brings us back to Manuel. It was stated earlier that Manuel is "undoubtedly" an outsider. And it cannot escape our notice that Juan Gabriel and Manuel are names that end identically. The final syllable "el" (like the third person pronoun "él", he, the one who is not "I") thus takes on the burden of exclusion and marginality, and Juan Gabriel also becomes an outsider.

Can it be, then, that the distinctive thing about Juan Gabriel is the maximum indistinctness of the tension between two poles? If so, we would have, obviously, in Juan Gabriel, the main character of the group, the one whose history the text proposes to emphasize.

That his first entrance is limited to a brief mention is not something without classical precedents. On the contrary: it is only proper to the modesty consecrated by the tradition of the best manners.

1/10/75

ONTOLOGICAL DETERMINATION/INDETERMINATION: There is another piece of evidence that we ought to bear in mind: it is not Juan Gabriel who had decided the question for himself: Juan Gabriel appears in the text and therefore it is the text that concedes him the privilege of the brief word.

Could that be the "good" thing about Juan Gabriel? I mean his insertion in a norm of "classical" behavior. The question is appropriate: it is evident that Juan Gabriel has something "good" about him because the text itself tells us, in the most unusual of its sentences, "Juan Enrique has what's bad in me", and one can only understand this verbal monstrosity as referring to Juan Enrique as an opposite of Juan Gabriel, not as his twin. If it were this last, no doubt the text would have behaved differently, i.e., "Juan Enrique and Juan Gabriel have what's bad," or some other equivalent statement.

But let us examine the monstrosity itself: "Juan Enrique has what's bad in me." The introduction of a categorical ethical judgment—

someone has something "bad," someone is "bad"—is already disturbing, and not only because of its single direct reference to Juan Enrique: moral qualifications applied to one are spread implicitly to all. But this disturbance opens before us a vision of the abyss when we see that someone is "bad" in relation to a "me." Who is this surprising "me"? Where does he come from? At what level is he situated?

The text does not reveal the least awareness of the mess it gets into by recording this minimal particle of sound. Because the "me" refers us back to an "I" which is a model of intrepid candor: it is affirmed with absolute certainty, but God only knows where it may be. (The same goes for "Elizabeth Hagen" and Cecilia.)

ETHICAL DETERMINATION/INDETERMINATION: But let us accept provisionally that Juan Enrique has something "bad" and Juan Gabriel something "good;" in other words, according to assertions proposed from some unfathomable dimension, one is part angel, the other part devil.

Let us then see what sort of dealings they have with the world. Juan Enrique is "famous" (probably not beyond the circle of his friends and his cousins, but that's beside the point); "famous" as somebody who is "ambitious," "successful," "a sure-fire success" in "life". He values Gloria because she "admires him" and because "she will be very useful to him." We don't know which will be her major service: whether the "sex," "the interest in his things," or the "etc." We like to think that it is the "etc." because of its marvelous capacity to extend the series of services to infinity, even going so far, through gradual shifts in meaning, as to end with a complete modification of the species of what it enumerates. The "etc." is frankly seductive.

1/11/75

Unquestionably, Juan Enrique is the man who reaps the laurels. Of course, he is also the man who wants to reap the ones he doesn't: "he is somewhat envious" of Manuel's "innocence."

Juan Gabriel, on the other hand, reaps the leftovers. We have already seen that Valentina goes out with him "to try to forget the dark boy." But although it is reasonable to leave a margin for unforeseen events of some sort, this "dark boy" is not contemplated in the group, as one might say: Valentina "wants to forget him", so that his present existence is doubtful,

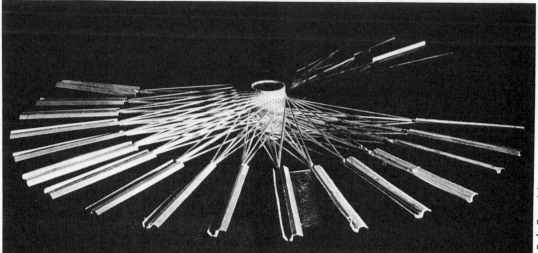

Alejandro Otero, *Another Ring for saturn*
(Model)

Paolo Gaspapini

to say the least, and would have to fade out. (In this, Juan Gabriel turns out to be more fortunate than Manuel, whose own "dark boy" is none other than Juan Enrique.) Juan Gabriel "starts" going out with Valentina for certain reasons. It is important to emphasize the temporal intention of the verb "to start." The verb describes the first of several stages in a process. We know that an apparent evil may be a blessing in disguise, just as we know that an apparent blessing may be an evil in disguise. That is, we know that things don't always turn out as it seemed they would. Life is full of surprises which elude human foresight. This apropos of what follows: we don't know why Juan Gabriel *continues* (if he does continue) to go out with Valentina, a fact that shows the possibility of developing along unforeseen lines to be latent in him.

The motives for "starting" are reduced (or expanded) to "curiosity". Since curiosity killed the cat, Juan Gabriel's latent development will not be free of danger.

Led by his curiosity, Juan Gabriel finds Valentina "interesting." What we know about her could well serve as an explanation for this: in her way and despite her youth, Valentina has "experience": she is the only character who knows something about lost illusions, who shows the traces of a frustrated project. One could say then that Juan Gabriel finds Valentina's "experience" interesting. Is this disinterested? We could easily suppose that he is interested in acquiring that experience to make it his own, in order to accelerate his own growth. What is most likely, however, is that Juan Gabriel himself is incapable of accounting

for any such ulterior motive. Perhaps the very idea of considering its mere possibility terrifies him. In any case, Juan Gabriel has bound himself to a race against time. More we cannot say.

But if the text attributes to him something "good" (by implication), it is in relation to his own lack of awareness of secondary motives; a lack of awareness that presupposes, on the part of the text, the nonexistence of such motives. That is, Juan Gabriel's goodness would lie in the gratuitousness of his acts. His interest would be disinterested. He is the object (although only in the instance of replacement) of a sexual passion—Valentina's. But it is not said that he himself experiences any sexual passion at all, nor is it said that he experiences any other type of passion. He would be, like an angel, above it.

3/23/75

SEXUAL DETERMINATION/INDETERMINA-TION: The treatment of sex characterizes on various levels. Of the three male characters, only Juan Enrique appears explicitly activated by his sexual impulses. "He goes around with Gloria," among other things, "for sex." Of Juan Gabriel, as indicated above, it is not said that he himself experiences any sexual passion at all, but the interpretation that he takes it from somebody else without having to be begged is admissible (even if we don't know for sure in what way he accepts it): Valentina starts going out with him "for sex."

The expression "for sex" is rendered only and about Juan Enrique and Valentina, for which reason we can discern a patent connection between the two. One and the other would be the only openly-sexed characters in the text and it is clear that the text does not remain impassive before the question: for a moment it calls Valentina Barbara; it tells us that Juan Enrique "has what's bad" in that "me" who has not been, (and won't so easily be) found out but who, in the final analysis, must have something bad when it is so positively affirmed. One could say, moreover, that the text applies a punitive measure for their effrontery and applies it in the very form of naming it: "for sex" is a fairly ugly expression due to the implacable coldness with which it excludes everything it does not include. Besides, it tells us that Juan Enrique "goes around" with Gloria. And the expression "to go around," in this context, doesn't bother to hide its contemptuous connotations. One guy "goes around" horny, another "goes around" only with whores, another "goes around" with the clap. With Valentina, on the other hand, it is more delicate: for her, the euphemism "to go out" is used, which points to the social externals of what two people of the opposite sex do together, indicating that they "go out", to dance, to the movies, to dine in restaurants, and carefully avoiding, out of decorum, allusion to what they do in private, which is the very opposite of going, consisting rather of coming. The difference between "to go around" and "to go out", to sum up, would be that he who "goes around" is going badly, and he who goes badly comes off badly, while he who "goes out", comes to eventual matrimonial consequences. The expression "to go out" is, in this way, more inclusive (not just anyone goes out and marries willy-nilly), and, doubtless, Valentina has been graced with it because her "paleness" and her "fleeting virginity" were borne in mind. Also, because her partner is Juan Gabriel. As far as Gloria is concerned, she "goes around" with Juan Enrique, as he with her. Her motives are well-known. Yet we can't help but consider one, which is particularly significant in relation to these lines: Gloria in interested in Juan Enrique's "things". If this were a euphemism, it wouldn't be as delicate as the one we've just examined above. Some would judge it downright obscene. In truth, we could judge it only naughty. And if it is that the text has turned naughty on us (in this rare instance), we can assume that it is due to its identification with the object that occupies it: Gloria herself must be naughty, a fact that would make her, suddenly and without our ever having suspected it, irresistibly appealing. But the text resists her, scowls, and judges harshly: she "goes around" with Juan Enrique because he is "famous" for his "successes", because it "gratifies" her "to be seen with him." For the text, thus angered, Gloria is a real bitch.

Now, when Valentina starts going out with Juan Gabriel "for sex" and "to forget the dark boy," an immediate relation between both statments is externalized. What is that relation? Without doubt, the absence of the "dark boy" has left a sexual need unsatisfied. The dark boy's things must have been as interesting to Valentina as Juan Enrique's to Gloria. Perhaps both men's things could be equally interesting to both women. We have postulated the fadeout of the dark boy. We must then postulate the exclusive permanence of Juan Enrique. With Juan Enrique the interest or effectiveness of his things is associated with a sweeping path, transgressive in a dark or perhaps perfectly clear sense. With the dark boy, the same parts are associated with "darkness," the only trait accorded his person. The text emphasizes in said trait the myth of Mediterranean virility, recorded some time ago by Plato. For Socrates, "the swarthy are of manly aspect," while "the white are children of the gods, divinely fair." *The Republic*, Book V, Section XIX, Loeb Classical Library, reed. 1963, Vol. 1, p. 513. Except if one were thinking of the Araucanian Indians, in which case the sexual transgression would be associated with a social transgression, comparable in its effects to that illustrated by Juan Enrique, thus delineating a singularly revealing and unbearable universe. To conclude: Juan Enrique's things will have to be decisive in the structure in movement of this network that is the group.

For our own uneasiness, we are not given the slightest hint of the interest Juan Gabriel's things have. It may be because of his classical modesty.

Nor of Manuel's. Let us remember that Manuel is "intelligent", "idealistic;" that is to say, a man endowed with virtues rather than things. Nevertheless, we cannot declare positively that his virtues are in fact appreciated as such. Because we are told he "is a naive fellow; intelligent, idealistic, but naive." And the reiteration of his naiveté would seem to contradict the sense of the adversative conjunction; it would seem to tell us that an intelligent man would never be idealistic if it weren't that he is naive, and doubly naive.

Finally, whether the cause of civil war is in pride, child of wealth, or in necessity, daughter of want, here there are two women for three men, and three men for two women, so we are heading for trouble. ⟐

Two Stories

ANTONIO SKARMETA

Translated by Edith Grossman

Born in Antofagasta, Chile in 1940, Antonio Skármeta was teaching Latin American Literature at the University of Chile and creative writing at the University of Chile and creative writing at the University of Santiago when Salvador Allende's government was overthrown in a military coup.

Skármeta, who now lives in West Germany, has published five collections of his own stories; El entusiasmo (1967); Desnudo en el tejado (1969), which was awarded the Casa de las Américas prize: Tiro libre (1973); El ciclista de San Cristóbal (1973); and Novios y solitarios (1975). His novel Soñé que la nieve ardía was published in Italian, French and German. Skármeta's novel for juveniles, Chilento!, translated by Hortense Carpentier, was published by William Morrow this fall.

The following stories originally appeared in Joven narrativa chilena despué del golpe, a collection of stories by Chilean writers reacting to the coup of 1973. Edited by Skármeta himself, the anthology was published in 1977 by The American Hispanist Press.

In the next issue of REVIEW, Skármeta will present a selection of new writings by Chilean authors currently living in Chile or in exile.

The Phone Call

He heard the voice on the streetcorner outside the *lycée*, and although he could not tell which of the two men had called to him, he knew they were police. As they approached him he put his right hand to the pocket with his cigarettes and made a rough calculation as to how many he must have smoked during the morning.

He had to transfer his briefcase and raincoat to shake the hand that one of them held out to him.

Despite the fact that the young man pressed his hand with a warmth that went beyond routine courtesy, the teacher trusted his forebodings.

While he endured the strange effusiveness of the clean-shaven young man, he tried to catch the eye of one student he could trust among the crowds that poured out the door of the Institute. But merely having thought something so indiscreet made it clear that he was shaken. As soon as the man let go of his hand the other one immediately grasped it—he too was clean-shaven and wore a kind of rosette in his lapel.

"Sergeant López," explained the younger man, watching him expectantly as if this whole act of smiles and handshakes had a key that the teacher should have deciphered by now. "Gentlemen," he said then, "I was already detained for a month and was freed because there was no case against me."

"Yes, Professor, yes," the nonchalant, clean-shaven young man droned in a monotone, adding a hint of understanding to his smile in the emphatic way he moved his chin up and down. And in the silence that followed he maintained his smile, as sharp as a razor, while the sergeant with the rosette folded his arms and watched the traffic on the Alameda.

"Don't you remember me, Professor?"

Wrinkling his brow the teacher tried to catch hold of something familiar in that featureless face. He pretended to think, and feeling in his jacket pocket he found his glasses and brought his right hand to his heart intending to take them out. He felt that the gesture was illegal. The sergeant could not help watching him, and it was then that the professor said:

"My glasses."

Burdened down with his leather briefcase and his raincoat, he had to bend over like an invalid to put them on. Then he stared again into the empty features of the other man.

"Come on, Prof," he said, urging him on

with a very Italian gesture, don't make me look bad."

The teacher carefully squeezed his nostrils.

"A student, right?" The young man looked with pleasure at the man he had called Sergeant and he nodded, asking for more with his eyes. "I would guess, because of your age, a student during the last five years."

"Exactly, I graduated in '70."

"'70," repeated the professor, disturbed as much by the date as by a certain intention in the young man's voice. His cheeks were burning. His face must have been as red as if he had swallowed a vinegary wine. "So many things," he heard himself saying incoherently, "one becomes old and my memory..."

"Fuentes," he interrupted, "Miguel Angel Fuentes, Number 17."

"Of course, Fuentes, Fuentes," murmured the teacher.

"In the examination I had to analyze that poem by Nicanor Parra. You always said that you were just like that character in the poem about the old teacher."

"Ah! Yes, yes, yes. Of course!"

"I was in the class that gave you the complete works of Neruda at the end of the year. Leather bound on bible paper."

"I remember, of course I remember."

"It was very nice because we all signed the first page, do you remember that?"

"Of course, Fuentes, of course!"

The sergeant nodded his head too, as if he wanted to testify to the accuracy of the professor's memory, but at the same time he was distracted—perhaps he wanted to go to the Hippodrome or the Santa Laura Stadium in one of the microbuses. The teacher felt his ankles thick and spreading, as if he were sinking into asphalt made of honey. Twice during this last silence he was on the point of putting out his right hand to show that he was in a hurry and to speed up the denouement. But on both occasions the glances exchanged between the sergeant and the clean-shaven man stopped him—it was as if they had nudged each other or exchanged small, imperfect signals.

Their courtesy was infinite, charged with premonitions, blind and imprecise.

"And Neruda died!" Fuentes went on, shaking his head. "You never can tell! A very good poet, don't you think so, señor?"

"Very good, yes, very good."

"The Nobel Prize, too."

The old teacher noted a warning in the corners of the young man's mouth. I smoked five cigarettes in class and one during the break, he thought. There are fourteen left, only fourteen. He anticipated their plan of attack: first weakening his defenses, then taking his

measure, wounding him, and finally closing in. Thirteen, he thought, when the sergeant raised his hand to give him a light.

"I was already detained," the teacher exhaled along with the smoke. "I was interrogated. There was no case, Fuentes."

"Yes, I know, Professor. How could I not know about you when I was in your class for a whole year!" He placed a sincere hand over his heart and gave a grave, ceremonial weightiness to his chin. "It's just routine, no need to be alarmed. Every once in a while the sergeant and I take a little walk around here. No problems with you, Professor. Right, Sergeant?"

"No problems."

The clean-shaven young man offered him his hand along with his sincere look, and when his palm pressed against the old teacher's he put his left hand over both of them. Fraternal, in a fraternal way. The sergeant only said "Pleased to meet you."

As he crossed the street the professor transferred the briefcase full of student papers to his right hand and dried the perspiration on his hands by wiping them against his raincoat.

In the Indianapolis he squeezed the yellow plastic slug before he went to exchange it for coffee. He moved it in his fist intently, as if it were a die, and then he quickly gave a coin to the cashier and his voice sounded hoarse as he asked for a slug for the telephone. He put it into his fist along with the one for coffee, and he looked for a place at the table next to the telephone. He hung up his raincoat and put down his briefcase. Although he didn't use sugar he stirred the coffee a good deal before deciding to taste it. As he brought the cup to his lips the steam clouded his glasses, and he took the first sip with his eyes tightly closed.

When he took out his handkerchief to clean them off his body turned slightly to the right, and that was when he saw the fat man, hardly a meter away, with Las últimas noticias opened to the racing page.

He finished wiping his glasses, he raised them to the sunlight that filtered through a discolored brown curtain, and he even improved upon the transparency of one lens by removing a tiny bit of dust just below the frame.

Then he finished the rest of his coffee in one swallow, and since he knew with absolute certainty that his intuition was infallible, he picked up his raincoat and the briefcase and didn't make the phone call. 🦅

Man with Carnation in His Mouth

I feel yearnings, desires,
But not with my whole being.
In my soul something
Cold, heavy, mute,
Something is always there.

—*Fernando Pessoa*

The girl walked past the trees with the urgent speed of a woman alone in a public place—dignified, cautious, distracted, as if being alone were shameful and the mouths of all the men were ready to kiss her neck or nibble her lips.

She assumed the appearance of someone with a destination until she had crossed the width of the square. When she reached the other side she stopped, permitting herself the luxury of a long sigh. Her shoulders lost their rigidity, her chin was lowered by a smile, and her elbows loosened with a gesture of self-encouragement. Once again she had surprised in herself the child of tensions and formalities which she scorned—self-consciousness, the misery of expressions applied to her face as if they were make-up, the egotism of useless dignity. She thought: "That's how I walked home from school, that's how I went to the movies on Sunday, that's how we all walked. As if being alone had turned us into prostitutes."

The men and women in the square raised their wrists and concentrated on the time. They compared watches, they peered down side streets, they looked at the sky waiting for all that restlessness to fasten onto something. They were together, but in the way people are together when a lively party is over: they toy with the arm of the phonograph when there is no music left that could possibly make anyone happy. There were only seconds to go and, like someone dropping a letter into a mailbox, nobody wanted to let the year go.

They looked at the corners again. They kept looking up at the sky, they raised their wrists to their ears, and the girl felt the flower behind her ear trembling with the breeze they created.

Then she knew there was a man standing behind her.

And at the very moment when everyone embraced, she also knew that he was the one who embraced her: not with the frontal, strident, emphatic embrace of the New Year, but with half an embrace, a suggestion of an embrace, like someone leaning on a familiar shoulder, but gently, as if he knew that the shoulder was fragile.

She wanted to hold on to the ignorant, merry silence, to remain a prisoner in that anonymous capture, to surrender to the rest of the scene: the other people, the decorations of unreal lights, the city, Portugal and the galaxy, but she had already turned her head and was looking curiously, with some tension in her eyes, at the features of the boy who only gave her a distracted, relaxed, casual smile as if he had been leaning on her shoulder for three nights now and, bored with chatting, had devoted himself to consideration of the small eccentricities of the passersby, their shouts and greetings, as if he were a connoisseur of shouts and greetings.

With a good deal of dexterity the young man curved his tongue around the stem of the carnation that he had in his mouth, and with a strange pirouette he rolled it to the left-hand corner. He held it there with a tightened jaw.

That was when the girl mentally censored her "Happy New Year" and let her own words speak for her.

"By the way, that's my shoulder," she said.

"Yes, I know," mumbled the young man (younger than she was), without looking at her (but getting ready to look at her). "I leaned on yours because mine doesn't interest me anymore."

In order to speak to her he had to hold the stem of the carnation between his teeth. She raised her free hand and tapped the flower with her finger.

"It seems you're a vegetarian."

"No, I don't eat them. I just leave them there in my mouth."

The crowd in the square surged feverishly toward the corner on the left. From a side street, preceded by horns blowing in time to the refrain "A people united can never be defeated" came a column of students and workers. They let themselves be carried by the movement of the crowd down the narrow street until they had joined the front ranks of the march. An old man with a pointed nose, thick glasses and a noticeable limp held the pole of an enormous red flag. Although the people applauded him enthusiastically as he passed, the man seemed removed, surrounded by his own halo of small glory, hearing a symphony composed just for him.

They marched a little in front of him without letting go of each other, while in the square they were singing rounds to the beat of that same refrain. There were bottles bubbling over everywhere. They were passed out of car windows or brought in by men on bicycles decked out in flags. The popping of champagne corks stood out from the sound of shouts, songs and horns carried by a breeze that was almost warm, just as if it weren't winter.

The young man moved her toward the Piquinique Restaurant, and motioned for her to sit at the snack bar. They asked for two sandwiches and a good red wine.

"Well," he said, "my name is Jorge."

"Carmen," said the girl.

They shook hands and waited for the wine in silence, glancing at each other with amused smiles and vague gestures. She concluded that it wasn't the young man's style to ask questions, although it certainly was hers. But in the end she didn't ask any questions either. When the wine arrived they drank the first glass with the speed of accomplices. The girl savored the taste and the warmth inside her cheek. He collapsed with laughter onto the counter and hid his face in his arms. He shook for a few moments while she poured two more glasses of wine and then he raised his head, wiping his damp cheeks. He put the carnation in the space between his irregular front teeth and nodded to himself, making the effort not to laugh anymore.

"I'm very happy," he said in Spanish.

"That's obvious," said the girl.

"I was in jail for a year. My old man was in jail for five years until he escaped. He died in France."

With her eyebrows the girl invited him to raise his glass. The steaming sandwiches were put on the counter and they ate them hungrily. When there were only a few scattered crumbs left and the waiter had emptied the bottle into their glasses with professional skill, the boy said:

"Now I'll pay and we'll go home. You'll go to bed with me.

He waited for her reaction to the news with excessive attention—not his style. He stretched his lips until she could see all his teeth crowned by the red carnation in the space in the middle.

"I don't want to," said the girl.

"Don't you like me?"

"No, it's not that: I do like you."

"Then what is it?"

"I don't want to."

The young man pulled his hair.

"It's that you're angry with me because I didn't take the carnation out of my face."

She was sorry there was nothing left in her glass. The young man passed her his, and the girl took a sip, suddenly serious. She picked up a crumb with one finger and put it in the palm of her other hand.

"I made a promise when fascism fell that I would spend all of New Year's Eve with a carnation in my mouth," he said, gently picking at his ear. "I can go to bed with you but I won't be able to kiss you or anything because of this little problem."

The girl scratched her head. She knew that in the way she smiled and looked at him, she was disappointing him.

"I can't," she said.

The young man paid the bill, pulling wrinkled bills of small denominations out of his pocket.

They walked without touching among the remains of noisy demonstrations and repeated slogans in a silence which he accentuated with his bent head and his hands thrust deep into his pockets. A few meters from the hotel the girl decided to offer him some consolation.

"I have a five-year-old son. He's with me in the room."

He kicked an imaginary ball and shrugged his shoulders.

"And your husband's there too?"

"No. I'm a widow."

"And so?"

They were at the door. She said:

"Good night."

He said:

"Good night."

And he turned a rounded back to her.

The last thing the girl saw was the color of his tousled hair as it blended in with a No. 11 Graça streetcar that was chugging away at the corner. She took out a cigarette dexterously and lit it with precision.

The maid was in the bed reading a love story.

"Everything was fine, Señora," she said in anticipation. "Just perfect."

"He didn't wake up?"

"He didn't even move."

"I don't know how to thank you."

"Please, Señora. Was the square nice?"

"Yes," she said.

"Did you take a little walk?"

"Yes."

"New Year, new life, right?"

"It was very nice."

The maid yawned involuntarily and tried to hide it by humming a little song. The girl unbuttoned her blouse and put her cigarette on the edge of the ashtray.

"What time do you leave?"

"10:00. Wake me at 8:00, please."

"Certainly. And where are you going Señora?"

"To Rumania."

In the doorway the girl clasped the woman's hand.

"You've been very nice. I'm grateful."

"See you tomorrow, Señora."

The maid went downstairs and made preparations for putting out the light at the reception desk. She had just locked the vestibule when she saw a young man with a carnation in his mouth peering in through the street door. Without knocking he motioned to her with a bent finger to raise the latch. With curiosity and some reservations the woman put her ear to the door.

"A señorita," the young man said through the glass. "I don't remember her name. The one with the little boy."

"Yes," said the maid, "the Chilean."

The young man looked at her gravely and blinked rapidly. With a clumsy gesture he tried to smooth back the hair that fell over his forehead, but couldn't.

"That's right," he said. "The Chilean. I have to go up to see her."

"She's already gone to bed."

"That's all right. It doesn't matter. Open the door."

The maid lifted the latch and the young man climbed up the first few stairs.

"Look, she's probably sleeping."

"Which room?" called the young man from the second floor.

"Eleven," said the maid, walking over to the staircase.

The young man knocked at the door but he didn't wait for an answer. He turned the knob and burst into the room. The girl was naked except for the underpants that she was slipping down over her hips. Without hesitating the young man came toward her and took the flower out of his mouth. He put it in the vase, next to the other carnation. He looked at the young woman's small breasts and stuck his hands back into his pockets.

"All right," he said before he left the room, be a little clearer next time." 🌎

Setúbal, Portugal, 1976

Translator's note: According to the author, the carnation was the symbol of the revolt against the fascists in Portugal.

Introducing Darío Restrepo Soto

THOMAS HOEKSEMA

Introduced and translated by

Thomas Hoeksema

Darío Restrepo Soto was born in Cartago, Colombia in 1943. He currently lives in Medellín, Colombia where he combines a writing career with a job installing and repairing appliances. He had intended to pursue a technical career, preferably in electronics, but had to forego these plans due to singular difficulties with mathematics. However, he retains a strong interest in the literature of science, especially the science fiction of Ray Bradbury, and the "Gothic literature" of H.P. Lovecraft.

Darío Restrepo began writing as a child and has persevered in it to the extent that his various occupations have permitted. He has published in various reviews and literary supplements throughout Colombia, including *Mágazín Dominical, El Espectador, Hora del Mundo, Universidad y Cultura, Unaula* and *Clave de Sol.* Currently, he is preparing a book of short stories and a novella for publication.

Darío Restrepo cites as profound influences on his work, the fiction of William Faulkner, Malcolm Lowry, and Samuel Beckett. Of the contemporary Latin American writers, he prefers the work of Julio Cortázar and Gabriel García Márquez. Reflecting on the extent of influences in his work, Darío Restrepo stated that "the principal task of the writer, and also the most difficult, is to free himself as much as possible from influences, and initiate 'his own search'."

The publication of "Isabel" marks the first appearance of Darío Restrepo Soto in English translation. 🌎

THOMAS HOEKSEMA teaches English at New Mexico State University, Las Cruces. He has translated poetry by Isabel Fraire and José Emilio Pacheco, among others.

Isabel

DARIO RESTREPO SOTO

Translated by Thomas Hoeksema

Weary of enduring a miserable life, I sought employment with a respectable company, and immediately upon entering, the secretary addressed me with some coarse flattery, but the worst thing was that I had to wait a long time, seated in a red chair, beneath her penetrating eyes which did not leave me for an instant, as if they had burned traces on my clothes, which I had washed and ironed carefully the previous night, and, in order to avoid her gaze, to feel, in a manner of speaking, alone, I had to turn my attention to the magazines that overflowed the small table with their accounts of persecution, atrocities and massacres, meanwhile the time passed, the time passed and I felt my discomfort increasing, because few situations can be worse than seeking employment for the first time, intruding on a totally strange world, and nothing was more unusual than the red antechamber where the grillwork of a ventilator glowed brightly, quiet in the ceiling, except for an occasional humming that seemed to be diminishing, and I, raising my head each time, saw only a trembling as if a finger or some similar object were obstructing the mechanism, and then, lowering my eyes, I had to rest them for an instant on those of the secretary who now displayed a large, red tongue dangling outside her mouth, a tongue I scarcely believed could exist, and again turning to the magazines, to the notices marked off by white and gray photographs, I passed over, inadvertently, the same account two or three times when a shrill voice called me from the interior of the adjoining office, that is, the office off the antechamber, and said, come in Miss, and the secretary, confirming the request, said, he's talking to you, Miss, please go in, and she gave me a last look, a final smile, and a parting grimace I would say, because her tongue still hung far outside her mouth reaching toward her upper lip, and, stifling nausea, I stood up and moved rapidly through the half-opened little door, proceeded over the carpeted floor to where a fat, short man was seated at a desk with his hand extended, and I offered my hand in return be-

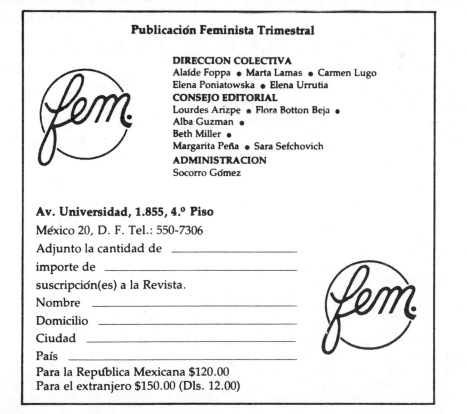

cause I had heard that it was proper, and observed with horror that my right hand was missing, my distress being greater since that was the first time I realized it, that is, so many years living without a hand, the most important one, and only now did I come to miss it, and since the air conditioner poured cool air between the curtains, I took advantage of it to observe how hot it was outside, my dear, and extending rapidly the left hand, and seating myself in the leather chair that was at the front of the desk, I related some amusing things, things I had learned from a child, little songs and things like that, not giving him time to reflect on my defect, an intention that most certainly I seemed to have succeeded in because he began the questions, the tests, and at that point one had to react quickly since there was only a short pause from one question to the next, which caused, when I delayed a little, when I vacillated, two or three questions to run together, depending on my slowness and his speed, which was doubled at every opportunity, although I believe, considering it all, that the interview proceeded very well, since the man's face revealed a sincere interest and I said to myself, the job's mine, I will be like common, ordinary people, those that I view with envy every morning, and I am through with sleeping amid garbage cans and being abused every minute by beggars, and also, at times, by members of high society, many of whom gladly pick among the rubbish, everything was going, I repeat, according to my desire, and even more so when he directed me to stand, to confront the most important part of the interview, the formal ritual of the departure, and I realized I was lacking legs, a defect which, joined to that of my right hand, transformed me into a despicable being, an invalid of the lowest state, and again I reproached myself and cursed myself a thousand times for not carefully considering these matters before, and I scratched my face with my only hand until feeling an intense burning, which I always do in moments of extreme misery, and because of which, I imagine my face is not very pleasing to see, I scratched my face, I say, which is not pleasing to look at, I groaned, I reclined deeply in the chair, groaning, and my two stumps waved in the air, the remains of my shattered thighs was the last thing I saw when the chair collapsed, and then with a rapid motion in the air, the blow, absorbed by the carpet, the open roof, and the plump hands of the man, the hands of that fat man probing among my clothes, which the night before had been washed and ironed most carefully, while his tongue, very red and large, hung, flaccid, within a few inches of my face, and I who had always feared that a tongue would enter my mouth, deep into my throat, choking me, tried to avoid it, without failing at the same time, to be alert for whatever question could be put to me, because I still had a faint hope of obtaining that job, and it would be unforgiveable to spoil everything at the last moment through inattention on my part.

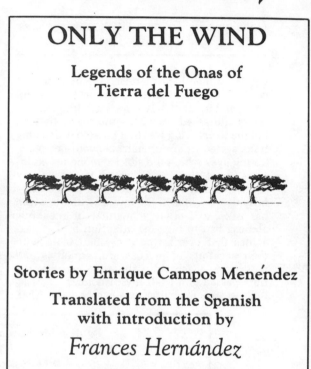

For a Small Tribute to

Guillaume
Apollinaire

OCTAVIO ARMAND

Translated by Carol Maier

F

or what is dust along the road
But ashes of the dead?

1

Apollinaire wrote erotic novels and a Pythagorean poem—quality in quantity, the lithic in the sycaleiptic—on the number 69.

2

He had an eye for appearances and the reverberation between image and object. Also for names and the reverberation between word and thing. For example, it's possible to borrow this compliment from him: Linda, I speak a truth every time I say your name.

3

A poetry of sight. And of play. But of *play played out*. Magic: myriad of images: mirage: the baroque. As if the eye were a law of capricious symmetry and what it observes added a scandalous healthy arbitrariness.

4

Because reality is a scandal if our eyelids (don't) erase it. Eyelids: the implacable bourgeoise of the eye until surrealism did away with the dream as bureaucracy and gave in to the dream as liberation. A science of the eye, grounded more in Freud than *The Dioptrics*. Ocular and oracular. Ontology and optics: presence. A tautology that sums up, always awkwardly, certain laws of identity. I am referring to the true lens of images, imagination. Len(til)s = sense(less). As if to say: the eye's eye.*

> Lower your other eyelid
> Neither because of the sun nor because
>   of the land
> But for this oblong fire whose intensity
>   will increase
> Until one day it becomes the only light

*Look out! The following visual information will appear in this essay either by photographic reproduction or the reader's imagination. There is a passive reader, an active reader and a Kodak reader. (1) The drawing of Guillaume Apollinaire, Artilleur. (2) Apollinaire with his head bandaged. (3) Saint Sebastian. (4) *The Assassinated Poet*, cover by Cappiello. (5) A sea-urchin. (6) A leper. (7) The calligram "Heart Crown and Mirror," which up-dates the tradition of the *inhabited mirror* and complements the fourteenth fragment of this tribute.

5

I(S(L(A(N(D(S=E)Y)E)L)I)D)S)

6

It was Apollinaire—in a poetic drama—who launched the word *surrealist*. The work: *Les Mamelles de Tirésias. Drame surréaliste en deux actes et un prologue.* Male and female, blindman and seer. Tirésias, prophet. Tirésias, surrealism. Along with the gift of that word, Apollinaire suggested its context. The word as parable. Surrealism is an excess. Not a plague, although at times it may have been/ may be a plague. Not a plagiarism, although at times it may have been/ may be a plagiarism. Excess: reality as scandal.

7

> This is the law of the plague of leprosy in a garment of woollen or linen, either in the warp, or woof, or any thing of skins, to pronounce it clean, or to pronounce it unclean.
>
> *Leviticus 13:59*

8

An esthetic of surface that is not a superficial esthetic. An esthetic of reaction that is not a reactionary esthetic. Revolution of the surface: revelation.

9

When I think about the poet of *Alcools* or *Poèmes à Madeleine*, I think of half an orange. Of colors breaking from things, bombarding us, rescuing us from all the monopolies of habit and death. I think of L,I,N,D,A: name/ image/lover. Of the sun, of naked gods, oneirocriticism. I remember that my terrible, childish calligraphy was highly expressive and find that his Calligrams, a childlike and genial reversal of my infantile awkwardness, also express me. His words are like thoroughly visual bridges, joyously syllogistic. His mind: joyous; his rhymes, visual. His poetry, a great Mirabeau bridge. All of us who cross it carry less death to the other side. Because Apollinaire pulls children from our heads as the magician pulls rabbits out of his hat. Which proves that we are old pretentious top hats

and that **(1)** nevertheless
        (2) therefore

children and rabbits are still possible. I am a top hat.

I am   **(1)** a child,
      (2) or a rabbit,   whatever the *assassinated poet* says.
      (3) or a poem,

Cartesian logic in dizzy, radiant reverse. The *trompe-l'oeil* as mirror. The top hat as a head now openly irrevocable, rhapsodic, more

> **TRUTH WILL ALWAYS BE NEW.**

inclined to the rituals of Malabar than to stupidity or headache.

10

In his *Calligrammes* Apollinaire shows—demonstrates—an *excess of surface*. He shows us that the poem can be departure/deployment, thus freeing us from a profundity which is above all descent, collapse, gravity. There are alternatives. It is possible to enter matter through its surface, which is like arriving at logic through paradox, or to remain on the surface. Extasis of extension against extasis of intensity. It now occurs to me—surprise/analogy—, that leprosy also is an excess of surface and that, as such, it provokes an inverted extasis of extension: disgust. What's certain, however, is the leper's attraction. Of course disgust is fascinating. It does not seem possible that a human being could be present in such

---

> **GUILLAUME WHAT HAS HAPPENED TO YOU**
> **I AM LAZARUS ENTERING THE TOMB**

---

excess. But he is, as if buried in his own skin, dead on the surface. Leper: Narcissus. Here again, the *trompe-l'oeil* as mirror. Like a mummy without a pyramid or death, the leper also shows us—demonstrates—something of our destiny. He is a Calligram. It does not seem possible that a poem could be present in that double excess—of means/of meaning—which is the Calligram. But the poem is there, as if pierced by its own visibility. (All this: a parable about the baroque.)

11

Calligram: leprosy. Apollinaire: an accursed poet.

> **How frightening to see yourself outlined in the agates of Saint Vitus**
> **You were extremely sad the day you saw yourself in them**
> **Looking like Lazarus dazed by daylight**

A poet of reverberations. Wilhelm de Kostrowitzky and Guillaume Apollinaire. Guillaume Macabre and Louise Lalanne: male and female: Tirésias. That double LL binds him to Tragedy and the Comics: the double LL is also Superman's girlfriend. It's forward and reverse: Croniamantal and Latnamainorc. Kostro: artilleryman and poet (Apollonian (and Dionysiac (Pythagorean (and Priapean). An assassinated poet.

12

> **What doubtless remained longer than leprosy, and would persist when the lazar houses had been empty for years, were the values and images attached to the figure of the leper as well as the meaning of his exclusion, the social importance of that insistent and fearful figure which was not driven off without first being inscribed within a sacred circle.**
>
> Foucault: *Madness and Civilization*

13

> **Mme. de Kostrowitzky et Weil occupaient maintenant au Vésinet une grande villa où Angelica faisait régner la violence et le désordre, terrorisant son amant et sons fils qui, régulièrement domicilié chez elle, passait souvent la nuit dans des hôtels de la gare Saint-Lazare.**
>
> André Billy: *Oeuvres Poétiques d'Apollinaire*

(Three Mirrors)

The mirror is a plagiarism: it steals our faces. A masked man hides from his face: he covers it. A facetious one hides from his face: he takes it off. The mirror steals our faces—effaces us—by multiplying them. Narcissus repeatedly condemns himself to life disguise: mask, facetiousness, mirror. Text, surface and relation in the following mirrors owe a great deal to Baudelaire, Apollinaire and Claude Lorrain. One surface is denied from excess, another from insufficiency, a third from symmetry. Narcissus—he/I/you—dies on each of these surfaces: celebrated/egoistic/fascinating.

* * *

VIOLENCE / DISORDER / EXCLUSION / LAZARUS /

Vrorrim	mirror	mirror	mirror	mirror/
Vrorrim	mirror	mirror	mirror	mirror/
Vrorrim	mirror	mirror	mirror	mirror/
Vrorrim	mirror	mirror	mirror	mirror/
Vrorrim	mirror	mirror	mirror	mirror/
Vrorrim	mirror	mirror	mirror	mirror/
Vrorrim	mirror	mirror	mirror	mirror/
Vrorrim	mirror	mirror	mirror	mirror/
Vrorrim	mirror	mirror	mirror	mirror/
Vrorrim	mirror	mirror	mirror	mirror/
Vrorrim	mirror	mirror	mirror	mirror/
Vrorrim	mi	GUILLAUME MACABRE		rro/
Vrorrim	mirror	mirror	mirror	mirror/
Vrorrim	mirror	mirror	mirror	mirror/
Vrorrim	mirror	mirror	mirror	mirror/
Vrorrim	mirror	mirror	mirror	mirror/
Vrorrim	mirror	mirror	mirror	mirror/
Vrorrim	mirror	mirror	mirror	mirror/
Vrorrim	mirror	mirror	mirror	mirror/
Vrorrim	mirror	mirror	mirror	mirror/
Vrorrim	mirror	mirror	mirror	mirror/
Vrorrim	mirror	mirror	mirror	mirror/

VIOLENCE / DISORDER / EXCLUSION / LAZARUS /

***Dear reader: (1) Put me in the mirror. As imitation, literature will reveal its more sinister nature: facetiousness. Because you look for yourself in that literature and find only the opacity of an insistent but alien I. Don't give up. (2) Put yourself in the mirror. Verisimilitude: use inverse symmetry, ЯƎᗡАƎЯ. The mirror isn't enough, is it? (3) Break the mirror.

15

In this day and age it's not easy to allude to the possible force of the *accursed poet*. That tradition seems worn out; and the imperialism of analysis seems to guarantee its discontinuity. It is more probable now that the marked be marketed; that the leprosy be lucrative; that accursed poets be candidates for one prize or another. In *The Assassinated Poet*—poetic autobiography, allegory on allegory/ a very twentieth century *Divine Comedy*—, which is to say, in the very book that suggests the presence of the accursed poet in the assassinated poet, the following warning appears.

> Today poets are only good for taking money they don't earn since they no longer work at all and the majority of them (except the songsters and a few others) have no talent and therefore no excuse. As for those who have a bit of ability, they're even more infuriating, for even if they come to nothing or no one, they make more noise than a regiment and badger us with complaints of their own accursedness. There is no longer any reason for all these people.

Nevertheless, the death of Croniamantal (and Apollinaire) seems to belie the implacable logic of cynicism and analysis. Poetry against Prose. The death of the Artilleryman/ Poet is certainly grotesque; no less so the murder of Croniamantal/ Latnamainorc. If leprosy's black tradition is suggested in the final image (photo) left by the former, the final scene (image) of the latter, de(scribed) as if with a sea-urchin, with bristling, recalls the black, hair-raising prose of Lautréamont.

> Then some men in the crowd shouted: "Shut up, you scum! Step back, ladies!"
> The women moved aside quickly and a man balancing an enormous knife on the flat of his hand threw it so it landed in Croniamantal's open mouth. Other men did the same. The knives stuck in his stomach and chest, and soon there was nothing left on the ground but a corpse covered with spines like the shell of a sea-urchin.

Leprosy: scum. An excess of surface: a corpse covered with spines like the shell of a sea-urchin. Prose: poetry.

16

"I have to sculpt him a statue, a profound statue in nothing, like poetry and glory." This small tribute to Guillaume Apollinaire, like the statue in nothing that the Bird of Benin sculpts to Croniamantal—a statue in nothing is and is not an empty statue—is a hole just the size of his spirit.

17

He was capable of the Bestiary and the Dictionary, medieval world and Renaissance world, symbol and definition. But his Dictionary—of theatrical vocabulary, for example—is more like Bierce than Menéndez Pidal. And his Bestiary is sometimes laced with a certain black humor, a certain Umour. Which is logical. His Bestiary is from this century which (1) tames the bestiality of the unconscious through analysis and (2) ridicules the bestiality of beasts with zoos. Today's true Bestiaries are the Rorschach blots—the great octopus/the great leprosy—or language itself when it turns from the intentionally confessional and reveals the unconfessable.

(1)

> **THE OCTOPUS**
> **Throwing its ink toward the sky,**
> **Sucking blood from what it loves**
> **And enjoying the taste,**
> **That most cruel monster is me.**

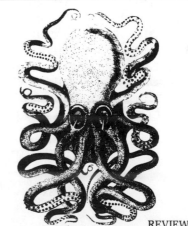

THE LION
Oh lion, unhappy reflection
Of unfortunate, fallen kings,
Now you are born only in cages
In Hamburg, among Germans!

18

**THE BESTIARY ACCORDING
TO FOUCAULT:**
In medieval thought, the legions of animals, which Adam had named for eternity, symbolically represent human values. But at the beginning of the Renaissance, relations with animality are inverted; the beast is freed; he escapes from the world of legend and moral illustration to acquire something fantastic, peculiar to him. Through a surprising inversion, it will now be animals who spy on man, possess him, reveal to him his own truth.

19

I have seen a few photos and drawings of Apollinaire. One drawing shows the Artilleur Guillaume de Kostrowitzky in 1914, surrounded by his pipe, saber and cannon. Everything in this ingenuous drawing tends toward the symbolic. Contemporary perspective is not spatial but analytic; not the work of painters but scientists. For that reason, this ingenuous drawing, pursued relentlessly by analytic perspective, tends decisively toward the symbolic. It has a Priapean theme. But within that sym-

IT WAS THE YEAR OF THE UNIVERSAL EXPOSITION, AND THE NEWLY BORN EIFFEL TOWER GREETED THE HEROIC BIRTH OF CRONIAMANTAL WITH A SPLENDID ERECTION.

bolic tendency there is an explicit symbol which paradoxically—in 1914—does not turn from the strictly concrete and everyday. Artilleryman Kostrowitzky is dressed in his uniform. A photo, taken later, will show a variation of this drawing, this uniform. Its reverse. Or more precisely, its negative. Kostro, as he was known to some of his friends, has his head bandaged picturesquely. The soldier is now wounded. At 4:00 on the afternoon of March 17, 1916, while reading the *Mercure de France,* he had been seriously wounded in the head. A trepanation was later performed to relieve pressure on his brain. Through the bandages—negative of his shattered helmet/ of his uniform—seeps the excess of surface mentioned earlier. Among those bandages Kostro seems delirious. As if his throat has been slit. A *beheaded sun.* The Adamic poet changed into John the Baptist. It is not difficult to imagine this: he also looks like a leper. One of those

**ABOVE ALL,
ARTISTS ARE MEN WHO WANT
TO BECOME INHUMAN.**

lepers who layer patches of cloth on their broken skin until they become premature mummies, doubly detested Pharaohs. That photo then is like the mummy of a mummy. From drawing to photo/from uniform to bandage/ from Kostrowitzky to Apollinaire/ from poet to soldier/ from soldier to wounded soldier/ to leper/ to assassinated poet. Metaphors upon metaphors. Mummies of mummies. An excess of surface. Metaphors from Apollinaire, who made metaphors from typography. His Calligrams: a kaleidescope of words. The poet is a small god. The magic of the poet is analogous to the miracle of the gods.

> **He is a leprous man, he is unclean: the priest shall pronounce him utterly unclean; his plague is in his head.**
> Leviticus 13:44

20

> **And the Lord said furthermore unto him, Put now thine hand into thy bosom. And he put his hand into his bosom: and when he took it out, behold, his hand was leprous as snow.**
> **And he said, Put thine hand into thy bosom again. And he put his hand into his bosom again; and plucked it out of his bosom, and behold, it was turned again as his other flesh.**
> Exodus 4:6-7

21

FLASH
CURIOUS COINCIDENCES IN THE
LIFE OF KOSTROWITZKY

At the very moment they were opening the head of the inventor of the word surrealist, his poetic biography, the Assassinated Poet appeared. On the cover, designed by Cappiello: a figure with his head bloodied. Title of the last section of Calligrams, by the same author: "The Star-Studded Head."

22

Wizard: exorcises punctuation and traces its configurations, like a mandala. From the gestures, rhymes and rhythms of orality to the simultaneity of figurative writing. A modern poet. But there is a medieval presence in the visuality of his Calligrams. The autographic is a great leap toward the past: to the monastery, the manuscript. Kaleidoscopic perspective, the autographic/figurative typography that lets us see the poem in/through the words—like *illuminations,* according to Rimbaud's Anglicism—, have the capacity for diffusion and mystery of great stained glass windows. The book as cathedral. The Calligrams achieve from without, or from their typo (topo) graphy, what Rimbaud's Illuminations achieve from within. Moreover: they achieve from without exactly what they achieve from within: surpass as surface, surprise with tautologies.

Thanks to Guillaume Apollinaire it will be possible to say that our century had its jugglers. At least one. Certainly: a very modern juggler. A juggler of technology, of typography. *Minstrel* and *grand master of troubadours.* With him, the functional achieves a surprising expressivity and Gutenberg's invention seems like a poetics. With him every city is Paris and Villon still walks them all. Thanks

> **MEN OF THE FUTURE DON'T FORGET**
> **ME**
> **I LIVED AT THE TIME OF THE LAST**
> **KINGS**

to the *assassinated poet* and some other martyrs of the word—I'm thinking of the Boustrophedon of a Cuban novelist, a certain Orator of Ionesco—the faith lives on. That faith is language when it is something more than a great lie. A faith with its relics, its engravings. One of them—a verbal Saint Sebastian—looks like a sea-urchin. If we move closer, we'll see Croniamantal. An open mouth and a knife. No: a mouth full of knife. That mouth, open or full of knife, still has something to tell us.

Selected Poems
GONZALO ROJAS

Translated by Christopher Maurer

Selected by Octavio Armand, these works by Gonzalo Rojas, who was born in Chile in 1917, comprise part of the anthology of Latin American Poetry that began appearing in REVIEW 21/22 and will be published eventually as a book with the support of the Center for Inter-American Relations

THE LITERATI

They prostitute it all,
   they spend their soul in talking round,
explain it all, talk on and on
like oiled machines,
stain everything drooling their metaphysics.

I would like to see them on the southern seas
one night of royal wind, their heads
empty in the cold, smelling
the world's loneliness
with no moon,
no explanation,
smoking in helpless terror.

LOS LETRADOS

Lo prostituyen todo
con su ánimo gastado en circunloquios.
Lo explican todo. Monologan
como máquinas llenas de aceite.
Lo manchan todo con su baba metafísica.

Yo los quisiera ver en los mares del sur
una noche de viento real, con la cabeza
vaciada en frío, oliendo
la soledad del mundo,
sin luna,
sin explicación posible,
fumando en el terror del desamparo.

BED WITH MIRRORS

That mandarin did it all on this bed with two mirrors, two mirrors:
   he made love, he had the arrogance
to believe himself immortal, and lying here he watched his face between his feet
and the bottom mirror gave him back the face of the visible;
and so he developed a thesis between two half-lights: the upper
against the lower, and reclining almost in the air
he came to build his great wooden flight.

The shrillness of the days and the dry dust of the functionary
were no match for the portentous spell:
ideograms of flesh, butterflies of different wires, many and many
were the daughters of heaven consumed in the flames
of these two lewd sleepwalking mirrors
disposed in the intimacy of two meters, closed one upon the other:
the one so that the other might tell the other that the One is the Beginning.
Neither the yinn nor the yang nor sperm alternating with breath
took him from this liturgy, swift were the scenes
in the stillness of the paroxysm: shining the black ship sailed
in its oils and the canvas of its varnishes,
and a current of the air of angels went from the Height to the Depths
without noticing that the Depths were the Height for the brain
of the mandarin. Neither the yinn nor the yang, and this gets lost in the Origin.

CAMA CON ESPEJOS

Ese mandarín hizo de todo en esta cama con espejos, con
                                    [dos espejos:
hizo el amor, tuvo la arrogancia
de creerse inmortal, y tendido aquí miró su rostro por los
                                    [pies,
y el espejo de abajo le devolvió el rostro de lo visible;
así desarrolló una tesis entre dos luces: el de arriba
contra el de abajo, y acostado casi en el aire
llegó a la construcción de su gran vuelo de madera.

La estridencia de los días y el polvo seco del funcionario
no pudieron nada contra el encanto portentoso:
ideogramas carnales, mariposas de alambre distinto, fueron
                                    [muchas y muchas
las hijas del cielo consumidas entre las llamas
de aquestos dos espejos lascivos y sonámbulos
dispuestos en lo íntimo de dos metros, cerrados el uno contra
                                    [el otro:
el uno para que el otro le diga al otro que el Uno es el
                                    [Principio.

Ni el yinn ni el yang, ni la alternancia del esperma y de la
                                    [respiración
lo sacaron de esta liturgia, las escenas eran veloces
en la inmovilidad del paroxismo: negro el navío navegaba
lúcidamente en sus aceites y el velamen de sus barnices,
y una corriente de aire de ángeles iba de lo Alto a lo Hondo
sin reparar en que lo Hondo era lo Alto para el seso
del mandarín. Ni el yinn ni el yang, y esto se pierde en el
                                    [Origen.

LATIN AND JAZZ

In the same air I read my Catullus and listen to Louis Armstrong, again I listen to him
in the improvisation of the sky, the angels fly
in the august Latin of Rome with their free, slow trumpets
in a chord now timeless, in the hum
of arteries and petals so that I can go in the torrent with the waves
that come out of this chair, this table, this matter
that is me and my body in the minute of this chance
to which I tie the wind of these syllables.

It is the birth, the openness of sound, the splendor
of movement, crazy the circle of the senses, the suddenness
of this harsh smell of sacrifical blood: Rome
and Africa, opulence and the whip, the fascination
of leisure and the bitter stroke of the oars, the frenzy
and the sad fortune of empires, vaticination
or death-snore: this is jazz,
the ecstasy
before the crash, Armstrong; this is the ecstasy,
my Catullus,
                    Thanatos!

LATIN Y JAZZ

Leo en un mismo aire a mi Catulo y oigo a Louis Armstrong,
                                                    [lo reoigo
en la improvisación del cielo, vuelan los ángeles
en el latín augusto de Roma con las trompetas libérrimas,
                                                    [lentísimas,
en un acorde ya sin tiempo, en un zumbido
de arterias y de pétalos para irme en el torrente con las olas
que salen de esta silla, de esta mesa de tabla, de esta materia
que somos yo y mi cuerpo en el minuto de este azar
en que amarro la ventolera de estas sílabas.

Es el parto, lo abierto de lo sonoro, el resplandor
del movimiento, loco el círculo de los sentidos, lo súbito
de este aroma áspero a sangre de sacrificio: Roma
y Africa, la opulencia y el látigo, la fascinación
del ocio y el golpe amargo de los remos, el frenesí
y el infortunio de los imperios, vaticinio
o estertor: éste es el jazz,
el éxtasis
antes del derrumbe, Armstrong; éste es el éxtasis,
Catulo mío,
                    ¡Thánatos!

ADULESCENS, TIBI DICO

Secret notebooks scribbled
and frenzied pages typed
for your exclusive pleasure.
                    Jack Kerouac

Your flowers are sons of nothing, they are the waves
    inexplicable in their labyrinth;
if one is smell, the other is storm
but all of them come out of your mouth,
because inside you is a tree that grows
outward and hangs you on its perfume
and your nose rots from excess and fatigue.

Why offer a symbol to every fallen leaf,
why weep for the ruins before you make the world
with your blood, why is your life a why
like a wide beach where you shout where
till all the shipwrecked come out and the air
fills with the monsters you invent?

Invent yourself a coast where the sea is you
so that you can know questions and answers,
and your face will not fall over the cliff
a passenger in your smoke.

ADULESCENS, TIBI DICO

Libretas secretas garabateadas
y páginas frenéticas mecanografiadas
para tu exclusivo placer.
                    Jack Kerouac

Tus flores no son hijas de nada, son las olas
  inexplicables en su laberinto;
si una es olor, la otra es tempestad
pero todas te salen por la boca,
porque tienes adentro un árbol que to crece
hacia afuera, y te ahorca en su perfume,
y tu nariz se pudre por exceso y fatiga.

Por qué ofrecer un símbolo a cada hoja caída,
por qué llorar las ruinas antes de hacer el mundo
con tu sangre, por qué tu vida es un por qué
como una inmensa playa donde tú gritas dónde
hasta que salen todos los náufragos, y el aire
se te llena de monstruos inventados por ti?

Invéntate una costa donde el mar seas tú
para que así conozcas preguntas y respuestas,
y no caiga tu rostro al precipicio,
pasajero en tu humo.

OROMPELLO

Let no one say I loved the clouds of Concepción, that I was here this murky
   decade, in Bío-Bío of the poisonous lizards,
as though in my own house. This was not my house. I went back
to the dirty ridges of Orompello to be punished, after I had
gone around the entire world.

Orompello is the year '26 and the stubborn paving stone and the horse carriage
when my poor mother what will she give us tomorrow for breakfast
and the day after tomorrow, when the twelve months, because no, it isn't possible
that these children with no father.
                    Orompello. Orompello.

The trip itself is absurd. The living end is someone
who cleaves to his moss in Concepción south of the stars.

The habit of being a boy, or this is going to burst with the street and everything else,
with memories and clouds I never loved.
                    Nightmare of lying
in wait for my childhood.

OROMPELLO

Que no se diga que amé las nubes de Concepción, que estuve
[aquí esta década
turbia, en el Bío-Bío de los lagartos venenosos,
como en mi propia casa. Esto no era mi casa. Volví
a los peñascos sucios de Orompello en castigo, después de
[haberle dado
toda la vuelta al mundo.

Orompello es el año veintiséis de los tercos adoquines y el
[coche de caballos
cuando mi pobre madre qué nos dará mañana al desayuno,
y pasado mañana, cuando las doce bocas, porque no, no es
[posible
que estos niños sin padre.
                    Orompello. Orompello.

El viaje mismo es un absurdo. El colmo es alguien
que se pega a su musgo de Concepción al sur de las estrellas.

Costumbre de ser niño, o esto va a reventar con calle y todo,
con recuerdos y nubes que no amé.
                              Pesadilla de esperar
por si veo a mi infancia de repente.

THE SUN, THE SUN, DEATH

Like the blind man who weeps against an implacable sun
I try to see the light through my empty eyes
burned for ever.

What use to me is the lightning bolt
that writes by my hand, what use the fire,
                                        the
depth
of the depths,
            what use the World?

What use the body, this body that makes me eat,
sleep, enjoy, despair,
palpate the pleasures in the shadow
of the shadow?

EL SOL, EL SOL, LA MUERTE

Como el ciego que llora contra un sol implacable
me obstino en ver la luz por mis ojos vacíos
quemados para siempre.

De qué me sirve el rayo
que escribe por mi mano, de qué el fuego,
                                         lo
hondo
de lo hondo,
          ¿de qué el Mundo?

¿De qué el cuerpo, este cuerpo que me obliga a comer,
a dormir, a gozar, a me desesperar,
a palpar los placeres en la sombra
de la sombra?

LOST PORT

All is narrow and deep
on this weightless soil, the flowers
grow on knives, face down in the sand
you can hear a volcano; when the rain
soaks it, the unknown
clears up, a fantastic
chair appears in the sky,
and the God of lightning is sitting there
like a mountain of aging snow.

All is narrow and deep, the people
leave no tracks because the wind
sweeps them into its north and its void,
so that suddenly
I go out on my balcony and no longer see anyone,
I see no house, no blond women,
the gardens have disappeared,
it is all invulnerable sand, it was
an illusion, there was no one
on the shore of the planet, no one
before the wind.

Then I run to the waves, I sink
into their kiss, the birds
make a sun above my forehead,
then I take possession of the air
and of the rocks of time
in the name of the wind, the blue stars,
Valparaíso, the wind.

PUERTO PERDIDO

Todo es estrecho y hondo
en este suelo ingrávido, las flores
crecen sobre cuchillos, boca abajo en la arena
puede oírse un volcán; cuando la lluvia
la moja, se despeja
la incógnita, aparece
una silla fantástica en el cielo,
y allí sentado el Dios de los relámpagos
como un monte de nieve envejecido.

Todo es estrecho y hondo, las personas
no dejan huellas porque el viento
las arroja a su norte y su vacío,
de manera
que de improviso
yo salgo a mi balcón y ya no veo a nadie,
no veo casa ni mujeres rubias,
han desaparecido los jardines,
todo es arena invulnerable, todo
era ilusión, no hubo
sobre esta orilla del planeta nadie
antes que el viento.

Entonces corro hasta las olas, me hundo
en su beso, los pájaros
hacen un sol encima de mi frente,
entonces tomo posesión del aire
y de las rocas temporales
en el nombre del viento, las estrellas azules,
Valparaíso, el viento.

MY ZITHER

My zither O my lovely
girl enjoyed so often in my feasts
of flesh and fruit, let us sing today for the angels
and play for God this swiftest flight this fit,
let us undress now, let us climb inside
the most tumultuous kiss
because heaven is watching us and taking pleasure
to see us free as naked beasts.

Give me again your body, its bunches of dark grapes so that the light
can flow from them. Let me bite your stars, your fragrant clouds,
the only heaven I know, let me
travel over you and play all your strings like a new David
so that God himself will go with my seed
like a multiple pulse through your precious veins
and burst in your marble breasts and destroy
the harmony of your waist, my zither, and pull you down to the beauty
of mortal life.

CITARA MIA

Cítara mia, hermosa
muchacha tantas veces gozada en mis festines
carnales y frutales, cantemos hoy para los ángeles,
toquemos para Dios este arrebato velocísimo,
desnudémonos ya, metámonos adentro
del beso más furioso,
porque el cielo nos mira y se complace
en nuestra libertad de animales desnudos.

Dame otra vez tu cuerpo, sus rácimos oscuros para que de ellos mane
la luz, deja que muerda tus estrellas, tus nubes olorosas,
único cielo que conozco, permíteme
recorrerte y tocarte como un nuevo David todas las cuerdas,
para que el mismo Dios vaya con mi semilla
como un latido multiple por tus venas preciosas
y te estalle en los pechos de mármol y destruya
tu armónica cintura, mi cítara, y te baje a la belleza
de la vida mortal.

EPITAPH

It will be said in parting that I loved the savage birds, the howl
enclosed here, the tablet
terse with not dying, the flowers:
                                    here lies
Gonzalo when the wind
and some poor women cried for him.

TEMPUS ABIRE TIBI EST

Time for you to go. Lusisti satis. You played
enough, ate
Romanly and drank.
Tempus abire tibi est.

EPITAFIO

Se dirá en el adiós que amé los pájaros salvajes, el aullido
cerrado ahí, tersa la tabla
de no morir, las flores:
                              aquí yace
Gonzalo cuando el viento,
y unas pobres mujeres lo lloraron.

TEMPUS ABIRE TIBI EST

Tiempo de que te vayas. Lusisti satis. Jugaste
bastante, comiste
romanamente, y bebiste.
Tempus abire tibi est.

CHAPTER AND VERSE

It was for this that man came into the world, to fight
the serpent that advances in the whistle
of things, in the glow
and the frenzy, like a glittering dust, to kiss
the bone of madness from the inside, to put
more and more love on the sheet
of the hurricane, to write on his love act
the lightning of continued being, to play
this game of breathing in danger.

It was for this that man came into the world, for this the woman
from his rib: to pay the interest on this suit,
this skin of lust, to eat this glowing perfume
for short days that fit inside a few decades
in the nebula of the millennia, to put on
the mask again and again, to inscribe himself among the just
in keeping with the laws of history or the ark
of salvation: for this, man came.

Till he is cut and thrown away, he came for this, till they clean him
with the knife like a fish, till
he is un-born and without bursting returns to his atom
humble as stone,
                    then he falls,
keeps falling for nine months, rises
suddenly, passing from the worm
of old age into another butterfly,
a different one.

VERSICULOS

A esto vino al mundo el hombre, a combatir
la serpiente que avanza en el silbido
de las cosas, entre el fulgor
y el frenesí, como un polvo centelleante, a besar
por dentro el hueso de la locura, a poner
amor y más amor en la sábana
del huracán, a escribir en la cópula
el relámpago de seguir siendo, a jugar
este juego de respirar en el peligro.

A esto vino al mundo el hombre, a esto la mujer
de su costilla: a usar este traje con usura,
esta piel de lujuria, a comer este fulgor de fragancia
cortos días que caben adentro de unas décadas
en la nebulosa de los milenios, a ponerse
a cada instante la máscara, a inscribirse en el número de los justos
de acuerdo con las leyes de la historia o del arca
de la salvación: a esto vino el hombre.

Hasta que es cortado y arrojado a esto vino, hasta que lo desovan
como a un pescado con el cuchillo, hasta
que el desnacido sin estallar regresa a su átomo
con la humildad de la piedra,
                              cae entonces,
sigue cayendo nueve meses, sube
ahora de golpe, pasa desde la oruga
de la vejez a otra mariposa
distinta.

THE HELICOPTER

It is there again the helicopter circling and circling the house
hours and hours, it never breaks
the seige, there it is
still, in the clouds the horsefly with that celestial
order, it turns and turns on our scent
till death.

It investigates everything from up there, it scrutinizes even the dust with its tiny
antennae, takes down everyone's name, the moment
we enter the room, the steps
taken in the darkest thought, it casts the net
and pulls it back with the thrashing fish, it cripples us.

Butcher machine whose rotors pursue us till after
we fall, dirty machine,
mother of the crows that betray, no abyss could compare
to this hallow country, this puking
sky with this poisonous hawk, this puking air
morbid with the hum of fear, this puking
life in the trap
of this tin clapping, in the murk
of noise and goo.

EL HELICOPTERO

Ahí anda de nuevo el helicóptero dándole vueltas y vueltas a la casa,
horas y horas, no para nunca
el asedio, ahí anda
todavía entre las nubes el moscardón con esa orden
de lo alto gira que gira olfateándonos
hasta la muerte.

Lo indaga todo desde arriba, lo escruta todo hasta el polvo con sus antenas
minuciosas, apunta el nombre de cada uno, el instante
que entramos a la habitación, los pasos
en lo más oscuro del pensamiento, tira la red,
la recoge con los pescados aleteantes, nos paraliza.

Máquina carnicera cuyos élitros nos persiguen hasta después
que caemos, máquina sucia,
madre de los cuervos delatores, no hay abismo
comparable a esta patria hueca, a este asco
de cielo con este condor venenoso, a este asco de aire
apestado por el zumbido del miedo, a este asco
de vivir así en la trampa
de este tableteo de lata, entre lo turbio
del ruido y lo viscoso.

COAL

I see a swift river shine like a knife, split
   my Lebu* into fragrant halves, I hear it,
I smell it, I caress it, I travel back over it in a child's kiss as then,
when the wind and the rain rocked me, I feel it
like an extra artery between my temples and my pillow.

It is him. It is raining.
It is him. My father has come home wet. It is the smell
of wet horse. It is Juan Antonio
Rojas on a horse fording a river.
It is nothing new. The torrential night collapses
like a flooded mine; the lightning makes it shudder.

Mother, he is almost here: let us open the door,
give me that light, I want to receive him
before my brothers do. Let me take him a good glass of wine
so he will feel better and hug me and kiss me,
and stick me with his beard.

There he is, he is coming home
muddy, raging against his bad luck, furious
from exploitation, dead of hunger, there he is
under his Castilian poncho.

Ah, immortal miner, this is your house
of oak, which you yourself built. Come in.
I have been waiting for you, I am the seventh
of your sons. No matter
that so many stars have crossed the sky of these years,
that we have buried your wife in a terrible August,
for you and she are multiplied. No matter
that the night has been black
for both of us.
                "Get inside, don't stand there
looking at me, not seeing me, under the rain."

* Lebu—port town near Concepción where Rojas spent his childhood

CARBON

Veo un río veloz brillar como un cuchillo, partir
mi Lebu en dos mitades de fragancia, lo escucho,
lo huelo, lo acaricio, lo recorro en un beso de niño como entonces,
cuando el viento y la lluvia me mecían, lo siento
como una arteria más entre mis sienes y mi almohada.

Es él. Esta lloviendo.
Es él. Mi padre viene mojado. Es un olor
a caballo mojado. Es Juan Antonio
Rojas sobre un caballo atravesando un río.
No hay novedad. La noche torrencial se derrumba
como mina inundada, y un rayo la estremece.

Madre, ya va a llegar: abramos el portón,
dame esa luz, yo quiero recibirlo
antes que mis hermanos. Déjame que le lleve un buen vaso de vino
para que se reponga, y me estreche en un beso,
y me clave las púas de su barba.

Ahí viene el hombre, ahí viene
embarrado, enrabiado contra la desventura, furioso
contra la explotación, muerto de hambre, allí viene
debajo de su poncho de Castilla.

Ah, minero inmortal, ésta es tu casa
de roble, que tú mismo construiste. Adelante:
te he venido a esperar, yo soy el séptimo
de tus hijos. No importa
que hayan pasado tantas estrellas por el cielo de estos años,
que hayamos enterrado a tu mujer en un terrible agosto,
porque tú y ella estáis multiplicados. No
importa que la noche nos haya sido negra
por igual a los dos.
                    —Pasa, no estés ahí
mirándome, sin verme, debajo de la lluvia.

AND TO BE BORN IS HERE
AN UNNAMEABLE FEAST
To José Lezama Lima (1910-1976)

You breathe by words ten thousand times a day,
   you swear by love and loveliness
and purify your lungs ten thousand times
biting the gust of the foreign wind,
but it is all in vain: death, the palate,
the verbal bird that flies from your tongue.

THE WORD

An air, an air, an air,
   an air,
a new air:

        not to breathe it
        but to live it.

Y NACER ES AQUI UNA
FIESTA INNOMBRABLE
a *José Lezama Lima (1910-1976)*

Respiras por palabras diez mil veces al día,
juras por el amor y la hermosura
y diez mil veces purificas tus pulmones
mordiendo el soplo de la ráfaga extranjera,
pero todo es en vano, la muerte, el paladar,
el pájaro verbal que vuela de tu lengua.

LA PALABRA

Un aire, un aire, un aire,
un aire
un aire nuevo:

no para respirarlo
sino para vivirlo.

Villa-Lobos in Winter

by Paul West

If he was anyone other than himself, he was Bach, and then only while composing on graph-paper, using little squares instead of notes. Only when he was that deliberate was he Bach.

"I claim to be *all myself*," he liked to say. Once he said "What is folklore? *I* am folklore!" And he even claimed he was afraid of becoming the best composer in the world. He invented his own uniqueness and saw how far it had taken him, in spite of killjoys and uremia, right into his early seventies. He was a primitive modern, he was sure, fond of examining the webs which spiders rigged a hand's breadth from the window screens of the well-to-do, as if in homespun parody. Always, he preferred the webs to the screens, as being more vital and complex. "They *radiate*," he chortled whenever outside, peering at the windows, "in wider and wider arcs, whereas the parallels in the screens will eventually have to meet."

Those were his great days, when his mind roamed, while he composed, through run-down mansions swathed in muslin decked with the sucked-dry abdomens of insects of all kinds. One of his favorite pranks was to conduct choirs of children with two flags while he stood on the cabin roof of a tiny red and yellow railroad locomotive, its brass dome a stunning blob of light. No one had seen anything like him in the whole history of the world, and he knew this, and he was glad.

"*Ah!*" or "*chuf!*" the children sang untidily, but what a shaded "*ah!,*" what a thrusting "*chuf!,*" each time reducing him to tears because every child had a voice and every human was a child suppressed. Decade after decade, all of life teemed before him, and all he could think was how abundant the world was, how lush, how thick, how swollen, pouring and sprouting wherever he looked. What a privilege, he said, to be immersed in such a lavish show. How could it ever end?

One day, though, when he was seventy-two, his luscious plenty shrank all of a sudden to the image of a jungle bird with stained-glass wingspread, orchids for plumage, and a tusk for a beak: a private, wild emblem, brittle and shrunken, of which he could make nothing at all. Mother Nature halts, he told himself; she's bound to start up again. Surely she will not fail just because I am weakening?

There was a new, blank place in his head, where lurked all the things he sensed he could no longer recall. Under his quaking hand, the net of graph-paper awaited his choice of a square, his inking it black or red; but now his fingers refused to move, and the usual hum failed to come into his throat. He had reached a choric pause, he told himself; but pausing had never been part of his natural idiom, he who had been the maestro of onrush, as careless with his finished manuscripts as with money. Some enormous subtraction worked its will on him, erasing and numbing until he felt a mere vestige of whoever he had been. He felt like the human equivalent of a misquotation: gibberish on legs, but for the life of him he couldn't put his finger on the wrong word.

He tried groping back to his old self, there in his head somewhere, but it was like obsolete heraldry, unable to stir the present or quicken his gift.

He remembered how he had learned to play the violin, as a child, by holding it vertical, cello-fashion. So that was one memory not gone. He remembered how his first composition had had a certain roundness, so he'd called it "Pancake." Another memory intact! Then he remembered how he had gone on to music shaped after the Paris or Manhattan skyline or the sawteeth of a mountain range: all on squared paper, in which an outline became the contour of a tune as naturally as grapes grew fat. Then, without warning, he couldn't remember what he'd remembered; he knew only there had been remembering.

Gone for ever, and he didn't know it, were Negro chants gleaned in Barbados, where he'd once been stranded, trying in vain to reach New York, and the bombardine, a brass instrument rather like a tuba. Gone too were the valleys of the Amazon, the stark Matto Grosso, along with masks, jaguars, blowguns, totems, potions, interviewers, and the snazzy tunes in those restaurants where he'd first earned a living. He strained to recapture something, but all that came was a red flush.

I have no technique for now, he told himself. I'll wait, and afterwards. . . . But afterwards refused to come. An hour became a day, stretched into a week. His skin dried and cooled. His eyes lapsed into pleasurable nonfocus. His head felt light and snuff-dry as balsawood, and he longed for a wind—ah, he remembered winds!—a green jungle wind, such as never was, to blow him into kingdom come. He wanted to be exhaled somehow into the noonday broil.

In fact, Villa-Lobos had discovered unseasonal time, the texture of in-between, when humans get the blues, cattle yammer, and birds of paradise lean sideways until they keel over. He was undergoing, without knowing it, what rituals are supposed to preclude. We camouflage time, not so much its passing as the sallow chasm between *tock* and *tick*. When the world is not a festival, it cannot be endured. He wept, self-searingly, with what remained of his mind, unable to use the lull, turn it into an event, or otherwise get through it.

What he felt had no formal structure; ennui, after all, was not a string quartet.

Nor was there a pulse, a heave, a bleat, to it. Ennui was not the jungle either.

Nor was ennui quite the word, anyway, any more than it was the blues, or cafard, or tedium, or funk. The blight that swelled inside him, heedless and furry, was another form of life, like something extraplanetary found in Caipira, where the little train ran. Had he been able to make comparisons, he might have likened the hiatus to *Rudepoêma*, the almost unplayable piano piece he'd written for Artur Rubinstein. As it was, however, he weakened hour by hour, and could only manage to accept the hiatus, much as he'd accepted the gift of his life—raw, as well as abrupt and slight—at eleven, when his father died.

This time, no other death could energize him, though. He was more deeply enmeshed in Mother Nature than ever. His cells were too far gone to wish to be free, and with what was left he dreamed he was being tweaked or strummed, but the only sound was the pale green squeak of the heart machine in the emergency ward. He groaned like a small animal.

It was November, 1959, but winter only north of the other tropic. Yet his warmth had gone: the head-lava, the mulled aroma of his joy, and all he could hear was a pulse not his own, and far away, that of a zombie who could remember nobody's face and nobody's name, behind his oxygen mask, in a hospital under the sun, in Rio.

PAUL WEST's books include *Words for a Deaf Daughter* and, most recently, *Gala*, his eighth novel. Harper & Row will soon publish his new novel, *Stauffenberg*, about the bomb plot against Hitler.

Arauco Redivivus in Pablo Neruda

JOHN FELSTINER

What I offer here is a kind of *catalogue raisonné*, tracing the Araucanian theme throughout Neruda's poems, prose, memoirs, speeches, and interviews from 1938 until his death in 1973. It seems that over the years, he more and more called to mind Chile's indigenous people and their terrain, as if sinking a taproot for his poetic imagination. Like many writers, he ended up discovering—if not actually creating—a past within the past he inherited. Simply to trace that emerging consciousness of Araucanía carries us deep into Neruda's work, and also provides a model of the mythopoeic impulse at its most resolute.

When I first heard Neruda's voice he was speaking of Araucanía, at the 1966 International P.E.N. conference in New York. He was their principal attraction, and had not visited the United States for over twenty years. In that time he had been elected a Communist senator, gone into exile from Chile, and published the *Canto general*; during the Cold War, he had become a renowned poet nearly everywhere except in the U. S. To this New York audience, then, speaking a lucid, deliberate French, he said: "I come from a country that a poet founded." And he went on to tell about Alonso de Ercilla, the conquistador whose epic *La Araucana* (1569) celebrated the Indian resistance to Spanish domination. I was struck, not only by the notion itself, but by the fact that a contemporary poet could think in these terms. What Ercilla had done for Chile, Neruda was attempting for modern Latin America. His remark did more than *épater el gringo*; it continued a thirty-year process of redeeming his own poetic birthright.

Chile's Araucanian people, particularly the Mapuche, do present a compelling historical example. Even before the Conquest, they had stopped the Incas' massive imperial hegemony at the Bío-Bío River. Pedro de Valdivia attempted to conquer them, but was killed in Arauco province in 1553, and although a few years later the chieftains Lautaro and Caupolicán lost their lives, Araucanía remained independent. For more than three cen-

turies, despite periodical campaigns of pacification and reduction, they held out between the Bío-Bío and the Toltén further south. Then long after Chilean independence, during the War of the Pacific with Bolivia and Peru, troops were sent down to subdue the Indians. A treaty was signed at Ñielol Hill in 1881, and land ceded for the founding of a frontier town called Temuco, far south of the Bío-Bío. After that, pioneers flooded in to clear the forests and extend the railroad.

Neruda was born in 1904, scarcely a generation later, and after his mother's early death, was brought south at age two to Temuco, where he grew up. His father, a trainman, sometimes rode him off to isolated spots with the line crew. As Neruda recalled years later in "Infancia y poesía": "We cut rock at Boroa, wild heart of the frontier, scene of fearful battles between Spaniards and Araucanians." But between the boy and the actual Mapuche of his Temuco childhood, there was no intercourse. "They lived totally apart," he once said in an interview, and they spoke a language he did not understand. A line of autobiographical verse that Neruda wrote for his sixtieth birthday expresses the sense of being close yet cut off from a native people: "I grew up spurred by silent races."

To give them a voice and a name, then, became a clear obligation for Neruda—an obligation whose poetic and political aspects developed mutually from 1938 on. "My land without name, without America," he says in the first book of *Canto general*. "But speak to me, Bío Bío," it goes on, "Yours are the words that slide / in my mouth." And Book One finishes by breathing the New World into being:

> listen to the Araucanian tree.
> There is no one. Look at the stones....
> There is no one, it is only the trees.
> It is only the stones, Arauco.

With *Canto general* Neruda became an Orphic poet, investing the word with a power to summon people, places, things. Therefore it makes a difference when he actually begins to speak the name itself: *Arauco, Araucanía, araucano, La Araucana*. And this difference gives us a valuable, because specific, demonstration of Neruda's historical imagination at work.

1938 *I belong to a piece of poor southern earth verging on Araucanía* ("La copa de sangre," *Selección de Pablo Neruda*, 1943; *Obras completas*).

Various elements were working in Neruda to make the year 1938, and this piece of writing, particularly significant. He had just returned from Spain, from the struggle for the Republic and the death of García Lorca; in Chile a Popular Front president was being elected. Neruda traveled around to speak about Spain and recite his poetry; on one occasion, his reading of *España en el corazón* to the Santiago porters moved him and them so intensely that he began to feel "in debt to my country." During that winter, both of his parents died. On the night his father died, Neruda wrote the first poem—"Almagro," on the explorer of Chile—of what developed into *Canto general de Chile* (1943) and then *Canto general* (1950). A few months later he composed "La copa de sangre." This prose meditation announces his deep tie to "my very own terrain," his "unending bond with a certain life, region, and death."

Years earlier, in the *Anillos* of 1926, Neruda had written on the "Province of Childhood," recalling its shadowy woods, incessant rain, mournful train whistles, and saying to it: "Let it be you that I now go back to for refuge." But this impressionistic prose-poem stops with a sensuous, emotional affiliation to the South as nature rather than as history. "La copa de sangre," while it also evokes the rainy landscape, deals with local ritual and his parents' death. Along with "Almagro," it makes the first movement of Neruda's historical imagination towards Chile. "When I return from far off," he says, "I sense...a patriot urge, a savage tricolor wind in my investiture; I belong to a piece of poor southern earth verging on Araucanía."

1940 *The unconquerable rivers of Araucanía know the news now* ("Oratorio menor en la muerte de Silvestre Revueltas," *Canto general*, Bk. XII).

By late 1938 Neruda had a kind of epic in mind, and had proposed it (unsuccessfully) to his publisher, Editorial Ercilla. Between then

Rogelio Navarro

and early 1940, he wrote other poems that eventually joined "Almagro" in the *Canto general de Chile:* "Oda de invierno al río Mapocho," "Botánica," "Atacama," "Océano," "Himno y regreso." They gave him ways of addressing *patria mía* in intimate terms, and calling up its physical genius. He read these poems, some of which evoke the South specifically, at a July 1940 ceremony on leaving Chile to become Consul General in Mexico. Then in October at a Mexican composer's funeral, Neruda read the "Oratorio," assuring his listeners that Araucanía's "unconquerable rivers" would pick up the lament.

1941 *Araucanía* (a magazine).

The theme must have been on his mind, for in January he published from Mexico City a patriotic-cultural magazine, calling it *Araucanía.* On the cover he put a blooming Indian woman with a toothy smile—for which desecration Chile's Foreign Minister rebuked Neruda.

Around that time, in an interview (*Books Abroad*, XV, 12), Neruda was quite clear about his poetic project: "I want to counter-balance the effect of the great poetry of the classics, such as Ercilla and Pedro de Oña"—Oña being the author of *Arauco domado* (1596).

Early in 1941 he also wrote a poem about Chile's northern desert, and another about the South. "Quiero volver al Sur" begins, "Sick in Veracruz, I remember a day / in the South, my land..." Having named several towns in Araucanía, Neruda says: "I want to go / behind the wood along the fragrant / Toltén River... to stretch out alongside cow dung, / to die and revive chewing grain." Then in 1942, still in Mexico, he wrote two more poems about Chile, one of them pervaded by longing for the South—its rain, woods, people, "your antarctic Spring."

1943 *One of the greatest dramas of human liberty: Araucanía's struggle against the Spanish empire* ("Viaje por las costas del mundo," *Viajes*).

Before leaving Mexico, Neruda wrote a rambling account of his journeys over the years. An imaginative research rather than a documentary record, the "Viaje" contains his first full telling of the Araucanian story. "While the Aztec and Inca oligarchies, after a brief struggle, were giving in to the invader... our native land taught a lesson inchoate then, but alive today more than ever." With war at its height in 1943, Neruda calls the Araucanians "the first national front against an invader; they came victorious through a bloody campaign that lasted 300 years and was borne into history and poe-

try by the marvelous *caballero,* the splendid poet, the *hidalgo* don Alonso de Ercilla."

This section of the "Viaje" goes on to link Araucanía with the poet's own genesis: "The warriors' agony, the end of a race that seemed immortal, made it possible for my parents... to come with the first pioneers in an old hackney, crossing stretches of hitherto unknown land, to the new frontier capital settled by Chileans. It was called Temuco and that is the history of my family and my poetry. My parents saw the first locomotive, the first livestock, the first produce in that virginal region of cold and storm."

1943 *Arauco's grating shadows* (a speech in Lima, *Obras completas*).

Neruda's return from Mexico took the form of a triumphal progress. He read the "Viaje" in Colombia, and in Lima he spoke about Peru as "the womb of America," a latent, forsaken force "we have the duty to discover." He also speculated about Inca influence on Araucanía before the Conquest. "When my land felt waves of fertile Inca conquerors who brought the woven touch of garments and liturgy to Arauco's grating shadows; when the animistic throbbing of watchful southern forests touched the sacred turquoise and the vessel brimming with spirit, there is no telling how far the vital waters of Peru ran through my country in its awakening, immersing it in a telluric ripeness whose natural expression is my own poetry."

However orotund the language and fanciful the logic, Neruda clearly means to extend his poetic roots throughout Latin America. The Incas' spiritual genius and the Araucanians' natural genius merge in the wandering bard. Such was his frame of mind on making a pilgrimage to Machu Picchu, a week after giving this talk. In the Inca ruin, as he later said, "I felt myself implicated... Lautaro was related to Cuahtemoc.... We had something to do with those high endeavors of the American community." So *Alturas de Macchu Picchu* (1945) spoke for the Quechua slaves who built the city, and Neruda's epic project opened to embrace an entire continent.

1948 *A good New Year, for you, for all / men, and for the land, beloved Araucanía* ("Feliz año para mi patria en tinieblas," *Canto general*, Bk. XIII).

In 1945, Neruda was elected senator from the northern provinces, joined the Communist Party, and wrote *Alturas de Macchu Picchu*. When Chile's president turned against the Left, Neruda spoke out, and in February 1948 had to go into hiding within Chile. During the next year he moved from place to place, writing the rest of *Canto general*. His New Year poem appeared clandestinely, "for my country in darkness."

1949 *There is no one, it is only the trees. / It is only the stones, Arauco* ("Los hombres," *Canto general*, Bk. I).

Nothing short of a creation myth could ground his epic deeply enough, given the gradual evolution of Neruda's historical and geographical imagination since 1938. Thus from Book One's opening:

> Man was of earth, a vessel, an eyelid
> of tremulous mud, a form of the clay,
> was a Carib pitcher, Chibcha stone,
> imperial goblet or Araucanian silica.

Then follow poems on Latin American plants (such as "the araucaria with bristling lances"), animals, birds ("the Araucanian ring-dove"), minerals, rivers, the last of which is the Bío-Bío:

> Where a child went unnoticed, you
> told me the dawn
> of the earth...
> a story the color of blood.

Finally, in "Los hombres," Neruda moves from the Caribbean down through Mexico and Peru to where

> At the base of nameless America
> Arauco lay among dizzying
> waters...
> Only the snowdrifts are seen
> and the storm rebuffed
> by the rugged araucaria.

Book One closes as this passage modulates into a kind of whispered fugue, regressing to the merest stir of aboriginal life:

> But look at the warrior within the leaves.
> Among the larches a cry.
> Jaguars' eyes amid
> the heights of snow....
> Look at the warriors' emptiness.
> There is no one. The songbird trills
> like water trickling at night.
> The condor crosses its black flight.
> There is no one. Do you hear? It's the step
> of the puma on air and leaves.
> There is no one. Listen. Listen to the tree,
> listen to the Araucanian tree.
> There is no one. Look at the stones.
> Look at the stones of Arauco.
> There is no one, it is only the trees.
> It is only the stones, Arauco.

1949 *Araucanía, branch of torrential oaks, / oh unforgiving homeland* ("Se unen la tierra y el hombre," *Canto general*, Bk. III).

Neruda made *Alturas de Macchu Picchu* Book Two of the epic, and in Book Three recounted the Conquest. Here he placed "Almagro," written over a decade earlier, and then a new poem about the Spaniards' hardships, where a stark terrain seems to act in the name of a staunch people: "First the earth resisted. / Araucanian snow / like a bonfire of whiteness / burned the invaders' steps." And the next poem, "Earth and Man Unite," bespeaks the same identity: "Araucanía, branch of torrential oaks."

The primitive bond between earth and man, which Neruda himself had realized in "La copa de sangre" (1938), led him in this poem to distinguish his own ancestors from other, more "advanced" American Indians:

> My Araucanian fathers had no
> plumy luminous headdress,
> did not recline on nuptial flowers
> or spin gold for the priest:
> they were stone and tree, roots
> in the shaken shrubbery,
> leaves shaped like lances...
> the fathers of stone became shadow,
> fused with the forest, the natural
> darkness, became light from the ice...

With this intensely recreative energy, Neruda animated a dormant mythology in which "earth and man unite." At the same time, he may also have been discovering the historical grounds for his own *residencia en la tierra*, his early attempts to find a residence on earth.

1949 *Arauco loomed up. Adobes, towers / ...Arauco began boiling its dish of blood and stones* ("Valdivia," *Canto general*, Bk. III).

The poet invests his native forebears with a heroic pathos, while the Spaniards appear merely brutal:

> Valdivia thrust the dripping spear
> into Arauco's flinty
> gut, sank his hand
> in the wound, and clutched
> the heart of Araucanía...

Yet it was "Thus," Neruda says, "the war for the fatherland was born," and he follows this poem with a grandiloquent address to Ercilla:

> Stones of Arauco and free-flowing
> roses, regions of roots
> encounter the man arrived from Spain.
> Gigantic lichen winds through his armor.
> Shadows of ferns beat down his sword.

In heroizing Araucanía this way, Neruda had significant precedent. For the early Chilean patriots, rejecting Spain, had turned south for an alternative myth. As Simon Collier observes, in

Ideas and Politics of Chilean Independence: 1808-1833, they savored *La Araucana* and adopted "our fathers, the Araucanians," idealizing their pride and valor. Bolívar called them "proud Republicans," precursors of the struggle for independence. Naturally Neruda's epic drew on this tradition, though for different reasons: to set Chile off from a growing U. S. hegemony; to confirm his Chileanhood against the government that exiled him; and to settle his imaginative roots.

1949 *Arauco was a cold womb* ("Surgen los hombres," *Canto general*, Bk, IV).

The epic's fourth book, "Los libertadores," colors in an Edenic scene, a matrix from which native resistance emerged: "Araucanía's hazelnut / hung out blazes and clusters." In these poems, Neruda feeds a primitive mythos into an epic mold, envisioning the damp, profusely forested region of his childhood quite explicitly as mother earth. Out of her "inmost dampness, / amid the hairlike bristle / of giant fern," the poet's "Araucanian fathers" arise:

> There the chieftains sprouted.
> From that black dampness,
> from that rain fermented
> in the volcanoes' cup
> the lofty breasts sprang out,
> the clear plant-arrows...
> Arauco was a cold womb.

Clearly the Indian earth may be female, but her salient defenders are not.

Along with Lautaro and Caupolicán, the sacred names of Arauco and Araucanía occur throughout this part of *Canto general*, more for their magic than anything else. And so it goes later in the epic. About González Videla, the president who banished him, Neruda says: "in the spot that light reserved for purity, / in the white snow-covered land of Araucanía, / a traitor smiles from a rotted throne." Chile's native people personify the heroic infancy of the nation—by now Neruda has made the theme his own, and will give it various turns for the rest of his life.

1951 *The natal honey of Araucanía* ("A la memoria de Ricardo Fonseca," *Obras completas*).

What touched off and then sustained Neruda's affinity was not some programmatic concern for the people themselves, as in doctrines of nativism, primitivism, or indianism. Instead, just as he was impelled to identify his own genius with Chile's, he made the Araucanian theme into something no less personal than political. Shortly after publishing *Canto general*, for instance, he elegized a fellow

Southerner and Party member this way: "the wild hive nourished your childhood: / the natal honey of Araucanía." And in 1955 he eulogized the naturalistic writer Mariano Latorre for his fidelity to the people and the soil: "he has heard the secret murmur of tutelary *maitenes* and araucaria fronds.... his true crown from now on lies in the Araucanian hills."

1954 *The heart's end of Araucanía* ("Infancia y poesía," *Obras completas*).

For a fiftieth-birthday ceremony, Neruda recollected the earliest influences on his poetry, among them that of Araucanía, a tacit presence in the ambience (and the nomenclature) of his childhood. In "Childhood and Poetry" he retells the story told in 1938, about a ritual cup of hot lamb's blood he was given to drink. Here the ritual shows how colonizers of the South were affected by Araucanía; how "powerful emanations from the virgin earth permeated Nordic and Mediterranean blood, making an Araucanian substance out of it."

Later in the talk Neruda singles out someone "who had a great influence on me: Orlando Masson"—a fighter against injustices, such as "Indians being killed off as if they were rabbits." "I do not believe," writes Neruda, "that the Araucanians used to be sullen, or timid, or wayward. After independence in 1810, Chileans set themselves to killing Indians as enthusiastically as the Spanish invaders had. Temuco was the heart's end of Araucanía."

This "romantic man" had literary as well as political influence, for he "wrote and printed the first book of poetry between the Bío-Bío and the Magellan Straits... *Flores de Arauco*. I read those verses with great emotion," Neruda says, and adds that Masson's newspaper also printed his own first poems.

1956 *Araucanians, / ...enemy friends / of the Spaniard Ercilla: / another poet comes singing* ("Oda al trigo de los indios," *Nuevas odas elementales*).

After the *Canto general* and Neruda's exile, he became even more of a public poet than before. References to Araucanía became more vague, as in the "Ode to the Araucanian Araucaria" (1956), "To Louis Aragon" (1959), and the proem to *Piedras de Chile* (1961). But in "Ode to the Indians' Wheat," Neruda movingly recovers the sense of living near a diminished people:

> in the red summer
> of my childhood
> the earth moved:
> a boulder,
> a thorny tree,

a ravine:
it was an Indian,
an Indian coming
on horseback.

...

The Indians' wheat,
the last of it, stunted,
the tattered gold
of wretched Araucanía.
I saw the caciques come,
hard faces,
thin mustache,
threadbare poncho,
who did not smile at me
because to the last king
I am a stranger.

...

Indian women,
seated like earthen pitchers,
gazed out of time...
and the Indians
seated like sacks of earth,
and the sacks of wheat
like ghosts
of ancient Araucanía.

1958 *I kissed my blood in your mouth, / my heart, my Araucanian one* ("Testamento de otoño," *Estravagario*).

The love for Matilde Urrutia, now his widow, confirmed Neruda's bond to the South where she also was born: "from rainswept ceremonies, / from ancient lands and martyrs, / the Bío-Bío sings on / in our blood-stained clay." Again in *Cien sonetos de amor* (1959), the poet finds the South's stubborn clay in her (XXIX), and what he owes her is "like a natal / root from Araucanía" (LXIV). Then again in *La barcarola* (1967) he sees Matilde "lying in the grain, / in the March threshing, in the mud of Araucanía."

1962 *That art of rain with its terrible, subtle power over my native Araucanía* (*Las vidas del poeta*, 1).

In this first version of Neruda's memoirs, Part One ("Boy From the Provinces") begins with the rain; then it reverts to the early struggles and "the pacification of Araucanía"—that is, the eventual dispossession of the Indians. We hear about train rides through the isolated territory, and "Araucanians with their ceremonial dress and ancestral dignity waiting at the stops to sell lambs, chickens, eggs, weavings.... Each stop had a more beautiful name, almost all descended from the old Araucanian lands.... Labranza was the first stop, Boroa and Ranquilco followed. Names redolent of wild plants, their syllables captivated me." Thus later in the memoir, when Neruda's

friends tell him Paris is the place to continue his career, he wonders what use that will be for "a semi-Araucanian poet like me."

1962 *In* La Araucana *we see ... our patrimony* ("Latorre, Prado y mi propia sombra," *Obras completas*).

Neruda once explained what Ercilla's epic meant to him poetically. It certified not only the national birthright but the "vibrant natural catalog of our patrimony. Birds, plants, waters, customs, ceremonies, language, arrows, aromas, snow, and tides that are ours, all were named at last in *La Araucana*, and by means of the word began to live." But later in the same talk he added that "despite *La Araucana's* painful pride, our Indians are still illiterate, landless, and barefoot."

1963 *Called* chahual (puya chilensis), *this ancestral plant was worshipped by the Araucanians* ("Premio Nobel en Isla Negra," *Una casa en la arena*).

Neruda had the poet's precise love for the proper names of things. He once seized the occasion of not receiving the Nobel Prize to describe his retreat from publicity on the Chilean littoral, where Spring was coming. Next to a "great dying flower [an *agave americana*], here is another huge one springing up. Nobody outside my country will recognize it; it exists only on these antarctic shores. Called *chahual (puya chilensis)*, this ancestral plant was worshiped by the Araucanians: now ancient Arauco is gone. Blood, death, time and then Ercilla's epic harp completed the old story: the tribe of clay that woke abruptly from the earth's crust to defend its homeland against invaders. Seeing its flowers surge up again over centuries of obscure deaths, layers and layers of forgotten blood, I believe that the earth's past is blossoming against what we now are." This is Neruda's clearest, strongest statement of the complex hold, through nature and history, that Araucanía had on him.

1964 *Before I could talk they brought me / to the rain of Araucanía* ("Primer viaje," *Memorial de Isla Negra*).

Neruda never knew his mother, but knew he had lost her, and perhaps that loss infused the rainy childhood landscape he came to write so much about. "Where the Rain Is Born," Book One of his sixtieth-birthday verse autobiography, dwells on the rain as if for its amniotic quality. A poem on "The Austral Earth" pictures the child "lost in the entrails' green / obscurity... alone / in the natal forest, / the dark depth of Araucanía." Here Neruda also touches carefully on the names of places, flora, and fauna native to the region, which lends a slight irony to his saying, a few poems later: "I grew up spurred by silent races."

1969 *The Araucanians turned into root!* (*Aún*, V).

At the 1966 P.E.N. conference in New York, Neruda appeared as a poet whose universality stemmed from his insistent Chileanness. In the same vein, he spent his sixty-fifth birthday "looking backward," writing a long self-reflective sequence called *Aún*. Poem IV summons "the branched-out Ercilla": "he alone showed us ourselves ... entangled himself in us till now." Much of the book celebrates places in southern and central Chile, but poem V concerns the dispossession of the Indians: "The Araucanians turned into root! / had their leafage cut away, / leaving only a skeleton / race ... and ourselves were the thieves."

1970 *We are not the descendants of Spanish soldiers and Araucanian women* (*Seven Voices*, ed. Rita Guibert).

Imaginatively closer to the Indians' past than to their present estate, Neruda held an interesting view of Chile's Araucanian parentage, which he expressed in an interview during his 1970 presidential campaign. After summarizing the "patriotic war" and Ercilla's "invention" of Chile, he mentioned a "curious exception": Chileans descend not from conquistadors and native concubines, like other mestizos, but from Araucanian warriors and captive Spanish women. While the national anthem may bear him out ("With his blood the proud Araucanian willed us a legacy of valor"), I believe the historians do not.

1971 *I return ... to Araucanía's lilac gardens* (Nobel Prize remarks).

While Ambassador to France, Neruda was interviewed by *L'Express* (13 September 1971). He began talking about the Mapuche of his childhood, who came into Temuco to sell goods and in the evening departed, "the man on horseback, the woman on foot. We had absolutely no communication with them, did not know their language, except a few words. Nor did they speak Spanish." Neruda again described Araucanía's fierce resistance to the Spaniards, adding that "The Indians made them swallow liquid gold, saying 'So now you've got your gold!'" (Oddly enough, this detail was omitted when a Chilean magazine, *Ercilla*, picked up the interview.) He went on to say that the Mapuche, whose language was "one of the world's most beautiful," were finally being given full citizenship by Allende.

In December Neruda travelled to Stockholm for the Nobel Prize. "I come from an obscure province," he said in his formal speech, calling his poetry regional and rain-filled. Some informal remarks he also made in Stockholm point once more to the fusion of personal and historical sources in his poetry: "I return to childhood streets, to the South American winter, to Araucanía's lilac gardens ... to mourning Indians the Conquest left behind." And this reference led him to say he represented all "the forgotten of the earth."

1973 *Against my people's enemies my song is rude and hard as Araucanian stone* (preface, *Incitación al Nixonicidio y alabanza de la revolución Chilena*).

In 1971 an essay collection appeared, *Don Alonso de Ercilla, Inventor de Chile*, whose title and introduction Neruda had contributed. Then in late 1972, ill and politically anguished, he wrote the *Incitación*, a defense of Chilean autonomy. Beginning with Whitman, it ends by invoking Neruda's precursor Ercilla, for "the same ancient struggle / comes from the depth of Araucanía." As the book's penultimate poem, "Don Alonso Speaks," Neruda places a florid strophe from *La Araucana* about "Chile, that passionate and fertile land, / Never submitting to a stranger's hand." Then he ends with "We Speak Together," rhyming tercets that interweave his own lines with Ercilla's:

> Whatever plot or violence is planned
> Will find this Chile, this my native land,
> Never submitting to a stranger's hand.

It was no less fitting a gesture, at the close of his career, for coming at the brink of tragic civil war.

1974 *One day we shall see Araucanian universities* (*Confieso que he vivido*, 7).

Neruda died on September 23, 1973, just after the military seizure. The eight posthumous books of poetry do not mention Araucanía, but during his last year he had been revising and expanding the 1962 memoirs. About his Mexican consulship of 1940-43, he added two paragraphs. One describes the short-lived magazine *Araucanía*, with its smiling Indian woman on the cover. The other makes a brave prediction about the forgotten Chileans: "One day we shall see Araucanian universities, books printed in Araucanian, and we will realize how much we have lost in clarity, purity, and volcanic energy." The prophecy, though even less likely now than when he wrote it, bears out the ideal of Neruda's Araucanian genesis. ◥

JOHN FELSTINER is Professor of English at Stanford. His book on translating Neruda's *Alturas de Macchu Picchu* will be published by Stanford University Press in the Spring.

Xul Solar: Star-Spangler of Languages

NAOMI LINDSTROM

In 1969, Leopoldo Marechal observed that Xul Solar's continuing impact on the Buenos Aires literary scene had far exceeded his visible achievement as a creative artist.[1] In Marechal's characterization, Xul is one of those figures who "started out as men of letters and ended up as true legends of Buenos Aires" (G; 67). Xul (1887-1963) holds an official place in literary history as one of the group of innovators who accompanied Jorge Luis Borges through his 1920s enthusiasm for avant-garde experimentation. Xul was a poet, a painter, an occultist and a spirited participant in the group's festivities. He published in the emblematic avant-garde magazine *Martín Fierro* and in the literary supplement Borges edited for *Crítica*: however, his published production is too slight to support his literary fame.[2]

Xul's mythic status derives in part from his lack of interest in completing artistic works that would bear and perpetuate his name. His strategy was to disseminate ideas into the general cultural environment, where all innovators could act them. Borges calls him the "father of writings, of languages, of utopias, of mythologies" and praises his "generous friendship" in sharing his newly-generated schemes with fellow creators (S; 7). Macedonio Fernández cites Xul's linguistic assistance on the former's *Museum of the Novel of Eterna* (1967).[3] Enrique Villegas and Manuel Peyrou recall Xul's ceaseless attempts to force all around him to confront basic issues of language and communication (G; 52, 80). Xul "insisted on speaking in his own language, *neo-criollo;* instead of saying 'I'm going right away' he'd say 'I'm instagoing (G; 52). Anyone hoping to communicate with him had to master the basic rule of this language, the playful amplification of Spanish words with a wild variety of prefixes, infixes and suffixes. When this strategy succeeded, Xul provoked his friends into verbal invention they might never have tried otherwise.

Even when Xul committed his new ideas to paper or canvas, he preserved their open-ended character. He invites the reader or viewer to attempt his own elaboration of the constituent elements. For example, after the exposition of a schematic representation for esthetic and cosmological principles, Xul adds: "This sample only set forth *partia* (partialities) and some more or less botchy upgrapplings with shimmerloose blurrinesses" (S, 39). The author looks to the "polemical playing-field" as the space in which concepts are refined; his readers should feel free to join the fray.

The innovator's incessant tinkering with the fundamental mechanism of language led Macedonio Fernández to proclaim him "the exquisite star-spangler of heavens, and of languages."[4] Going to visit Xul was like frequenting a "workshop called 'Languages Repaired Here,'" (MNE, 47) from which one might emerge with the most fancifully refurbished structures.

II

One area of discourse Xul is especially eager to "repair" is the language available for critical and theoretical discussion. He evinces a deep dissatisfaction with the standard terminology of rhetorical analysis, art criticism, musicology and esthetics. Needless to say, the need to reform critical usage has long motivated crusading efforts by purists and eclectics alike. Xul, however, stands somewhat outside this tradition. He has no interest in limiting the meanings of terms, in introducing new terms for greater precision of reference or, indeed, in any remedy meant to decrease the uncertainty inherent in language. Rather, he sees existing critical discourse as too precise, too "telling" in the sense of telling the reader what everything means. Consequently, the reader is left with very little to do in the way of creative interpretation.

Xul proposes, as remedy, something Macedonio Fernández calls "the brilliant Lesson of Xul Solar, the man who can make language hold its tongue, who can cure it of its nasty habit of 'non-stop talking' (PR; 164). Macedonio claims to have learned from Xul that the author should use a language that leaves a good deal unsaid. Xul's technique for "silencing" language is simple, but involves a radical departure from what one conventionally expects as responsible behavior: the writer or speaker should feel free to invent new words or use existing ones in unusual contexts. Having done so, he should then abstain from explaining what the new or decontextualized word might mean. The reader or listener must then take an active role in the process of producing meaning.

Xul's journalistic criticism follows the above-described "Lesson." Interdisciplinary in the extreme, Xul saw all art forms as superficially differing manifestations of the same underlying mechanism. Hence, in discussing the work of a painter, he randomly mixes terms proper to the discussion of several disparate media: "Musical necessity made him surrender control over lines of movements and masses and let it govern them according to its own rhythmic despotism.... Poetic necessity, finally, sought to base the whole composition on a subject it would dictate, determining exactly which elements and media should be employed...."[5] This shuffling of terms from context to context, frequent in Xul's work, serves two functions. Its specific goal is to move readers away from their habit of compartmentalizing artistic production into separate media. More generally, Xul demonstrates that, contrary to what this culture believes, one is not completely and helplessly dependent on predetermined meanings to make sense of discourse.

Using extant terms, though, sets limits on innovation, for each comes bearing a certain semantic weight. Xul's next step, then, is to create new words not yet contaminated with conventional meanings. Of course, the creator of the neologisms must himself refrain from imposing a definition. The invention of compound forms especially appeals to Xul, for the reader must decide what semantic relation obtains between the juxtaposed elements. He also makes free use of Greek and Latin prefixes to form neologisms, in fanciful mimicry of scientific discourse. Words borrowed from other languages and those invented for the occasion by the author himself also serve to "open" Xul's discussion to the reader's input.

An example of this reformed critical language is a statement Xul distributed to those attending his 1953 exhibition of paintings (S; 38-39). The theme of the declaration is another attempt to jettison genre classifications based on media. Xul proposes a new typology, purely tentative and heuristic, to show how a more global approach to taxonomy might work.

The text immediately announces itself as the work of an eccentric reformer. Like many before him, Xul modifies Spanish spelling, moving it toward a more perfectly phonetic system. *Qu*, for instance, is replaced with *k*, and *y* with *i*. However, the reformer himself is not consistent, including an occurrence of *que* as well as the improved form, *ke*. Also inconsistent is his deployment of a twelve-base counting system. The symbol *&* is once glossed as signifying ten and, shortly afterwards, is said to correspond to eleven. This apparent carelessness would seem to bespeak a conviction that the process of renovation matters more than the specific measures of reform.

Change continues to be in the foreground as Xul invents a number of new forms. In order to achieve compression, cumbersome noun endings are dropped: *preocupación* becomes *preocupa*, *explicación* is *explica* and *decoración*, *decora*. *Se clasifican (they are classified)* loses a syllable to become *se clasifan*. *Teor* can mean either theoretical or theoretically. The simplified forms in this statement represent no more than a first step toward Xul's eventual goal of linguistic compression. His ideal "panlanguage" would boil down the entire utterance "la miró cariñosamente (he looked at her lovingly)" to "lakermiru" and turn "la miró porque quiso (he looked at her because he felt like it)" to "la kiermirú" (S; 9). Faced with the pragmatic task of commenting on esthetic theory, Xul abstains from such feats of condensation.

In proposing the new esthetics, Xul compounds several previously-unknown nouns. In some cases, the overall meaning is apparent from the constituent elements. *Pensiformas (thoughtforms)* and *ideografías (ideographs)* clearly belong together under the heading of "pure abstract" art. *Modimodels (stylemodels)* are patently akin to fashion illustrations, the other entry in that esthetic class. These neologisms demand relatively little of the reader, but accustom him to the use of a type of compounding rare in Spanish—a type Xul is eager to introduce.[6]

The reader must truly struggle to devise coherent meanings for other, more enigmatic compound forms. One esthetic category, for instance, contains two entries that should, apparently, exemplify and so define it: *fotomontaje (photomontage)* and *realdetalles (realdetails)*. Since realism and would-be realism have already been assigned a place in the scheme, one must find some other feature common to *fotomontaje* and *realdetalles*. Some vague underlying notion such as "fragmentedness" must surely unite the terms. The author gives the reader remarkably little help in making this strange discourse coalesce into sense.

Xul also makes special use of Greek and Latin prefixes and suffixes. Their scientific associations enable him to create terms with an instantly "authoritative" ring, even though they have no existence outside the text in which they occur. For instance, he throws out a challenge to all future *filosofistas bellólogos (esthetological beautological philosophists)*. Rather than genres, schools or "isms," he speaks of *tipiescuelas (tipischools)*. The procedures used to realize a work of art determine its *tecnicarácter*. Clearly, Xul could have had recourse to such standard terms as *estheticians, types, schools, media* or *style*. His deliberate rejection of the vocabulary of art criticism underlines his determination to make a fresh conceptual start. The basic premises of discussion deserve a thorough rethinking. This drastic process can only begin when conventional terms, with their heavy accretion of fixed meaning, disappear.

Still more disturbingly aberrant is the creation of utterly strange-looking words that seem not to belong anywhere in the lexicon of Spanish. *Lalies* are the artist's technical means of expression. *Panbeldoike*, an improbable descendant from classical antiquity, designates a total esthetic doctrine. *Parties* are the biased and incomplete hypotheses set forth by a single theorist. To form these alien words, Xul takes elements from the most disparate sources and fuses them together without regard for any consideration other than euphony. Since no reader can devise an approach to these forbiddingly strange forms, Xul glosses them with patent ethical definitions.

III

Moving beyond purely linguistic renovation, Xul supplements his verbal exposition by having recourse to nonlinguistic systems of signs. His esthetic proposal uses two such systems: "Here I've worked it all out using twelve-base math and astrology." The reader finds each new category correlated to a numerical and a zodiacal sign as well as to artistic phenomena.

Here again, a considerable expenditure of imagination is necessary to make the suggested connections. It is unclear how the systems mesh: why, for example, Virgo should head the category containing photomontage and realdetails. Does the sign of Virgo somehow govern or regulate these artistic endeavors? Is the Virgo-ruled month of the year more propitious to their pursuit? Is Xul bringing together disparate signs in order to show how a global, totalizing system looks?

Xul's answer comes in a typically playful and indirect fashion. He gives his representational apparatus a curious credential: "it's taken from the PanTree, which is a neo improved version of the cabbalistic Tree of Life." His extravagant claims for his set-up border on caprice: "It's to show where exactly everything fits into the cosmos, its upgrowth is all in numbers that translate, in the circles, to planets; the straight lines give you the zodiac in bihour bits starting from midnight, using Cancer as your base value. (The dotlines are numerical equivalents for simple shapes, sounds, colors, etc.) Plug in letters instead of numbers and you start getting panlanguage out of pure logic." The same signs can serve to represent the four bodily humors, the four elements, advertising science, unrealized artworks and philosophical notions. Here Xul makes patent the arbitrary relationship between signs and whatever they may represent. The reader should not take the "PanTree" as holy writ, not to be tampered with. It offers him a variety of exotic, suggestive elements. To provide a meaningful structuring of those elements is the task confronting the imaginative reader.

Arbitrariness is kept continually in the foreground. For instance, Xul conventionally defines *Aries* as *ram*, but adds that it could also be *bulldog*. He names Virgo a second time as *Puella*, as if to point out that the use of any term is convention-bound. Random, too, is his offhanded use of medieval scientific terms. He offers no explanation for his equivalence of earth, melancholy, the nervous temperament, realism and photography. Even the overall structuring of his argument has an arbitrary character. At the outset, he suggests that the Western concepts of the "I" and of artistic individuality are fallacies, and that his scheme will show this to be the case. However, he not only neglects to demonstrate this point but actually includes a special category for art that "bears the stamp of an individual or is *sui generis.*" This "unreliability" emphasizes Xul's point that no reader should trust an author to do all his thinking and imagining for him. Irregularities and deficiencies in the "PanTree" program help irritate one into considering what he would demand from such a system. The ideal would be for the reader to attempt his own version.

The key to the strategy of the "PanTree" appears again in Xul's "Pangame." This project again involves an open invitation to create meaningful patterns out of the elements provided. The elements again come from a highly conventionalized system: the chess board with its squares and moveable pieces.

Traditional rules for board games bind players to rigidly determined patterns of activity. Xul's instructions are more like suggestions—they encourage spontaneous invention. Even to make sense of his directions requires an initial outlay of creative effort. The first item reads: "Playing time: ten minutes. Players get one musical note or two and a half degrees of arc..." (S, 16). One becomes increasingly aware of the game's openness upon reading "pieces may be stacked on top of one another, if you feel like it." What significance such stacking might have is left entirely to the discretion of the players.

The struggle to wrest meaning from the instructions, though, is nothing compared to the leap of imagination demanded to actually play the game. Xul puts forth these suggestions: "take the scorecard and write out words, turning the game into a coherent dialogue, a musical exchange in counterpoint or a dual-artist sketch; use shorthand to jot down the further poetic and pictorial possibilities."

Xul expresses the belief that pangame might eventually serve as a supplement to or replacement for natural languages. "The dictionary of 'panlanguage,' which I will come up with in time, is the chessboard of 'panchess.' The consonants are the tokens and the vowels and their combinations are the squares, one hundred and seventy-nine in all." (S; 9) Osvaldo Svanascini offers some elaboration of this seemingly extravagant statement. Svanascini sees pangame as part of Xul's campaign against the deficiencies of human languages. Xul criticizes existing languages as too ethnocentric, too encrusted with tradition, too slow to change. The chessboard, previously unused as a device for structuring meaning, would avoid these problems. The wildly radical character of Xul's proposal is what gives it a chance of succeeding.

The use of pangame as a language remains a nearly utopian ideal, perhaps realizable at some very future time. Meanwhile, however, Xul shows how "open" a message can be. He words his pangame instructions so as to avoid giving away the "point of it all." He effectively abolishes the factor, competitive strategy, that gives conventional board games the appearance of purposeful activity. Without either the traditional model for conflict or a new objective set by Xul, players must learn to posit their own goals. Pangame is a metagame. To play, one must constantly rejustify the entire endeavor. The question "What are we playing for?" is always present, eliciting an infinite number of valid responses.

The "how" of the game is also open. Xul recommends a special playing board, for which he gives these indeterminate guidelines: "thirteen squares down each side; the last repeats the first, like notes on octave apart." Rather than regulate which player goes first, he states: "the pieces go first, off the board." Most enigmatic of all is his final suggestion: "you can also play off two destinies against one another, plotting the moves to go with the players' horoscopes."

The instructions for pangame could stand alone purely for their heuristic value. They bring home how dependent one really is on author-determined meaning. But, in fact, Xul put his plan into practice and persuaded friends to participate. Svanascini recalls that Xul's special board and pieces "were finely crafted, but without the utilitarian perfection of ordinary games." This physical irregularity must surely be an objective correlative for the semantic indeterminacy at the heart of the game. For Svanascini, actual play makes manifest the game's linguistic or paralinguistic character: "When you played it with the author, when you picked up the little pieces, it could make you think ahead to a far-off time when language could be felt or thought so perfectly no words would be needed" (S; 16).

IV

Brief summations of Xul's linguistic strategy at first appear so contradictory as to refer to two different innovators. Macedonio Fernández credits Xul with the invention of a "language of noncommunication, his unintelligible neo-criollo." He predicts that "once the world gets hold of Xul Solar's language, anyone will be able to write unintelligible books" (PR; 70). Svanascini, on the other hand, insists that "For Xul Solar the desire for communication between all beings was absolutely crucial" (S; 46). Svanascini is certain that Xul invented languages "to bridge our severe communications gap" (S; 8).

There is no real reason why both sets of statements cannot be true. Macedonio emphasizes Xul's abolition of fixed, author or speaker-determined meaning from his speech and writing. Svanascini stresses the second half of the same operation. In the absence created by "making language hold its tongue," Xul leaves the field open for the structuring of new, surprising meanings.

This brings Xul's work close to that of certain present-day innovators. The theorists and creators associated with the magazine *Tel Quel* present an especially patent parallel. For example, Julia Kristeva's description of the "genotext" is very close to Xul's ideal:

Going beyond the "literary work" and the "book," that is, beyond a finished production of a closed message, the thing that today is called a literary work appears as a collection of texts: productions before meaning is fixed... The text is not a linguistic phenomenon; in other words, it is not the systematized meaning which appears in a linguistic corpus as a single level of structure. The text is its own process of generation; the engendering is inscribed within the linguistic "phenomenon" that is the printed text or phenotext, but it cannot be read except by retracing its steps vertically through the birth (1) of the pheno-text's linguistic categories, and (2) of the organization of the act of creating meaning. The process of generation will therefore be grasped in two ways: (1) creation of the material of language, and (2) the creation of the "I" which is in a position to make meaning appear.[7]

These are ideas close to Xul's heart. Like Kristeva and her colleagues, Xul demands a laying open of the mechanism that produces meaning. He shares the later-day critics' desire to make manifest "what happens when we read before we have interpreted what we read."[8] His ideal, like theirs, is a form of discourse characterized by plurality, the open interplay of elements and the possibility of infinite recombinations.

Xul's likeness to present-day innovative theorists shows why, despite his relatively insignificant output, he is such a fascinating figure, even a mythic one. He was quick to see what twentieth-century creation needed in order to move ahead. He realized the time had come to focus maximum attention on questions of meaning and communication. As a consequence, he would let no one around him take these matters for granted. To this purpose, he spoke and wrote near-nonsense, invented languages and paralanguages, supplemented speech and writing with signs from non-linguistic systems. In short, he played the role of the "star-spangler of languages." His flamboyant tactics, his sure grasp of where creation needed to turn and his sparse production entitle him to his current legendary status.

[1] Leopoldo Marechal, interview with Germán L. García in the latter's *Jorge Luis Borges et al. hablan de Macedonio Fernández* (Buenos Aires: Carlos Pérez, 1969), p. 67. Further citations from this work will be designated G with the corresponding page number.

[2] The largest available sampling of Xul Solar's work appears in Osvaldo Svanascini, *Xul Solar* (Buenos Aires: Ediciones Culturales Argentinas, 1962). Citations from this work will be marked S with the corresponding page number.

[3] Macedonio Fernández, *Museo de la novela de la Eterna* (Buenos Aires: Corregidor, 1974), p. 47. Further citations from this work will be marked MNE with the corresponding page number.

[4] Fernández, *Papeles de recienvenido* (Buenos Aires: CEDAL, 1968), p. 70. Further citations will be marked PR with the corresponding page number.

[5] Solar, text reproduced in Beatriz Sarlo Sabajanes, ed., *Martín Fierro (1924-1927)*; (Buenos Aires: Carlos Pérez, 1969), pp. 65-67.

[6] For a whimsical account of Xul's proselytizing enthusiasm for compound formations, see Fernández, MNE, p. 47. Macedonio calls Xul's presence a "taller 'Idiomas en compostura'," playing on the possible meanings of *compostura*: repairing, as one might repair a watch, and compounding.

[7] Julia Kristeva, *Semiotike: recherches pour une sémanalyse* (Paris: Seuil, 1969), p. 41.

[8] Veronica Forrest-Thompson, "Necessary Artifice: Form and Theory in the Poetry of *Tel Quel*," *Language and Style*, 4, 1 (1973), 15.

NAOMI LINDSTROM teaches Latin American literature at the University of Texas at Austin.

Alejandro Otero, *Light Catcher*
(Model) 1972

Carnival Triumph in Bruno Barreto's *Dona Flor and Her Two Husbands*

ANDREW HORTON

Bruno Barreto's recent successful film *Dona Flor and Her Two Husbands*, based on Jorge Amado's novel, not only begins with a depiction of carnival in a Brazilian city, but more importantly, it develops a comic spirit of carnival triumph in which the "impossible" becomes gloriously "real." Carnival, an integral part of South American culture, thus becomes, in spirit, a metaphor and means for personal liberation and "triumph" over the blocking forces of everyday reality.

Keep in mind the significance of carnival for any culture. An expression of a folk tradition, carnival is very much a democratic spirit celebrated in the streets and market places. Through the festive mingling of food, song, dance, laughter, sex, and clowning, it is a means of allowing every man to feel himself king for a day. Carnival is the social expression of the freedom of imagination and individual fantasy. According to Mikhail Bakhtin the importance of this phenomenon is that it manages to "... consecrate inventive freedom, to permit the combination of a variety of different elements and their rapprochement, to liberate from the prevailing point of view of the world, from conventions and established truths, from cliches, from all that is humdrum and universally accepted (*Rabelais and His World*, trans. by Helene Iswolsky, Cambridge, Mass., 1968, p. 34).

In literature this festive spirit of carnival triumph has found its clearest expression in the comic tradition. In Aristophanes, Chaucer, Boccaccio, Rabelais, Shakespeare and Moliere, we witness repeated examples of individuals who, in a spirit analogous to that of the sanctioned freedom of carnival, liberate themselves from confining situations and joyfully triumph over others, living out their elaborate fantasies.

In Aristophanes' *Knights*, for instance, a lowly Sausage Seller not only defeats the tyrant Paphlagon in verbal combat (abuse) thus ridding Athens of a feared ruler, but he succeeds in turning Old Man Demos (representing the Athenian people) into a vibrant young man in a carnivalesque-fantasy triumph that restores democracy to new life. Aristophanes' victory was, however, merely a "carnival triumph", for in reality Athens steadily lost the democratic glory that Aristophanes had known and appreciated as a young man. His comic art thus became his means of triumphing over the depressing political realities of his day.

Not all carnival triumphs are so complete or so effortless. Cervantes' Don Quixote touches both comic and tragic depths as he continually attempts to triumph over the dull mediocrity that surrounds him, only to have his fantasies collapse painfully each time. But Cervantes manages finally to raise the spirit of carnival triumph to a level far beyond that of street festivals and stage farce as Quixote's death insures the survival of his spirit through the power of recorded art (fiction). Why "carnival" triumph and not simply "triumph" or personal triumph? Because Cervantes' scope is so all-inclusive. As in the spirit of carnival, Cervantes' work embraces the sacred and the profane, the grotesque and the visionary, slapstick, farce, and pathos. Furthermore, Quixote's fantasies are, like the spirit of carnival, far beyond those of everyday reality. It would not be a carnival triumph, for instance, if Quixote had run successfully for political office in La Mancha and attempted to improve the quality of life through reasonable legislation. His life becomes a carnival triumph in the end because through his *unreasonable* (in the eyes of those around him) fantasies, he transforms the most mundane existence into a world of mystery, multiple possibility, and justice.

Bruno Barreto is one of a number of contemporary filmmakers who has brought the original and festive splendor of carnival triumph in a modern setting. Think of Jean-Charles Tacchella in France, for instance, who has made the theme of carnival triumph central to his popular *Cousin, Cousine* and *Blue Country*. As his loving "cousins" (by marriage only—not by blood) in *Cousin, Cousine* walk out of the boring annual family Christmas party and joyfully express their affection, leaving their respective spouses behind, the audience shares their sense of exhilaration, frankness, liberation. It is as if many filmmakers and writers in the late 1960's and 1970's have rejected the self-conscious pessimism of existential themes of alienation, "bad faith", and thus a modern tragic view of man caught in a chaotic universe. Instead, these artists have recovered a carnivalesque perspective on life as an open-ended and ultimately comic vision of life in the fullest sense.

Nowhere is this more true than in South America. The so-called "magic realism" of many South American writers and filmmakers is, like carnival, an inextricably fused blend of illusion and reality, myth and history, magic and everyday existence. Influenced not only by the almost "surreal" diversity of people, nature, and social classes of their native countries, these artists also reflect a great debt to the master author of illusion and reality and carnival triumph, Cervantes. Visible in the labyrinthine tales of Jorge Luis Borges, "magic realism" most clearly began to be recognized throughout Europe and the United States with the publishing of Gabriel Garcia Marquez's *One Hundred Years of Solitude* (1967). Bruno Barreto's *Dona Flor and Her Two Husbands* (1977) is strongly in this same tradition.

The film is based on the 1966 novel of the same name by the Brazilian writer Jorge Amado. A Marxist and one-time Communist, Amado has concerned himself in his fiction with celebrating his native Bahia in northern Brazil and with pointing to the many social injustices that divide his country. Bahia is a particularly festive area of a country famous for its celebrations of the carnival spirit. Amado's first novel was in fact titled *Carnival Land* (1932) and depicted social and political corruption against a colorful background of carnival and magic. Magic is not the stuff of fairy tales for the people of Bahia (or most of South America for that matter) but an integral part of their culture. *Candomble*, meaning "magic-religion", a fusion of African cult beliefs and practices with Roman Catholicism, along with pure magic (*macumba*), has become a part of daily "reality."

Dona Flor draws heavily from this tradition to depict a tale in which a carnival triumph is quite literally the theme and plot. The novel begins with Carnival:

Vadinho, Dona Flor's first husband, died one Sunday of Carnival, in the morning, when, dressed up like a Bahian woman, he was dancing the samba, with the greatest enthusiasm, in the Dois de Julho Square, not far from his house.
(translated by Hariet de Ónis. New York, 1967)

In a series of flashbacks we learn that Vadinho was a Dionysian rogue who gambled, ate, drank, and whored himself to his premature Carnival death. But for the last few years before he died, he was the loving though unfaithful husband of the beautiful Dona Flor. Their days together were joyfully occupied with love-making and eating the gourmet dishes Dona Flor, a cooking teacher by profession, prepared (recipes are included in the novel). The young widow mourns her husband for a year but then consents to an arranged marriage with the dull but respectable owner of a local drugstore. At first attracted to a bourgeois life of comfort and stability, she soon becomes destracted and then disenchanted. Amado then introduces a carnival triumph as Vadinho reappears to Dona Flor to reclaim his role as lover and husband. Dona Flor is shocked by his victory over death which, of course, only she can see. But as she grows accustomed to his "presence", she finally accepts the ghost-reality of her first husband as a healthy counterpart to her second husband's lifeless sobriety. The story that began on a Sunday in Carnival as Vadinho left the Triumph Bar, ends on a "rain-washed Sunday morning, with Dona Flor strolling along, happy with her life, satisfied with her two loves."

Again, the straightforwardness with which Amado presents such a "magical" triumph reflects a culture that accepts the supernatural as natural and the unusual as an everyday occurrence. And in the last paragraph of the novel, Amado reemphasizes this point:

...All this took place; let him who will, believe. It took place in Bahia, where these and other acts of magic occur without startling anybody. If anyone has his doubts, let him ask Cardose e Sa., and he will tell him whether or not it is the truth. He can be found on the planted Mars or on any poor corner of the city.

Dona Flor thus represents the theme of carnival triumph in its purest and most literal form. Vadinho as a Brazilian Dionysos carried the spirit of carnival to its extreme: exhaustion and death. Yet his carnival spirit could not be long suppressed by middle class conventions, a fact that Dona Flor finally recognizes and embrances.

Without having to be dogmatic, Amado skillfully succeeds in making us aware of a number of different ways in which carnival has triumphed. On the social level *Dona Flor* is a re-affirmation of a popular culture and its festive traditions. Psychologically his tale supports the individual's need for a healthy fantasy world to counter-balance the restrictions of social patterns, while from a Marxist point of view the novel suggests the sterility of bourgeois life without the vital spirit of the lower classes. Most importantly, however, Amado creates a work that is playful (illusion-reality), comic, and thus an enjoyable vision of fulfillment in an imperfect world.

It has been necessary to give a detailed introduction to the film because Barreto has faithfully captured the spirit and most of the substance and style of Amado's novel in his film. Barreto mirrors Amado's intentions when he says that in the film he wanted to "...do a comedy that was picaresque and casual, a film where the naughtiness and sensuality of the Brazilian people could be shown and felt." Barreto therefore was concerned with finding the most effective ways to transpose the novel to the screen.

Although only twenty-two when he shot *Dona Flor*, Bruno Barreto had already made two other feature films and seven shorts. Furthermore, many of these films were adaptations of literary works including his shorts *A Bolsa E A Vida* (*The Handbag and the Life*, 1971) based on Carolos Drummond de Andrade's *A Bolsa*, and *Emboscada* (*Ambush*, 1972) from Heberto's *Sale's Tale*, and his second feature, *A Estrela Sobe* (*The Rising Star*, 1975) taken from Marques Rebelo's 19th-century novel. Finally we can see he was well prepared to deal with the Bahia region since in 1967 he had shot a documentary *Bahia Visited* which won a prize in a Brazilian film competition.

As director and script writer Barreto brought an impressive amount of experience with him to the Amado project.

His success is apparent from the opening sequence. We open with a long-shot of the main square in Bahia, completely empty in the early morning. Bahia is thus established as the background against which the story will unfold, but more importantly Barreto gives us time to orient ourselves to an attractive but dilapidated old city which reflects the architecture of the "old" world falling into ruin. The mood is drab, somber, threatening. Barreto then switches to a table of men drinking beer outside a bar as the sound of a samba can just be heard in the background. As the music grows louder and the carnival celebrants come into view, one of the men—Vadinho—rises and joins the street celebrants. Vadinho (played by Jose Wilker) is tall and blond but featureless within his bizarre carnival costume which includes a native dress and a huge artificial phallus (much like that of an Aristophanic chorus!). Carnival fills the plaza. Suddenly Vadinho collapses and we learn he is dead. Dona Flor appears and begins to grieve for her husband as those around her already start to whisper about his decadent reputation.

The mood and themes of the film are captured visually in the opening without the need for much dialogue. Carnival is where the film begins, but the somber atmosphere of Bahia and the sudden death of Vadinho during his samba indicate immediately that *Dona Flor* is not a companion piece to the highly romanticized *Orfeu Negro* (*Black Orpheus*, 1958) made by French director Marcel Camus from the play by Vinicius de Moraes (*Black Orpheus*, for instance, begins with a postcard sunrise over Rio). Barreto effectively establishes a tension between the decay of the old city and the carnival spirit of its people, and with Vadinho's sudden end, between death and life.

For the flashbacks which retrace Dona Flor's life with Vadinho, Barreto has employed a variety of techniques to make the film a satisfying work in its own right rather than merely a filmed novel. Dona Flor, portrayed by the alluring actress Sonia Braga, remembers a life of love-making and culinary delights. This vision of a full and sensuous and fertile life is cleverly captured as she recalls Vadinho's favorite dish, marinated crab. She goes over the recipe as Barreto uses a close-up of the exotic ingredients being combined and cooked. As we see the sizzling stew in super close-up we hear Dona Flor mourning:

It was Vadinho's favorite dish,
I will never again serve it at my table,
His teeth bit into the crab,
His lips were yellow with the dende oil,
Alas, never again his lips,
His tongue, never again
His mouth burning with raw onion!

These last lines become a refrain running throughout the film as Barreto presents a series of scenes of the young couple making love. The words, of course, are Amado's, but the imaginative visual juxtaposition of the simmering food and the passionate sex is Barreto's successful coup. The healthy sensuality of all appitites, the basis of the carnival spirit, is thus realized more fully than it has been in earlier films such as the famous eating scene in Tony Richardson's *Tom Jones* (1965). Richardson's scene is simply one moment in a long narration whereas the combined food-sex imagery is central to Amado's and thus to Barreto's work in a way that suggests the importance of culinary and sexual imagery as a carnival spirit in Aristophanes and Rabelais.

Barreto also uses the samba music of carnival throughout the film as a theme representing Vadinho's spirit and thus, at times, as a suble counter-current to the "proper" bourgeois world Dona Flor enters upon her second marriage. The ending of the film is all the more triumphant because of the engaging rhythm and melody of the samba music composed by Chico Buarque. Dona Flor's carnival triumph is clear in the novel, but it is even more striking in the film. Having finally accepted the reality of her "dead" first husband, she begins to feel free to walk about in public with her two husbands. No one except Dona Flor can see Vadinho who is stark naked in his "new" life, and so unabashedly represents the sensual force he was in his first life. Barreto treats us to an ending in which Dona Flor emerges from the cathedral on a Sunday and enters the crowded streets, walking arm-in-arm with her two husbands. She smiles broadly, content with her new life, and pleased with the fact that her "secret" is unknown to those around her. The music increases as the camera pulls back to show the naked Vadinho, Dona Flor and the sober Teodoro melting into the crowd. Because it is the same shot we had in the opening of the film, the carnival triumph is made even more apparent: the somber empty square has been replaced by a crowded plaza filled with music as Dona Flor defies social convention and entertains her two husbands. After the film fades from the screen, the triumphant beat of the samba continues.

Much of the success of Barreto's film has to do with the straight-forward simplicity with which it is presented. The chance to include a "ghost" as a major character would be the green light for many directors to round up a special effects crew. But, as Amado suggests, magic is so much a part of the daily life of Bahia that his story is not to be taken as a trip into the supernatural. Barreto simply presents Vadinho as *there*. Unlike the Hollywood witchcraft and magic films in *The Exorcist* tradition, *Dona Flor* remains intensely human in perspective through its acceptance of an "ordinary" magic. The sense of carnival and human comedy derives from the situation (the return of a "dead" husband) rather than from tricks, special effects, an evocation of an unknowable force. In a simple style that quite apparently owes much to Bunuel's technique of presenting the surreal with casual ease, Barreto uses no self-conscious camera movements, cuts, or gimmicks to hold our attention. Instead we are treated to the human pathos and comedy of each scene: Vadinho sitting on top of a bureau laughing as Dona Flor's second husband makes feeble love to his wife, for instance, or to a shot of the three of them in bed, Dona Flor in the middle, uneasy about her predicament. Furthermore, Barreto's simplicity of style is refreshing and called for because of the innate appeal of Bahia, its people and culture. Especially for foreigners, the "reality" of this tropical city appears more unusual than the reappearance of Vadinho.

The final result is that Barreto has created a film that does justice to Amado's novel while emerging as a well-crafted, satisfying film in its own right. The theme of carnival triumph has been important in literature, but Barreto has taken advantage of film's unique capacity to capture this spirit in its Brazilian native variety both visually and through its sounds and music. Dona Flor recalls one of Vadinho's favorite expressions: "If God meant for man not to make love he would not have given him balls." While one reviewer spoke of *Dona Flor* as high class Brazilian porno, it is difficult to understand how such a label could accurately be given, for what Barreto succeeds in conveying is a full vision of human sensuality (and his grainy color photography also plays a role in this capacity) in which sex is one part of a vibrant force that embraces all of life. The problem with porno films, in fact, is that sex is seldom presented as a joyous experience that leads to personal fulfillment. The closing shot of Dona Flor and her *two* husbands is a powerful image of fulfillment. [And such complete satisfaction is the very essence of carnival triumph.]

ANDREW HORTON is an assistant professor of film and literature at the University of New Orleans and is a frequent contributor to many film journals.

escandalar

40-40 Hampton Street, Elmhurst, New York 11373

a literary magazine in Spanish will appear quarterly beginning with the January/March 1978 issue. A non-commercial, non-academic forum for writers/critics from diverse cultures and traditions. Poetry, narrative, essay, translations, reviews, interviews. Rigor and risk. The greatest range possible within the limitations set by circumstance. Currents and tendencies in contemporary art and thought. Literature, music, art, philosophy, cinema. In each issue: an aspect or figure of American culture. Contributions from outstanding Latin American and Spanish writers. New values. A magazine of orientation, adventure, exploration.

Contributors: Severo Sarduy, Alberto Girri, Harold Bloom, Marco Antonio Montes de Oca, Ramón Xirau, Fernando Savater, Mario Vargas Llosa, José Emilio Pacheco, Julieta Campos, Dore Ashton, Charles Simic, Jorge Ibargüengoitia, Alvaro Mutis, John Ashbery, René Char, Gabriel Zaid, Charles Tomlinson, Enrique Krauze, Saúl Yurkievich, Joseph Brodsky, Juan Sánchez Peláez, Jacques Roubaud, Roberto Juarroz, Denis Roche, Gonzalo Rojas, Salvador Elizondo, Elizabeth Bishop, Danubio Torres Fierro, Natalio Galán, Claude Esteban, Richard Howard, Carlos Germán Belli, Juan Liscano, Phillippe Sollers, Guillermo Carnero, Raúl Gustavo Aguirre,

Editor:
Editorial Board:

escandalar, *like the compass room, will be a space open to destiny. Destiny? Destinies: the three cardinal points of creation and knowledge: Heaven, Hell, Earth.*

Octavio Armand
Guillermo Cabrera Infante
Roberto Cantú
Lorenzo García Vega
Pere Gimferrer
Ulalume González de León
Octavio Paz
Julián Ríos
Mark Strand
Guillermo Sucre

... ...

Please begin my subscription to *escandalar* with issue No. ....

Individual:	$12/yearly	$20/two years
Institutions:	$16/yearly	$24/two years

Name ....

Address ....

....

* Please send your check or money order along with this form. Payable to escandalar, inc.

escandalar, inc. is a non-profit organization incorporated in the State of New York. *escandalar* does not depend on commercial support nor is it inclined to academic or ideological syllogisms.

Alejandro Otero

Venezuela, b. 1921

"He is the most important creative plastic artist in our part of America, precisely because of his relationship to architecture and his mastery of public space."

Pablo Neruda

Page 127 *Rotor*
Caracas, 1968

Page 128 *Delta Solar*
(*Detail*)
Washington, D.C.,
1977

Above *Delta Solar*
(Detail)

Left *Delta Solar*

The Artist's Choice: Four Views

ROBERT A. PARKER

Four artists from four disciplines...four nationalities...four decades.

The perspective from an artist's mind, like that from within a geodesic dome, suggests the strength and harmony on which all art is based. The struts and braces, the angles and lines of the dome have their equivalent in the materials of art and the form that the artist gives them. To understand the blending of these elements is to confront that elusive process of creating art.

The core of this process is choice. What influences choice? Here is an insight into the minds of four Latin American artists.

Alberto Ginastera, the Argentinian composer, has been called "the Mozart of the 12-tone system." Now 63, he is working on his newest opera, Barrabas, whose religious theme contrasts to the barbaric elements of its predecessors, Don Rodrigo, Bomarzo, and Beatrix Cenci. At his residence in Geneva, he receives a visitor in a dark business suit, white shirt, black and white tie, gold cuff links—much more the image of a banker than of an artist whose themes have prompted a gasp from the philistines. Persian rugs on the floor of the receiving room and modern paintings on the wall capture the blend of tradition and originality that have made some critics uncomfortable with his music but have characterized his works from the early ballets, Panambi and Estancia, to the operas that have earned him his international reputation.

Roberto Athayde, the 29-year-old Brazilian playwright, saw his one-character work, Miss Margarida's Way, mounted more than 55 times in Europe, Asia, and Latin America before its successful New York run in 1977. The play, which has certain political overtones, asks the audience to play the eighth-grade students of the authoritarian teacher Miss Margarida. One night, in a tiny espresso cafe that faced a theatre marquee bearing his name, the playwright discussed a growing need to leave the isolation of writing and become more involved in human relationships; his intent, he said, is to turn from writing to directing. With straight dark hair hanging in a pony tail to his shoulders, with a classic profile and deep flashing eyes, Athayde offered the image of one ready to step on stage—perhaps as a director, but conceivably also as the romantic lead.

Oswaldo Vigas, the Venezuelan painter, is perhaps better known in Latin America than in Europe or the United States. He is recognized both as an outspoken critic against the use of art as a mark of social status and as a creative artist who is strongly influenced by the primitive, pre-Columbian art of his continent. After a decade of study in Paris, the artist returned home to discover this fountain of inspiration that dates back a thousand years or more. His hair now grey at age 53, he retains the vigor which has helped him to lead the artistic effort "to confront the magic, the cruel, the complex realities of the continent." While the angular images of his paintings hung in the background at a recent one-man exhibit held in New York City, he shrugged off a corduroy jacket to free his arms, his hands for gestures that symbolized his own reaching out for cultural identity.

Luis Valdez, the Chicano playwright and director, brought the mythical world of El Pachuco to Broadway last spring. All too briefly. Pausing for a moment in his hectic rounds of interviews and public appearances—designed to save the work Zoot Suit from the critics' thunder—he discussed the problems of an artist whose culture marries two languages. His deep, vibrant voice filled a sparsely decorated room, where actresses once received their admirers at the Winter Garden Theatre. But his pride in his heritage thrust away those ghosts of the past. And his dress was as contemporary as his concerns, a red sleeveless sweater over a dark shirt, a strand of beads around his neck. He stressed, too, the problem of identity for the bilingual artist, underscoring his points with a dead cigar. At 38, Valdez was ready for the climax of his career, a Broadway hit. Was his Hispanic audience ready as well? Well, if not, Valdez would be back. Ever since the farmlands of California, he has learned to survive.

ALBERTO GINASTERA
The Artist as Original

Stravinsky once repeated a line attributed to Picasso: "I do not search; I encounter." This clarifies many things, but most of all that originality is an innate quality of the artist.

For centuries, the artist never thought of being original. Bach did not think so; nevertheless, he was original. And the same occurred with Mozart, with Chopin, with Brahms. They existed to create art; they did not seek originality. Ours is an era of transition, and we find ourselves with an original named Stravinsky. Now, Mr. Stravinsky did not wish to be original; he is original. And the same with Schonberg, the same with Bartok.

Each is original; each is also clearly different.

Today, young people, above all in Europe, want first to be different—and this is a disaster. Because instead of thinking of perfection or harmony, or the true depths of art, they are thinking of the ways they can do something different. This is fashion; this is avant-guard incompetence.

Originality is influenced first of all by environment. In fact, one reason a good composer always has a distinct personality is that it is formed culturally and spiritually by his particular society. A unique influence on me was my exposure to opera at the Teatro Colon in Buenos Aires—although it was a long time before I took up the challenge to create one, for the libretto, the staging, the acting require a knowledge that goes beyond the field of music.

Spiritual factors also affect the artist. Many persons do not believe this, but I am sure that they do. Faith does not affect art directly, of course, but it influences how one sees things and feels things. And it often serves as a fountain of inspiration.

Another influence that artists confront is folklore, but despite my ballets *Panambi* and *Estancia*, I believe there is little folkloric influence in my work, for Buenos Aires was always a very cosmopolitan city. But I have been teaching Latin American students for 10 years now in Switzerland, and it is distressing to see how many of them are so intent on using the folkloric tradition of their countries. For folklore is not an integral part of art. One may use basic rhythms from folklore, and also its forms, but this by itself is not artistic creation. One must transform those elements. The beginning of the *Rite of Spring*, for example, seems like a melody of Stravinsky's although it is really a popular song, I believe from Lithuania. However, for me, the time for folklore in music has passed, even for the sophisticated and spiritualized folklore by the likes of Stravinsky and Bartok.

What is advancing is an era of frankness in all art. When I am asked about the violence and sex in my operatic works, my response is usually that they are purely accidental, that I was attracted to the story in each case, and are not the stories of most operas concerned with love and death? But I should add that more significant themes in my operas are the anguish of man and his concern with death—which will also be themes of my new opera, *Barrabas*.

What we must remember is that sexual concepts have changed considerably, so what was concealed before can now be presented on stage. It began, perhaps, when Richard Straus wrote *Salome* at the turn of the century, when its staging presented a woman dancing and disrobing—even though the music itself was in the romantic tradition. From the perspective of our post-Freudian era, on the other hand, I wonder how a composer of today would write *The Barber of Seville*. Even as a musical comedy, it would have to be different: the sex would be lighter, the love not so pure. It would have to belong to our era.

However, an artist should never compromise with his audience. For example, the cello concerto I wrote for my wife concludes with probably the longest note I have written. It lasts and lasts, until what would be the final climax is transformed into an anticlimax by the length of the note. Then as it persists in the psyche of the listener, it is converted into another climax. And this climax, touching on something within us that sustains it, diminishes into another anticlimax. Nevertheless, it is so persistent that it begins to bother us, and although it is very soft, we say to ourselves, *caramba*, when is this going to end? And there is the climax. Understand? It is a very curious effect.

In art, what you never do is imitate. I tell my students that artists must know from the beginning what they wish to accomplish with a new work. And that they must get their technique up to date, that technique is like language and they must learn to speak the language of their time. Learning to use language, I say, is like learning to dress for the occasion. And should others not understand if the language is proper, then wait, for those who follow will understand. So basic is the need to dominate the technique of your day—and so I speak the language of Cervantes, but I do not speak as Cervantes did.

And the second thing is to look within yourself. To discover yourself. To be conscious of what you want to do or do not want to do. This is fundamental. Everything else is *ambiente*, the atmosphere that surrounds the artist: culture, history, folklore, the picturesque. No, above all, the artist—like Bach, like Stravinsky—discovers himself within himself. This is the source of originality. What is outside, his *ambiente*, comes later.

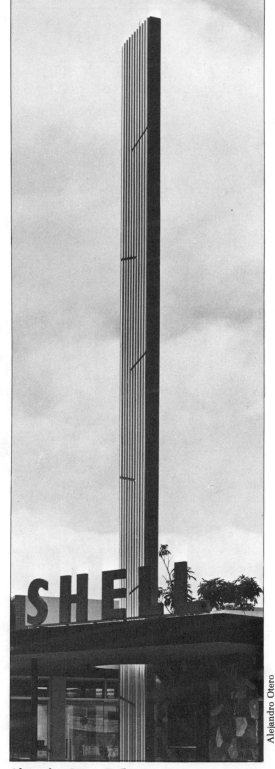

Alejandro Otero, Reflecting Stele
Caracas, 1958

ROBERTO ATHAYDE

The Artist as Alone

The fate of a writer is to be extremely lonely. You deny yourself the whole world, and then you turn around and recreate it in your own terms. As you sit there before a blank piece of paper, you feel a sensation of extreme power, but as you exert that power, as you exercise that fantasy, you begin to miss the real world.

Playing God is fun, that is, but you know you are not God, and you know you need the world around you. Otto Rank discusses this dilemma of the artist, that the intense act of creation awakens him to his need for the real world of other people, until he rebels against his own creative act.

That is what has happened to me at this point in my career. I can no longer commit myself to artistic works that do not involve other people. I wish to interact with others. After the lonely world of the artist, I feel entitled to broader social contacts, such as directing a play or a motion picture, in which you must commit yourself to other people's works, other people's demands.

The director, you see, is dealing with life, with people, with problems that involve their personal life. When you face a blank piece of paper, with an entire vocabulary to use, your decisions can be very arbitrary; but a director cannot do this, since he is dealing with human beings who possess their own world, their own personality, their own ego.

I am also interested in directing because I am interested in the present, and directing requires a spontaneous communication with your fellow beings. You cannot deal with people in the past. The past belongs to the intellectual realm, which is also the realm of the writer. The present offers an authentic experience, because that is all that truly exists. Whereas the past is an abstraction. The past may be extremely difficult to explain away, because it feels so alive in the present; but ultimately it can be said not to exist, to be just a reflection of the lonely intelligence.

Art may be thus said to exist on two levels, the psychological and the social. Of the two, the psychological is really the crucial one, because the nature of the creative act is that it takes place in solitude. The psychology of the lonely creator is paramount.

Now, having said this, I must also say that the social level is extremely important. Because the civilized standards by which we live are really social standards. And a work of art that reflects these social concerns cannot be downplayed. Because if you should reject such social concern in a work of art, you would really be betraying the civilization that you belong to. So this is one of the forces at play in a work of art, and when you blend these two concerns, the social and the psychological, you have created the strongest type of art.

To illustrate, at the risk of appearing immodest, my own play, *Miss Margarida's Way*, is really a very personal psychological statement about an emotionally complex school teacher, with a lack of any social comment. Yet you only have to consider it from a social perspective, with the implication that the schoolteacher in a classroom symbolizes a dictator and his oppressed people, and the play appears to be engagé. And so I am taken to be a political writer by many people in South America, particularly by those from countries with an authoritarian government. Yet the people who know me most closely consider me completely aloof from politics or social concerns.

The fact is, my social concerns exist on a personal level. In fact, that may be why my personal life can no longer be a life of solitude. However, those who say my directorial ambitions mean a loss of my creativity do not understand me. It may be a loss for others, but it is not a loss for me. It is a loss only for those who are extreme enough to believe that a writer's not needing to write is a loss. But it is very silly to think that way. I am totally incapable of thinking of myself as someone who *has* to write a new work. I think of myself simply as committed to living out my next bit of life, and that, I think, is burden enough.

OSWALDO VIGAS
The Artist as Committed

I became truly an artist when I discovered the visual forms that had existed on our continent before the Conquest. Like many painters, I had been intent on creating a cosmopolitan art that was directed toward the eye, that had no human or spiritual connotation, much less any philosophic comment on the condition of our continent.

But suddenly, I found I had something personal to give. It is not that I became interested in pre-Columbian elements; it is that they were suddenly inside me and needed to manifest themselves. My current exhibition offers homage to the idea of ancestors in our primitive culture. The figures represent a search for organic images that evoke our unity with the landscape; they suggest animal shapes yet also shapes that seem like vegetation in humanoid form.

The result is a baroque art which is very appropriate, for our history, our traditions in Latin America are baroque; even our jungles are baroque. Our great writers today—such as García Márquez—are baroque. So are the great artists since before the Conquest. When the aboriginals of our continent created their religious art—such as the images of the Aztec gods—they also created a decorative art, an art that reflected the joy of life and occupied space merely as decoration. This is a very baroque concept.

In addition, Latin America offers a surrealistic touch, for life itself is surrealistic. You can drive along a river in a brand new car, with the roar of a 747 overhead, and you can see a woman in a native dress washing clothes in the water, perhaps even wearing a snake as a collar around her neck. What else is this scene if not surrealistic?

For years, the problem of Latin American artists has been a denial of such scenes. They wanted to be cosmopolitan in order to be accepted throughout the world. But more and more, I myself want to be considered a regional artist. I feel weaker when I am aware of my cosmopolitan tendencies; I lose the earth that is under my feet. I am stronger and happier when I maintain contact with my roots.

For too long, Latin American artists filled their space without any philosophic, any religious, any social connotations. Everything was created strictly for the eye, since this pre-

sented no problem of conscience, no conflict, and could be accepted by everyone. But to be appreciated by the masses, you must descend to the level of the masses. And this results in the inevitable prostitution of the artist.

Picasso was asked once how to distinguish between two paintings: which one is art, and which one only fills space? He said that the one which is art contains conflict, reflects the human anguish within us all. Now, that struggle to be human includes philosophy, includes religion, and includes the great scandal of death—that we are going to disappear, that we are subject to the tyranny of time.

I foresee in Latin America an art that affirms our social, cultural, and moral values, that reflects the fact we are envied by people in Europe and the United States for preserving standards that have disappeared in their countries—such as those which concern the family, friendship, and all human relations—standards which are impossible to preserve in the great cities of the world. The result will be not an art produced in a classroom or laboratory but an art which is in contact with reality, which expresses the life style of a people.

The Latin American artist, like every artist, is destined to a life of discovery. Each day he must become like a child, expressing an innocence, a pride, a conviction that he possesses the truth. And he must remain a child to the end of his days. For to renounce art is to renounce life.

Of course, as we grow old, many of us strive to become more pure, more ascetic, more perfect, renouncing more and more each day, like a sailor who seeks to survive by throwing everything overboard, until he remains alone on his ship with no life jacket, no ropes, no anchor. And all the while he is steering, like Hemingway, toward *nada*, toward nothing. And this is death. This is the tendency toward *nada* that exists in all human beings.

But there is also another tendency—toward struggle, toward survival, toward life. And I do not believe it is the destiny of man to bow to death, to lower his head and submit. For how could the human species have done so and yet have survived on earth since prehistoric times?

Man has indeed created great machines, great methods of distruction in our times, and they link man to death. They are the products of technology, of reason. But art is the opposite. It is not a product of rational thinking, or an esthetic logic.

Perhaps this is the difference. That death is linked to rational thinking. That life, that art is instinctive, is natural.

It is a difference to which the Latin American artist can easily adjust.

LUIS VALDEZ
The Artist as Bilingual

I started life speaking only Spanish. My introduction to English was both a joyful and a traumatic experience. It was in school; and I just had to pick it up myself, from the time I was six to the time I was seven. I still remember not being able to speak the language the teacher was speaking, while everyone else understood. The experience left me with a tolerance for not understanding another language, as well as an ability to read people, to understand the sense, the feeling they are projecting. Because sometimes what people say is not what they mean.

And so, years later, in my travels with the Teatro Campesino, when I saw groups performing in their native language, such as Japanese, Rumanian, or French languages I did not understand, I appreciated a scene portrayed in its own language. Although I didn't get the word-for-word meaning, I sensed the quality of the language. You see, there is a deeper level to language, which has to do with the quality of its sound.

That is why to me there is a certain smugness in a person who says, "Well, it's not in English, so I won't pay any attention to it." How do you know it can't communicate to you, I ask. Because I have gone all the way in the other direction. Because I have embraced English, which is a beautiful language, which has something particularly energetic and dynamic about it.

But the Latin culture has its own values, too. In the theatre, Latins prefer a lot of color and physical movement, so that a perfectly natural expression of human emotion seems to the anglo eye to be overstatement, even hammy. And I have to be aware of this, as I deal with either Hispanic or Anglo audiences, or even with Hispanic or Anglo characters in my work.

There was a period in my life when I was very Anglo, when I wore a crewcut and a high school sweater, when I was not being my barrio self. I was called Louis or Louie, and I was happy chasing Anglo girl friends. But I lost my sense of self-appreciation. In fact, I got rather tired of myself. It was not until after high school that I let my moustache grow, and let it all hang out. Then I began to feel better about myself.

I know that my work for the Teatro Campesino has been criticized for being too concerned with identity. But the critics do not live in the world that I do, a world of two cultures. To tell you the truth, I do not know what would have happened if I had been born a foot taller and light skinned, rather than being short and dark. I do know that all around me as I grew up, I saw Chicanos who were tall and were accepted if they behaved Anglo. But when I tried to behave Anglo, it became an absurdity. People in the barrio said I was acting ridiculously, that I was never going to be a white man.

Today, I no longer want to talk about the Chicano, but about the Hispano. For there's a ring around the United States that includes Indian Americans, African Americans, Asian Americas, and European Americans. And as soon as this great mass of people wakes up and discovers that it is related to each other, things are going to change. We are La Raza. I am no longer just a Chicano, a child of the Sonoma desert.

Shelley, I think, once said that poets are the unacknowledged legislators of the world. I am not sure what role language is going to play in all this, but I don't see now a need for artists to be bilingual. They will simply communicate to the other world through their sheer artistry. The important thing is for artists on each side to make a statement, using all their fundamental tools, such as texture, tone, imagery, symbolism. What may happen first is that Hispanics in this country will find a way to make their statement in English—and will change English much as Blacks have changed English. And the language will benefit from this.

So I am working on a new vision of America. Just as the so-called conquest of Mexico by the Spaniards and the colonization of America by the pilgrims did not happen overnight, however, neither will the understanding between Latin America and Anglo America. It takes time for people to understand each other. The creation of one America may be a thousand year process, and we are only 500 years into it. There will continue to be problems, but we have to continue struggling to deal with them. And while it may be easy to become cynical, we must resist it. I know it is not going to achieve anything for me but take me back to a little town in California.

ROBERT A. PARKER, director of publications for an international public accounting firm, has written on a variety of cultural subjects for both U.S. and Latin American publications.

Island of Luminous Artifact

View of Dawn in the Tropics
by Guillermo Cabrera Infante
Translated by Suzanne Jill Levine
Harper & Row, 1979. $8.95

WILLIAM KENNEDY

The new work of fiction by Guillermo Cabrera Infante is, for him, a radical divestiture of literary ornament. After his first novel, *Three Trapped Tigers*, a bouillabaisse of styles, word games, cinematic ruptures, squiggles, scriptings, puns, poetry, parodies and other Finnegannigans which sprawled for almost 500 pages, this much-lauded Cuban author delivers up a work of understated social outrage.

The new book is *View of Dawn in the Tropics*, first published in Spain in 1974, and said to have been, originally, a segment of *Three Trapped Tigers*. If *Tigers*, as it was published, was Joycean, then the new work, standing alone, is Hemingwayesque, in the tradition of the vignettes of *In Our Time*. The power of the new book is not so much in its invention as in its poetic concision. It runs only 145 pages and consists of 103 prose poems, few of which exceed a single page and one of which is only two lines long: "In what other country of the world is there a province named Matanzas, meaning 'Slaughter'?" In keeping with his poetic mode, the author has indexed his first lines.

He is translated into an English that is both powerful, and, when necessary, elegant, by Suzanne Jill Levine, one of the two translators of *Three Trapped Tigers*. With this book Cabrera Infante becomes yet another contemporary Latin American novelist to write a fully politicized work. The dual theme is oppression and rebellion, one following the other as relentlessly as the night follows the day.

The book begins in Cuba's pre-history: "The islands came out of the ocean as isolated isles, then the keys became mountains and the shallows, valleys. Later the islands joined to form a great island, which soon became green where it wasn't golden or reddish...."

Nature poetry quickly fades with the arrival of the Ciboney Indians, who are the first inhabitants, but who swiftly become enslaved to the more savvy Tainos; and both fall prey to the cannibalistic warriors of the Caribs. And then come the whites, who reduce the Indian population from 100,000 to 5,000 in five years, not only by warfare but by disease, by terror that induces a great many suicides, and by killer bloodhounds, soon to be known in the hemisphere as Cuban hounds.

Cabrera Intante leaps forward like a spastic time-machine operator, giving us the first rumblings of uprising by black sugar mill workers, the execution of an unlucky poet accused of conspiring against the colonial powers, the retaliation against some anatomy students who, while in a cemetery, inadvertently scratch the glass on a Spanish journalist's tomb. Officials try the students for the crime, including two who were not in the city when the scratch was made. Eight students, all under 20, are shot.

So we are immersed, fragmentally, in what the author calls his vision of "the strategies of history." Rebellion grows, and traitorous Cubans join the Spaniards in trying to thwart it. The rebels shape a style, a uniform for themselves: "In the engraving, published in New York, you can see in the foreground four *mambíses*—that's what the rebels called their insurgent army.... The rider is black and wears his machete on his belt. Two of the riders are also black and, unlike the rider, they're barefoot. [One] black chats with a white *mambí*; he's wearing a kerchief on his head, while all the others wear palm-leaf hats." In a later era the rebels will wear fatigue caps and beards.

The book evinces a fascination with old photos, and Cabrera Infante's prose reveals beneath the stillness of the photos the fury and the failure that are the undying realities of the oppressed. But his prose is often in service of the odd moments when the horror is pushed offstage so that people may reveal their humanity. The meeting of two rebel generals is a case in point.

The generals pause in their war for a meal together—plantains, sweet potatoes and a roasted cow, their first meat in two months. The moment is cinematic: fat dripping from one general's chin, meat lying on a palm leaf on the grass. "The other general went to the river and took out of the water two brown bottles stoppered with wild cork. He displayed them from afar, one in each hand and up high, like two trout. What luxury, said the general. The bottles were sweating and they drank straight from the cold bottles while they ate and talked and laughed. It was like a picnic."

The picnic is interrupted in the next vignette by news of an enemy column approaching. One general leads his troops into the fight and has his brains blown away. His men strip him of his possessions to prevent his being identified and defiled, and bury him with a silver dollar to prove his identity at a later date, when the revolution succeeds, and when he can be exhumed and buried with the glory and pomp that befits his bravery.

Bravery of rebels in the face of what since the beginning has been the overwhelming power and cruelty of the oppressor is one theme of Cabrera Infante, whether it be men in the 19th century fighting for independence from Spain, or modern rebels in the Sierra Maestra, led to glory by an unnamed Castro. (Very few names are used, chiefly designations: the colonel, the old commander, the comandante, the chaplain, the boy.) Now the bravery means carrying dynamite, now tunneling under a cemetery in a doomed effort to kill a tyrant. Perhaps the plotters are boys, hiding in a house and pleading with the owner: "Please, sir, hide us. We are being chased by tyranny."

"This is also true: that's what they said," Cabrera Infante writes. "How they turned that terrible, but then personal, moment into a generalization, almost into an abstract thought, how they did it nobody knows, but it is known that they did it. They hid in a house on Hope Street and the police came and took them out on the street and killed them near the market. But that was later. Now what really matters, what is really moving, is to know that those three boys, persecuted, half naked said: 'We're being chased by Tyranny,' and not: 'We're being chased by the police'...and that's what made them heroes. Shouldn't one believe that if there is a poetical intuition, there is also a historical intuition?"

Whether it is the tyranny of the students murdered for scratching a foreigner's coffin, bestial torture by Batista's army, or the starving to death of a prisoner under Castro's revolutionary police, the burial of his body in secret, and the refusal to notify the mother of his death or the location of his grave, the depredations do not change except in particulars. Bravery recurs, rebels overthrow tyrant, rebels install or develop new tyrant, new tyranny creates new rebels.

Cabrera Infante, born in 1929, was raised with a sense of insurgency: his father was a founder of the Cuban Communist party. The son became a journalist, a film critic and a cultural commisar (head of the Council of Culture, director of the Film Institute) when the Castro revolution succeeded. From 1962 to 1965 he was with the Cuban embassy in Brussels and in 1965 he returned to Havana. Soon after, he chose to leave Cuba and live in London with his family. His rise to cultural eminence seems to have ended not only with disenchantment but with indictment—specifically an indictment in this work of Castro's arrogance of power, and of the debasement and murder of brave but deviant revolutionaries.

The Cabrera Infante vision of history is that it is a dismal horror with intermittent eras of light, which are the eras of struggle. Students of Cuban history will be able to identify battles and events, villains and heroes: Martí, Machado, Batista, Guevara, Cienfuegos; for it does seem to one observer of Cuban politics over the past two decades, that Cabrera Infante has been historically, as well as poetically faithful to the rebel and fascistic actualities; and surely they were the animating elements for him in the shaping of such a book as this.

But one need not be Cuban, or even try to play the matching game; for the author creates his island as a luminous artifact that reflects the history of almost all of Latin America: the perennial practical joke that time plays on ideologues of all stripes: evil dies, then bravery dies; and the sun also rises on the artifact.

"And it will always be there," Cabrera Infante concludes, "...that long, sad, unfortunate island will be there after the last Indian and after the last Spaniard and after the last African and after the last American and after the last of the Cubans, surviving all disaster, eternally washed over by the Gulf Stream: beautiful and green, undying, eternal."

WILLIAM KENNEDY, former book critic for LOOK Magazine, is a novelist and critic who has written frequently about Latin American fiction. His novels are The Ink Truck, Legs, and Billy Phelan's Greatest Game.

Crac!

The Magic Orange Tree and
Other Haitian Folktales
Collected, edited and translated by
Diane Wolkstein
Alfred A. Knopf, 1978. $6.95

BARRE TOELKEN

Diane Wolkstein's wide and well-deserved reputation as a collector and teller of stories is once more enhanced by the publication of this attractive and modestly-priced book. Although the collected texts are not provided in their original form, their translation is apparently accurate, their rendering as tales certainly effective, comfortable, and natural. Wolkstein makes clear in her introduction that the tales are not hers, but the property of much valued friends and acquaintances in Haiti who perform these narratives for each other under everyday circumstances and in the shared emotional and cultural contexts of real village life in Haiti. To that extent, the basic selection is theirs, not hers, although she admits to liking some stories better than others, to presenting some and not others. She is thus honestly and correctly listed on the title page as collector (though one must read the book carefully to pick up references scattered throughout the introductory passages to find out who the principal translators were).

In a very real way, Diane Wolkstein is a handsome example of what author Barry Lopez calls a Translator; not merely someone who brings words from one language into another with dictionary precision, but a person who can bridge cultures in such a way as to bring understanding—wit, humor, and moral meaning—along with the words. Wolkstein presents stories here that cover the whole range of Haitian village life, and they do not feature much of those pretty, childlike, quaint, primitive, or other easy characteristics usually attributed to folktales by elite readers. There is instead a tone of resignation to a world where chance, frustration, disappointment and meanness are so common that they provide motivation and meaning for everyday entertainments in oral tradition, and a world in which humor and resourcefulness are the primary defenses against the inevitable. The stories, of course, do not say these things; they embody them. This is hard and abstract stuff, masquerading as fun. Wolkstein handles it with sensitivity, not letting the heavy aspects get in the way of a good story, not letting the earthy and oppressive themes escape from these fine expressions of the human condition.

Although Wolkstein makes it clear she is not pretending to do a folkloristic, scholarly presentation, it may be interesting to provide a folklorist's response to her position. She refers to "folklorists, who make statistical samplings of all the stories they have gathered, [while story collectors] choose in the end those stories they believe in." Without defending aimless statistical analysis on the one hand, or decrying personal choice on the other, a modern folklorist would be moved to ask the question "Yes, but what dimension might have been added to this collection through the use of comparative methods in folklore?" Perhaps the fact that the story "Four Hairs from the Beard of the Devil" is an obvious version of "Jack and the Beanstalk" would not be considered momentous to the general reader, and merely listing that information in the headnote might certainly strike the reader as pedantic. But a folklorist would point out the interesting fact that here is an identifiably European story circulating among black Haitians. Has it developed particular Haitian characteristics that, by comparison with European aspects, might help

reveal even more fully the dynamic and creative dimensions of Haitian storytelling? Remarkable if it were not so. And is it entirely coincidental that the story features a helpful woman plucking hairs from her husband's beard while a young man hides under the bed (in a striking parallel to many ribald stories) while finding answers to dilemmas involving a limping virgin, a plugged well, and a guard standing at attention pointing his gun? Both Freud and European folklore have much to say about these features, but especially important is the question of what, if anything, they mean in Haiti; there is too much for coincidence, but too little in the way of commentary for a full recognition—and thus a full enjoyment of the story—to occur.

Another fine story, "Tayzanne," concerns a young woman who falls in love with a wonderful fish. Her family entices the fish to the surface and her father kills it with a machete, at which Velina combs her hair and weeps until she sinks into the earth. Wolkstein professes not to understand the story, but comparative reference to the folktales of other cultures might have suggested some possibilities: parental anxiety about exogamy, for one. A Tsimshian story from the Northwestern United States concerns a young woman who marries a frog and goes to live with him in a lake. Her family, incensed at what they consider to be an outrageously unnatural union, drain the lake of water in order to get her back, but her human "reality" has changed to a frog reality, and when she is deprived of water, she drowns in the air before their eyes. Now, it would be irresponsible to suggest a direct relation between the Haitian and the Tsimshian tales, and even more ridiculous to suggest that Wolkstein should have mentioned this particular example. But a brief look such as this might have suggested a possiblity for meaning. Do the Haitians believe unions of love ought not to be impeded by the tastes of parents? Do they believe, conversely, that anyone who marries totally outside the group is committing a dangerous and potentially deadly act? That is, in "Tayzanne," whose tragedy is it? Some comparative work might have helped to ask those provocative questions of the storytellers themselves, rather than saving the puzzle for discussion over coffee with friends back home. If there is any failing in this book, it is in this: that the reader, deprived of the contextual references available to Wolkstein, may never know how close to a fuller view he or she might have been with the boost of another paragraph or two of incisive folkloristic commentary.

But this book is not addressed to folklorists primarily; thus, while these comments are not mere quibbles, they should not be taken as derogatory to a fine collection of stories with other distinctive and helpful features. One outstanding part of this book's offering is the place it gives to women narrators, who are often overlooked (or are considered unapproachable) by male folklorists and anthropologists. Moreover, Wolkstein provides rich—if brief—accounts of the actual dynamics which characterize the narrations of both men and women, both of whom ask for attention by saying "cric?" and are urged on to tell their stories by the audience's response of "crac!" The lesser storytellers do not call forth this response as often as do the superior ones, testifying to an ongoing esthetic system that encourages the best performers and performances. Since these narrations often include songs, gestures, and even dance, Wolkstein has provided contextual and gestural description (it is so rich, one wants more of it) and, at the back of the book, transcriptions of song tunes in English and Creole.

Indeed, aside from the scarcity of folkloristic comparison—which, after all, will not be lamented by all readers—it is hard to imagine how this could have been a better book. The stories are warm and human, and are presented without condescension. Its illustrations, done by a self-taught Argentinian (but why not a Haitian? one wants to ask) are attractive and appropriate. Wolkstein's introduction ends with a hopeful "cric?" and the collection itself is, certainly, a resounding "crac!"

BARRE TOELKEN is President of The American Folklore Society and teaches at the University of Oregon.

Promise for Tomorrow

Latin American Women Writers: Yesterday and Today
edited by Yvette Miller and Charles Tatum
Latin American Literary Review, 1977
$7.50

MARGERY RESNICK

During this decade, scholars of Latin American literature have successfully applied a variety of contemporary critical modes elaborated by both Continental and North American critics to the study of Latin American letters. Unfortunately, however, feminist literary scholarship with its particular emphasis on the relationship between life and art has been largely ignored. As we examine bibliographies on Latin American literature, it is astonishing to

note the discrepancy between the superfluity of critical energy expended on a rather limited group of male writers, often of modest talent, and the almost complete absence of substantial research on Latin American women poets, novelists, and playwrights. The works of Latin American women authors have been studied superficially, if at all. Their biographies have never been written, their correspondence remains uncollected, and their works are often difficult to obtain in the original and inaccessible in translation.

Yet, feminist literary criticism in France, England and the United States has developed into a rich and cosmopolitan field where scholars have skillfully drawn on the disciplines of social history, psychology, anthropology and linguistics and have examined the applications of structuralist, phenomenological and Marxist methodologies to the study of women's writing. During this past decade imaginative critical studies have successfully destroyed the clichés that had earlier left many female authors invisible, while scholars within the academy have challenged the reasoning of those who insist that inclusion in the literary canon is based solely on a disinterested evaluation of artistic merit. Concurrently, the publication of carefully researched alternative literary histories has made previously unavailable writing by women accessible to a wide audience, and the achievement of recognized women writers has been reassessed by scholars committed to a thorough study of the cultural web that often provided women writers with a separate tradition. Furthermore, feminist critics have examined the spiritual, social and economic ambience in which literature is conceived, created, published and reviewed.

The extraordinary power of this approach which, as Adrienne Rich suggests, takes "the work first of all as a clue to how we live, to how we have been led to imagine ourselves, how our language has trapped as well as liberated us; and how we can begin to see—and therefore live—afresh . . ."[1] cannot be overemphasized. It appears at a time when literary criticism is too often characterized by esoteric discourse that vitiates the works it treats, and that fails to make larger connections between individual works and the broader issues of cultural history.

The much-needed application of feminist criticism, which emphasizes the disparity between the vitality of life and the tyranny of social myth, would surely challenge our sensibilities and our shared assumptions about Latin American literature and society. In this context, the publication of *Latin American Women Writers: Yesterday and Today* marks a venturesome step on the part of critics and publishers into a new literary exploration.

Latin American Women Writers: Yesterday and Today contains selected proceedings from the Conference on Women Writers from Latin America, held in March, 1975, at Carnegie-Mellon University. There are critical essays as well as a bilingual anthology of poetry by women poets of Latin America who currently live in the United States. The editors, Yvette Miller and Charles Tatum, have not attempted to impose a formal structure on the essays, and the book is intended to serve as a starting point for studying women's literature in Latin America. The essays provoke questions, and, in many cases, provide bibliographies so that the interested reader may begin to pursue the answers.

The volume tantalizes us by identifying fascinating areas yet unstudied. For example, Harold Hinds' article on Soledad Acosta de Samper presents a prolific journalist, an indefatigable traveller and keeper of journals, and founder of four women's magazines who has yet to be placed intellectually in the development of nineteenth-century Latin American literature. Hinds notes the grave contradictions between the author's feminist writing and her diatribes in support of traditional values, but only a more exhaustive study of this writer's works and circumstance will allow us to draw meaningful implications for the creative process itself. Moreover, detailed study of the periodicals of the day would be required to determine the extent to which Acosta de Samper influenced the elaboration of a feminine literary subculture. When, later in the volume, Raymond Williams interviews two contemporary Colombian women writers—Fanny Buitrago and Albalucia Angel—one wonders at the development of a feminist perspective in Colombia that allows these authors to agree: "There haven't been any women writers in the boom because it hasn't occurred yet to any editor: they just haven't hit upon the idea. . . . It's more a problem of a mafia. Among writers there is a kind of very tight cord, not only abroad, but also in Colombia. These solid groups are formed that are always willing to support each other, but they don't consider it necessary to include women because of their 'machiso' . . ." Later, Angel identifies *La Tertulia* organized by women in Cali as a source of strength. Is there any connection between the contemporary Colombian women's literary *tertulias* and those established and frequented by Acosta de Samper? Is the cultural milieu in which Buitrago and Angel write shaped in any way by Colombian women writers who preceded them? Buitrago and Angel see clearly

that publication, discussion and distribution of books depends on the power to select; such power, in Latin America, has always belonged to men. Yet, the sureness of vision of these writers has allowed them to be productive in spite of the socially imposed difficulties. The specific historical and cultural conditions that have made such confidence possible remain to be determined. These articles do, nonetheless, encourage interested critics to direct attention to these questions.

Essays on other female novelists—Silvina Bullrich, María Angélica Bosco, and Beatriz Guido (Argentina); Clorinda Matto de Turner and Mercedes Caballo de Carbonera (Peru); Teresa de Parra (Venezuela); Marta Brunet (Chile); and Elena Poniatowska (Mexico)—are important for their presentation of works and authors rarely studied. To critics used to mining ever more deeply the works of the anointed, these essays may seem superficial. To the curious reader, however, this process of identification makes possible studies which go beyond the obvious. Critics who consider the content of these essays will, if they are sympathetic to broadly based esthetic studies, ask the following questions: if we take this fiction seriously as a criticism of life, what will it tell us about the collective feminine language? Does a community of Latin American women novelists who share a literary experience through correspondence and meetings exist? Do national boundaries effect the writing of women in the same way they bear upon men's work?

The questions raised by the articles on drama are equally provocative. In her thoughtful article on Myrna Casas, Griselda Gambara and Luisa Josefina Hernández, Gloria Waldman analyzes the authors' presentation of social deformations from a distinctively female perspective. Eleanore Maxwell Dial studies the boldly experimental form adopted by Isadora Aguirre in her plays, and effectively destroys the notion of the passive, derivative feminine artist. In subsequent studies of female dramatists, critics will surely assess the difficulties of theatrical production in Latin America and the way that censorship affects the language of the stage in plays written by women. Information on the reaction of audiences to social criticism, on the limitations placed on "women's language", and on the cultural milieu in which these plays are produced and received has yet to be provided.

Disappointingly, the articles on poetry do little to broaden our perspective on Latin American women poets. An article based on Juana de Asbaje and Sara de Ibáñez simply offers meaningless parallels between two poets whose only reason for appearing together seems to be that they both write and that April, 1975, marked the joint anniversary of their deaths. Articles on Julia de Burgos and Gabriela Mistral are routine and predictable. By turning to less well-known figures, critics of poetry could have brought needed attention to the significant experiments in language produced by avant-garde female poets in Latin America.

Despite the flaws in this volume—the annoying insistence on translation of terms a person unfamiliar with Spanish would surely know ("señoritas" is replaced by young ladies, etc.), hyperbolic language that could have been avoided by rigorous editorial intervention, and the failure to explain the process of selection that determined the bilingual anthology of poets—the book serves as an important point of departure for feminist studies of Latin American literature. Its existence challenges readers to consider the possible rewards of future investigations in this field where the basic research has yet to be completed. The book's reader comes to understand the research difficulties faced by contemporary critics who are determined to study Latin American women writers of the past. It takes little to imagine the plight of researchers of the future who wish to study-twentieth century Latin American writing in its rich diversity, and find, instead, the omni-present names of those who form part of the "Boom" repeated as a litany in our books and journals. The publication of *Latin American Women Writers: Yesterday and Today* signals an alternative to patterns notoriously resistant to change. The volume is of primary importance since it forces us to question the narrowness of our experience as readers and critics.

The publication of *Latin American Women Writers: Yesterday and Today* indicates that the base of Latin American literary criticism is expanding so that productive insights of contemporary feminist criticism, which in its variety and richness stretches the limits of critical theory, can be incorporated into our journals and classrooms. The energy for this expansion derives from many sources. There is significant interest on the part of English, American and French scholars to extend the scope of feminist literary studies to cultures outside of their own. The development of the Women's Movement in Latin America provides an increasingly broad base for the study of the female experience in many spheres, including literature. Most important, as feminist literary study matures, critics utilizing this mode are gaining skills which enable them to tackle literary problems heretofore viewed as

impenetrable. *Latin American Women Writers: Yesterday and Today* supplies the interested reader ample material for embarking on this new critical endeavor.

[1] "When We Dead Awaken: Writing as Re-Vision," in *Adrienne Rich's Poetry*, eds. Barbara Charlesworth Gelpi and Albert Gelpi (New York: W.W. Norton & Co., 1975), p. 90.

MARGERY RESNICK is Director of Modern Languages at Massachusetts Institute of Technology.

The Phases of Julio

The Final Island: The Fiction of Julio Cortázar
edited by Jaime Alazraki and Ivar Ivask
University of Oklahoma Press, 1978.
$12.95

AMBROSE GORDON

The story is found in Cortázar's *Octaedro* and is entitled *Las fases de Severo*. It concerns one long night. Severo is seen by the reader and by a gathering of family and friends entirely in his bedroom and the phases are six in number: one, with hands crossed over his knees, sweating (copiously, prodigiously, until his pillows become like giant tear drops); two, leaping, first in bed, then about the room, then back in bed again, hunkered down, or on his knees, or flying into the air; three, lying perfectly still, not even eyes moving, while a swarm of moths is let into the bedroom and slowly settles on his face, covering it completely except for the eyes; four, assigning numbers to each of the increasingly nervous witnesses of these proceedings (those with low numbers are the most nervous); five, directing each of them to set his or her watch either back or ahead (some who set theirs back appear relieved); six, immobile, said to be sleeping, his face quite covered by a handkerchief held in place by coins sewed into its four corners.

Strange? Yes. But phases of what or of whom? How can we fit them together so that they will compose an individual or comprise a dramatic event? The narrator, somewhat unusual in Cortázar's fiction, is named Julio, and these come also in some fashion to be his phases.

I have continued to keep Severo's story in mind while trying to attend to the present book of essays, whose preface by Ivar Ivask announces that it is a "study in depth by twelve Cortázar specialists." In a short review it might be difficult to do justice to the reasoned arguments of each on such topics as Doubles, Bridges and the Quest for Identity, Games, Love and Humor, the Ambivalence of the Hand, the Erotics of Liberation, Vampires and Vampiresses, the Mythology of Writing, Ontological Fabulation, and so on. Fortunately, there is a different approach possible. It has occurred to me (perhaps impertinently) that the names of the twelve, some perhaps still little known outside their circle, all probably intimately known within, have come to represent (1) a gathering of apostolic witnesses to some venerated or nearly miraculous corpus and (2) (though it may be much the same) a partial guest list of those who were present at the house of Severo. The names are as follows: Roberto González Echevarría, Malva E. Filer, Martha Paley Francescato, Lida Aronne Amestoy, Sara Castro-Klarén, Margery A. Safir, Ana María Hernández—to which should be added Saúl Sosnowski, Saúl Yurkievich, Evelyn Picon Garfield, who has devoted a critical book to Cortázar, a Harvard Professor of Spanish, Jaime Alazraki, serving as joint editor, and a National Book Award winner for translation, Gregory Rabassa. What, I have asked myself, have these men and women added to my understanding of theis representative anecdote, the strange story of Severo?

Some, indeed, very little, and perhaps least of all Evelyn Garfield, who among them is the only one to take note of it. The story's atmosphere, she tells us, is "filled with the suggestive symbolism of a fantastic albeit possible situation." What symbolism and what situation? There is no answer given. Indeed, I am surprised that she does not say also about the atmosphere that it is dreamlike, especially since we have Cortázar's word for it that some of his stories began as dreams. In a lecture at Oklahoma, he revealed that he had dreamed *Casa tomada* "with all the details which figure in the text" and wrote it "upon jumping out of bed, still enveloped in the horrible nausea of its ending." Others are made from shreds of dreams. Near the beginning of *Las fases de Severo* the narrator explains, or tries to explain: "we felt . . . as if we were awaiting things already happened or that all that could happen was perhaps something else or nothing, as in dreams."

This is tantalizing, but it leads us nowhere as to meaning. Jaime Alazraki sees Cortázar's stories rather as mysterious metaphors. "We know," he writes, "we are dealing with vehicles of metaphors because they suggest meanings that exceed their literal value. . . . [It] is the reader's task . . . to determine the tenor." This approach, to my way of thinking, is more helpful. The only objection I would

care to raise (beside questioning the word "task") is that it suggests a single meaning to a single story. The idea of vehicle and tenor traditionally has been one vehicle, one tenor, the vehicle performing like a bicycle, never like a bus transporting an opera company. Cortázar's stories typically resemble versions of a myth, where (to quote González Echevarría) "The specificity of text vanishes as we . . . accept the plurality of potential readings that the myth contains." As is well known, myth and ritual are near allied. The action within these stories often calls to mind some curious ritual, understood in a certain way by those performing it (here Severo and his wife, and perhaps his older son and even some of the guests) but understood differently, if at all, by the onlookers, including the narrator and, of course, the reader himself.

Our first impression on coming to *Las fases de Severo* may have been that we are present at a wake, one of the many wakes in Latin American fiction. Upon arriving, the guests are invited into the bedroom but remain first for a few minutes in the diningroom. Thereafter, they shuttle between the two, drinking coffee and grapa and mate between their vigils at Severo's bedside. Instead of a corpse, however, we encounter a live performer, a very alert Severo even in his phases of seeming passivity—someone "in phase" who is following meticulously certain to us still unknown laws. According to one dictionary the word *severo* includes among its meanings "*exacto, puntual y rígido en la observancia de una ley*" (exact, punctual and strict in the observance of a law). What Cortázar has said, in an interview with Garfield, about buses and trains and streetcars comes to mind here: "A streetcar or a train is a bridge that moves. . . . But inside, they . . . are a 'no-man's land', because streetcars and buses are strange. In them . . . people are thrown together and moved along in space and time. This creates a kind of unity separated from all else." Cortázar adds: "that situation seems to me to be able to determine the function of certain unknown laws; certain things can happen there that do not occur outside."

A bedroom is also a kind of bridge—from sleep to waking, as it may sometimes be from nonbeing to being (birth, conception) and from life to death, including what the French call "la petite mort." Anything may happen in a bedroom, and anything that does will seem significant, partly because a bedroom is a kind of sanctum, a place of privacy, of secrecy—the exact opposite of a communal and festive diningroom. There is a transgression in merely looking in. These various bedroom happenings, including the erotic, are suggested by

Severo's phases, where he both suffers—supine, passive and helpless, perhaps almost voluptuously—and yet also leaps, cavorts and dances and, in still another phase, indifferently inflicts suffering upon his friends and relatives when he tags them with the fatal numbers. Speaking of what she calls "sadistic voyeurism" in Cortázar's fiction, Margery Safir explains how "spectators and participants are inevitably and simultaneously the same." She extends the relationship to the reader as well "since, given the montage structure . . . he must be an accomplice, a participant in constructing the text, while at the same time a spectator of the events presented." A bedroom—like a text—is thus also a labyrinth, where the reader-author, or doer-sufferer, is hero and monster together, both Theseus and the awaiting Minotaur.

The text turns at last upon itself; writing is such another peculiar, sacred activity. So González Echevarría remarks, concerning an early play of Cortázar, "If in other versions of the myth the birth of reason, morals or politics is at stake, what we have in Los reyes is the violent birth of writing. The catalogue of herbs that the Minotaur 'tastes" is a series of disconnected words, without syntactical and therefore temporal structure, linked to their individual origin through their stems. By killing the Minotaur, Theseus attempts to replace the perishable sound of individual words with the linear, durable cogency of discourse." (Perhaps also as critics attempt to replace the shifting, emphemeral text with a definitive interpretation?) González Echevarría adds: "This primal scene appears with remarkable consistency in Cortázar's writing." Is then Severo in his dream labyrinth, with his disconnected phases, his mask of living moths—Severo, whose death we perhaps witness at the end—a version of the monster? And is the narrator, to whom he assigned the disquieting number 2, who yet walks out into the dawn at the end of the story, is he the hero? Possibly. At the very least we sense a fatal bond between them. The critic concludes, sadly and mysteriously: "Like the labyrinth the text is empty at the end."

Alejandro Otero, Solar MIRROR I (Study) 1973

Mauro Rodríguez

So it is, and yet, one reflects, one must not read short stories too solemnly, Cortázar's least of all. In Los reyes the Minotaur is called the "lord of games," and Cortázar is that too. And Las fases de Severo? One thinks of the two Julio's the one within the story who gets his mortal bingo, the other who wrote the story and who is the subject of these essays, and of that final bit of dialogue when Severo's young son asks:

—It was a game, wasn't it, Julio?
—Yes, old man, it was a game. Go to sleep now.

AMBROSE GORDON, who teaches English at the University of Texas at Austin, is the author of The Invisible Tent: The War Novels of Ford Madox Ford.

Homesick at Home

Alejo Carpentier: The Pilgrim at Home
by Roberto González Echevarría
Cornell University Press, 1977. $16.50

DJELAL KADIR

To think that we may glimpse, however momentarily, the ambivalent and elusive ground between the two veils, that luring fissure between person and persona may be the temptation of greatest longevity in our history. The thought has seduced theologians, enticed venerable sophists, and has provoked fascinating experiments by authors who have been able to see the potential of such allurement. One thinks, for example, of Rousseau, of Wordsworth of The Prelude, of Proust, of Octavio Paz. Alejo Carpentier belongs to this constellation of provocative figures who would superimpose the autobiographical person onto the ficticious pseudo-autobiographical persona with deliberate imperfection, allowing the interstices to show and to become a siren song for the wakeful reader. Only, Carpentier, in the best tradition of Latin American letters, compounds the enticement by simultaneously approaching the problem not solely on the autobiographical—pseudo autobiographical plane but also at the level of hemispheric, national biography and fiction; that is, at the level of history and poesy. It is not surprising that many have floundered in Hispanic criticism on the seductive waters of this siren song. Roberto González Echevarría does not eschew the temptation but, deft reader that he is, he finds clear sailing. He confesses that the genesis of his study lies in an attempt to reconstruct a transition—one leading from the unfinished *Libro de la Gran Sabana,* an autobiographical travel journal, to an autobiographical novel, *The Lost Steps.* "Carpentier's displacement of the autobiographical 'I' of the travel journal onto the fictionalized 'I' of the novel seemed worthy of analysis," González innocently admits. But González is not an innocent reader. As one would expect, the problematics of that "reconstruction," much less of a deconstruction or of a reconciliation, become apparent to him from the very beginning. So, he confesses, "reconstructing the process by which *The Lost Steps* was written became as difficult a task as that of Carpentier's own narrator-protagonist in his search for origins." The reader who perseveres through the next three hundred pages of González's study realizes that the confession is not pure self-indulgence. The problematics described in the initial, modest undertaking emblematically embody the problematics of Carpentier's entire *oeuvre* and González skillfully rises to the occasion.

What emerges from this study, with disquieting clarity for this reader, is that Carpentier, the most Platonist among the Platonic writers of the contemporary novel, embodies the poetic principles of the most conservatively Aristotelian among literary theoreticians. I refer to Julius Cesar Scaliger, the Renaissance poetician whose misreading of Aristotle transforms literature into a poetization of history and whose portrayal of the poet as demigod and cosmogonist anticipates the Romantic and post-Romantic literary traditions. I should qualify this characterization of Carpentier by pointing out, as González aptly elaborates in the latter part of his study, that after 1953, when he begins to wax ironical, Carpentier undermines his own constructs predicated upon the relationship between writer, literature, and history and embarks on a revindication of the sportive, the playful vanguardism and its revolutionary spirit. González's greatest contribution may lie in his keen delineation of this transformation in Carpentier's work.

One senses in reading the Carpentier of the earlier works (before the mid-fifties) an anxiety of secondariness. While González's study constantly hovers over Carpentier's irrepressible desire for primacy, pointing out how Carpentier, in his attitude, is exemplary of a whole generation of Latin American intellectuals, González's discussion of it remains diffuse. However, the accumulated impact of González's observations, for the reader who experiences the book as a whole, does in fact accomplish the task. Thus, one comes away from the book with a gnawing realization that what Carpentier initially sought and then ironized consists of an attempt to transform the random and contingent secondariness of history (of Latin American history especially, and González is emphatically clear on that) into the primacy of form through the fixity of literary discourse. In the end, when "the pilgrim" is finally "at home," a monstrous realization that has plagued American writers since Columbus put pen to paper to describe the New World dawns on Carpentier as well: that discourse is itself secondary, recursive, and as cultural schema, as language, it floats as a predicate of the random, casual seas of historical contingency. Carpentier's latest works, then, speak to us not simply of a "pilgrim at home" but, as Chesterton would have it, of a pilgrim who finds himself "homesick at home."

The primacy of González's work at a very mundane level is the only unproblematic phenomenon. As the publisher hastens to point out on the dust jacket of the book, this is the first book-length study in English devoted to Carpentier. They also point out, with accuracy, that González carries off his task with éclat. However, they cannot, wonderful marketing creatures that publishers are, refrain from the hoopla of announcing that González's is an "experimental, post-structural approach." Such a claim, chronologically accurate, may be characterized (and I borrow the words of the late Lezama Lima, who, no doubt, is now gleefully lighting his sybaritic cigar on the fires of hell) as "priapic gossip on climacteric ears" for some academic circles. Reading González however, one comes away with the inevitable impression that the success of his study is not necessarily a function of any particular critical method. In fact, the intellectual rigor, tightness of argument, sharp critical insight, and a not infrequent Carpentierian flair of language evinced by the work would suggest that any critical method (and there is ample catholicity of methodology in the book) would have yielded equally rewarding results, and with the same éclat, given the critical capabilities demonstrated by the author of this study. ✒

DJELAL KADIR teaches in the Department of Foreign Languages and Literatures at Purdue University.

Reading the Spanish American Mind

Hispanic America and its Civilizations
by Edmund Stephen Urbanski
Translated by Frances K. Hendricks
and Beatrice Berler
University of Oklahoma Press, 1978.
$14.95

THOMAS J. KNIGHT

Hispanic America and Its Civilizations dissects the symbols and habits of creole, Indian, and mestizo culture and offers striking comparisons with their equivalents in the United States. By combining the perspectives of cultural anthropology and the history of ideas, Professor Urbanski, an internationally known Americanist educated at the National University of Mexico and now teaching in his native Poland, reconstructs the symbolic architecture of the Hispanic American mind. The implied question is: "How has Hispanic America been seen by its native peoples, its explorers, and its present-day inhabitants?" In one respect this English edition goes beyond the 1972 Spanish version by adding an intriguing chapter on the maps available to European explorers of the New World. More importantly, Urbanski offers some interesting speculations on reasons for the Europeans' conflicting visions of the New World as green hell or earthly paradise (religious mythology), on the backwardness of Iberian cartography (imperial security), and on purported predecessors of Columbus (especially Sánchez, who supposedly told Columbus the secret on his deathbed). Urbanski might have added that the Europeans held conflicting preconceptions as to whether the Indians were children of Satan or noble savages nearer Eden. He does, however, provide an entrée into the question of cultural interaction by analyzing "Americanist terminology" such as *Indias, Hispanidad,* and *Mexicanidad.*

In general, the colonial period is treated in anthropological terms: "The vital sources of Hispanic American civilization came from the union of Spanish blood with Indian and the Indians' acceptance of the language and religion of the conquerors. To the north the situation was entirely different. The rejection of English feudalism . . . laid the groundwork for a vigorous Anglo-American civilization. It did not face linguistic obstacles because almost all the settlers spoke the same language and lived apart from their Indian neighbors." Psycho-logical rather than ethnographic factors predominate: "The collective psychology of a people evolves from its customs, lifeways, and political convictions.... Hispanic American pride, stemming from Spanish pride of birth and race, was diffused throughout Hispanic America. Anglo-American dignity originated in the satisfaction produced by individual and collective achievements, not usually from lineage or past history." These differences are "racial" in the sense that Urbanski employs Manuel M. Valle's distinction between *morphorace* ("traditional racial typology") and *thermorace* ("ecological adaptation"). There are obviously dangers in this approach. One is that Urbanski's definition of Hispanic American society does not fit the Europeanized states of southern South America, the Indian states of the Andes, or the Negro states of northern Brazil and the Caribbean. A second is that the analysis of colonial settlement in terms of "sumptuous capitals" in Hispanic America and "centers of work" in Anglo America comes uncomfortably close to the Black Legend of Spanish exploitation and English productivity.

To his credit, Urbanski confronts these dangers head on. His description of Hispanic America as biologically mestizo and culturally Hispanic becomes considerably more elaborate in the discussions of "Indians and Indianism," "Creoles and Creolism," and "The Mestizos." The economic and political powerlessness of the Indians of Mexico and the Andes is contrasted with the cultural and intellectual force of the idea of Indianism generated by pre-Columbian artifacts and contemporary literary and political figures, although only Mexico is said to have generated practical consequences in Indian life as a result of "the indigenous consciousness." Creoles, who are less hostile to *Hispanidad* than Indians for both economic and psychological reasons, nevertheless produced a creole consciousness (*criollismo*) in opposition to the values of Iberian-born *peninsulares.* This creolism has been manifested not only in the literary modernism of many River Plate writers but also in the eventual abandonment of the *Hispanidad* campaign initiated by twentieth-century Spain.

Urbanski's view seems to be that appeals to *la raza* have minimal effect because Hispanic America is, in fact, mestizo not only biologically but psychologically. Octavio Paz's *Labyrinth of Solitude* is praised for its analysis of the isolation and paralysis of mind and will of mestizo America, a civilization waiting to mature, an American and Hispanic mind searching for a new creation myth and the meaning of its psychological history. In Urbanski's terms, "A melancholy dualism emanates from the mestizo spirit, and there is no easy remedy in the complexity of modern life." Thus mestizos flee, actually or intellectually, the Mexican and Cuban revolutions and their literary manifestations in the works of Azuela and Fuentes, Guillén and Carpentier, and even in the "magic realism" of García Márquez and Vargas Llosa. Urbanski should not be identified with the political and intellectual revolutionaries in any simplistic way, however, since for him ideology follows ecology, not political economy.

The Black Legend-like comparisons of Hispanic with Anglo-Saxon America therefore lead paradoxically to the conclusion that mestizo America may be closer to psychological health than pluralist North America. The Black Legend may have a happy ending because the ecological basis exists for resurgence and renewal. To be sure, because most Hispanic American settlers were gentry and Anglo-Saxon settlers were not, the "cultural orientation" in the former has been to educate only the elite, share wealth more unequally, and preserve vestiges of rank. Urbanski quotes Leopoldo Zea: "The Saxons are sons of modernity, and the Hispanics people of the Middle Ages." Manners and mindsets are therefore quite different south and north of the Rio Grande and the Florida Straits. The cultural transformation inevitably to be produced by the ecology of the Americas therefore progresses slowly in Anglo-Saxon America, whereas it has hardly come at all in Hispanic America.

Urbanski seems nonetheless to have reversed Turner's famous Frontier Thesis about the creation of North American democracy. The Anglo-Saxons have created a surface equality that isolates the Indians and Blacks and leaves their psyches separatist in orientation, whereas Hispanic America has the fertile confusion of Paz's culture ripe for transformation. Urbanski's treatment of "Blacks in the Americas," for instance, favors the Hispanic American orientation and is much closer to the approach of Frank Tannenbaum than of Carl Degler. The Anglo-Saxons are holding off vital changes by means of the affluence produced by a well-behaved but sterile "liberalism," whereas the "religious dogmatism" of Hispanic America is under serious challenge by revolutionary movements such as Christian or Indian socialism rooted in the psychology of the mixed majority.

As yet, though, Hispanic Americans are mired in a psychology which Urbanski believes has for long produced stagnation in Slavic and Oriental civilizations too: "In the preparation of this book my previous interest in Slavic and Oriental civilizations was of some scholarly advantage.... I found charac-teristics shared by Occidental Slavs and Hispanic Americans: a high-pitched emotionalism, a metaphysical outlook on life, and a weak sense of what might be termed 'practicality.' On the other hand, a contemplative attitude, generally enigmatic behavior, a tendency toward fatalism, and passiveness in certain stages of collective distress are idiosyncrasies shared by Spanish American and Oriental cultures." Urbanski's stated aim is to untangle "the physical and psychological coexistence of Amerindian, European, and African elements" and "to provide insight into their cultural and social significance within the framework of Americanist studies." In pursuit of this aim, he also presents a view of the Hispanic American future that is remarkably akin to that of such Mexican intellectuals as Paz, Fuentes, Cosío Villegas, and Caso.

THOMAS J. KNIGHT is Associate Dean of Liberal Arts at Pennsylvania State University.

Affirming History

Studies in Afro-Hispanic Literature,
vol. 1
edited by Clementine C. Rabassa and
Gladys Seda-Rodríguez
Medgar Evers College, 1977.

CONSTANCE GARCIA-BARRIO

Interest in the black in the history and literature of the Americas has soared in the past five years. Critical consideration of the portrayal of blacks in Latin American literature has resulted in the publication of several excellent books.[1] Another important outgrowth of scholarly inquiry is the annual Symposium on Afro-Hispanic Literature. Sponsored jointly by Medgar Evers College (CUNY) and the Center for Inter-American Relations, the symposia have provided a forum for provocative papers on Afro-Hispanic literature. The Humanities Division of Medgar Evers College has recently published *Studies in Afro-Hispanic Literature* edited by Clementine C. Rabassa and Gladys Seda-Rodríguez and including eight papers presented at the second symposium.

Although the essays differ in subject and critical approach, one finds a common concern among them: each treats an aspect of identity or alienation in black writers, or authors writing about blacks, or in the characters they create. Two of the essays, "Racial Attitudes of Gregorio de Matos" and "An Uncommitted Author: Jorge Issacs' Portrayal of Blacks In

María", measure the distance between the writer and the black characters he portrayed.

Carol Beane, in her discussion of *María*, notes that in nineteenth-century Latin American novels (*Sab, Cecilia Valdés, Francisco*), the characterization of blacks was dictated by the expectations of the readers: "... it was inconvenient and untenable to present blacks other than picturesquely." Beane cites Stanley Fish (*Self-Consuming Artifacts*, 1972) who describes two kinds of literary presentations: rhetorical and dialectical. Rhetorical presentations confirm the reader's viewpoint, satisfying him, assuring him that he's right. Dialectical presentations oblige the reader to painfully re-examine his convictions.

Beane analyses the rhetorical and dialectical elements in *María*. After thorough examination of the black characters—with particular attention to the intercalated "Historia de Nay y Sinar"—Beane concludes that the dialectical element is not developed, for had it been, a denunciation of racism would have resulted. Issacs uses a technique of distancing—intercalating the story, placing characters in settings and situations with which the reader cannot identify, telling the story through distorted childhood memories—so that the reader avoids questioning contemporary race relations.

If Issacs achieved distance through subtle literary technique, as Beane's incisive and original criticism suggests, for Gregorio de Matos, a seventeenth-century Brazilian poet, distance—economic, educational, emotional—from Afro-Brazilians was a way of life. In "Racial Attitudes of Gregorio de Matos," Nola Kortner Aiex points out that de Matos belonged to the upper class of Bahia. Proud, profligate, and patrician, he excelled at writing satire, much of which reflects his class bias. It is helpful, Aiex states, to keep in mind the medieval *jograis* and *trovadores* in considering de Matos, who shares with his thirteenth and fourteenth-century predecessors a preference for satirizing a particular person or group. He uses the time-honored technique of reduction to belittle the subject. He attacked the clergy, a traditional target, and the Portuguese, whom he considered rapacious. His barbed verses were also aimed at ambitious *mestiços* and *mulatos*. Aiex notes that he satirized mulatto men—whose social gains were an unpleasant reminder of changing times—but was usually kinder to mulatto women many of whom were slaves or prostitutes, thus representing no social threat. Aiex includes much material on society and customs in seventeenth-century Bahia, the milieu de Matos looked upon with such a sardonic smile.

Richard Jackson's paper, "Ethnicity and the Modernist Esthetic in Panama", shifts the focus of the identity-alienation issue. Jackson challenges Jahnheinz Jahn's position that the race of a writer should not be a factor in his inclusion among authors of Neo-African stylistic features and patterns of expression. Jackson, however, stresses the relationship between skin color and literary esthetics, noting that the studies of Martha Cobb and Antonio Ollíz Boyd have led them to similar conclusions.[2] To illustrate this Jackson considers the Modernist poetry of the Panamanian Gaspar Octavio Hernández (1893-1918). Hernández' poetry moves with Modernist musicality and color, but the poet assiduously avoids direct reference to his being black. Nevertheless, Jackson states that "... as a black modernist poet the ethnic dimension he brings to his works is extremely valuable to those of us who would like as much insight as possible into the esthetics of the black writer, especially one whose tendency is escapist." The question here—endlessly debatable—is if a writer does not give voice to his ethnic identity, how much can a reader learn about it from his work? How eloquent is the silence?

An essay by Gregory Rabassa, "Antônio Olinto and Brazilian Remigration", and another by Lorraine Ben-Ur, "The Affirmation of Black Heritage in Francisco Arriví's *Máscara Puertorriqueña*," deal with black heritage and national identity. Rabassa explains that the vital sense of African heritage among black Brazilians led to a movement of return to the motherland after emancipation. Antônio Olinto, a Brazilian literary critic and writer, was Cultural Attaché at the Brazilian Embassy in Nigeria in the fifties. After observing returnees from Brazil, he wrote *Brasileiros na Africa* (1964), marking their efforts to maintain their cultural heritage by forming associations of Brazilian descendants and teaching their children Portuguese. Olinto saw that some customs of the returnees set them apart even among their own Yoruba people.

Rabassa also comments on an historical novel written by Olinto, *A Casa da Agua* (1969), published in English in 1970 as *The Water House*. The novel is about a woman who, taken from Africa to Brazil as a slave at eighteen, returns years later as a grandmother with her family. The problem of re-migration—a double cultural identity—becomes clear when the woman's granddaughter asks "... are we Brazilians or Africans?", and the answer is "We are both, my child". Olinto's point, Rabassa states, is that the maintenance of the Brazilian heritage is a source of strength for the family; it "acts as a kind of kentledge to hold things permanently steady". Rabassa not only persuades one to read *A Casa da Agua*, but to reread Graham W. Irwin (*Africans Abroad*, 1977), Philip Curtin (*Africa Remembered* 1967), and Alex Haley.

While the characters of *A Casa da Agua* accept a double identity, those of Arrivi's *Máscara Puertorriqueña* live a tortured duality, as Lorraine Ben-Ur shows in her essay. Since the beginnings of contemporary Puerto Rican drama in 1938, three fundamental themes have emerged according to Ben-Ur: 1) the lives of rural (*jíbaro*), urban (*arrabalero*) and U.S. bilingual Puerto Ricans; 2) the desperation of poverty; 3) the ethnic complexity of the Puerto Rican people who are of black, white, and, to a lesser extent, Indian stock. *Máscara Puerto-rriqueña*, published as a trilogy in 1956, is concerned with the ethnic issue.

In Ben-Ur's view, the three plays represent a progressive *concientización* or awakening with respect to racial-cultural identity. Some critics have stated that the trilogy does not deal with racism, but Ben-Ur argues, convincingly, that the "psychological complex of the characters is but an interiorization of racial prejudice." In *Bolero*, the first play, a crisis moves Augusto, who lives with his white wife in the U.S., to re-establish long-broken ties with his black relatives in Puerto Rico. When they do not accept him and his wife also rejects him, he commits suicide. In *Sirena*, the second play, Cambucha, the voluptuous mulatto mistress of a businessman, Roberto, undergoes plastic surgery to make her features less Negroid. Roberto, displeased with the "new" Cambucha, ends their affair. In the final scenes, Cambucha tears at her face with her fingernails. In the third play, *Los Vejigantes*, Clarita, whose grandmother is black, rejects a white American suitor from the deep South who wanted to be sure of her racial purity.

In the trilogy, Ben-Ur feels, Arriví indicates the prerequisites for Puerto Ricans of different colors to sustain normal relationships: 1) equalization of class differences, 2) rejection of the North American model, 3) official support for the enduring values of African heritage. Ben-Ur's discussion of racial and cultural issues is balanced by analysis of Arriví's literary technique: use of the popular music motif, theatricality of flashbacks, dreams, and simulated dreams. Frantz Fanon's *Peau Noire, Masques Blancs* (1952) and Isabelo Zenón Cruz' *Narciso Decubre Su Trasero* (1975) prove useful in clarifying the issues treated in the trilogy.

The black in Puerto Rican literature and the qualities with which he is identified are treated in another essay: "Poe's 'Dream-land' in Black and White: An Approach to the Poetry of Palés Matos", by David Haberly. Haberly seeks to answer the question of why Palés Matos, a white Puerto Rican, chose to write "poemas negros", and how his poems should be classified. Haberly outlines three categories of black poetry: 1) *poesía de negros*, written by "genetically black" writers: 2) *poesía negrista*, which describes "black people and their world in the standard forms and language of Hispanic poetry: 3) *poesía negroide*, a complex category in which white writers may assume "...superficial characteristic defined as African", shifting themselves temporarily towards black identity, or black writers may adopt European values and forms. Haberly feels that Pales Matos poetry fits into none of the foregoing categories, but into a fourth which he designates "poesía de lo negro". He compares Poe's "Dream-land" with Palés Matos' "Tierra de sueños," stressing the many meanings of blackness in the latter. The blackness of night signifies: 1) values of the lost Puerto-Rican past; 2) sordid night life; 3) the depths of the poet's soul; 4) life for black Puerto Ricans. For Haberly, Palés Matos originality lies in his attribution of multiple meanings to blackness.

Haberly's suggested classification of black poetry, particularly *poesía negroide*, will certainly arouse controversy, but he does offer an entirely new interpretation of Palés Matos' black poetry. The essay also draws attention to Poe's influence on Hispanic literature.

While Haberly focuses on the significance of blackness in one poet, Kay Boulware in "Women and Nature in *Negrismo*" discusses a broad tendency in Caribbean poetry—the identification of black women with nature. Black nineteenth-century poets sang the beauty of European women, Boulware notes, but were generally mute when it came to black women. Only with the *negrismo* movement of the late 1920s and early 1930s did the black woman become a worthy literary subject. The Cuban poet Nicolás Guillén led the vanguard with "Mi Chiquita", a short poem praising a black woman who really knew how to cook, dance, and party. However, the qualities poets most often associate with black women are beauty, sexuality, and productivity. These qualities, Boulware points out, are frequently conveyed through images of nature. Sexuality seems to be the most consistently portrayed. A madrigal from Guillén's *West Indies, Ltd.* (1934) provides an example—striking in its simplicity, economy, and suggestiveness—of images of nature used to describe a black woman: "*sencilla y vertical/ como una caña en el cañaveral*". Although the many examples Boulware cites are from Caribbean poets, one finds that the correlation between woman and nature holds true in poetry of other Spanish American countries.

A still broader view is that of Lemuel Johnson[3] in "History and Dystopia in Alejo Carpentier and Wole Soyinka". The essay is an inquiry into the limitations and potential of human nature. Quotations from Sigmund Freud, George Orwell, and Wole Soyinka serve to preface the essay and to comment on the predatory behavior of men toward one another throughout history. This conception of history as a succession of violent acts set in motion by some "primal crime"—a sort of demonic domino effect—is explored in the works of Carpentier and Soyinka.

There is no evidence, Johnson notes, of a time of paradise and innocence in Carpentier: "The belief in and literature of a paradisiacal antecedent is . . . subjected to ironic and epigraphic treatment." In Soyinka's *A Dance of the Forests* (1963) and *Madman and Specialists* (1971), "Human inaccessibility to moral enlightenment" implies some ancient outrage. In Soyinka and Carpentier, Johnson points out, men can resist neither their instincts nor the force of history: "The weight of the intractable in Man and History finally results in weariness, which Carpentier measured in Ti Noel in cosmic and geological time. In *A Dance of the Forests* that intractability is incarnate in the Slave Dealer." Johnson notes that although hope of perfectibility of man underlies the works of both writers, one's final impression is that of a determinism which makes this ideal unattainable. The vision is *à la* Bosch, *à la* Breughel, as far as the eye can see into man's past—or his future.

This collection of essays represents a unique contribution to criticism of Afro-Latin American literature. While each deals with a different aspect of identity or alienation, together they show a cross section of scholarly concern. Three different genres—novel, poetry, theatre—are treated, and the perspective is interdisciplinary: literary analysis is accompanied by historical and sociological data. Notes and ample bibliographical references equip the reader to pursue the interest that these essays will surely awaken.

[1] See Richard L. Jackson, *The Black Image in Latin American Literature* (Albuquerque: University of New Mexico Press, 1976); also Miriam DeCosta, ed., *Blacks in Hispanic Literature: A Collection Of Critical Essays* (Port Washington, New York: Kennikat Press, 1976).

[2] Martha Cobb, "The Black Experience in the Poetry of Nicolás Guillén, Jacques Roumain, Langston Hughes," Ph.D. dissertation (Howard University, 1974).

Antonio Ollíz Boyd, "The Concept of Black Esthetics as Seen in Selected Works of Three Latin American Writers: Machado de Assis, Nicolas Guillen, and Adalberto Ortiz," Ph.D. dissertation (Stanford University, 1975).

[3] Johnson is the author of a book, *The Devil, the Gargoyle and the Buffoon: The Negro as Metaphor in Western Literature* (Port Washington, New York: Kennikat Press, 1969).

CONSTANCE GARCIA-BARRIO teaches at West Chester State College in Pennsylvania.

Mauro Rodriguez

Alejandro Otero, Solar Wing
(Study) 1975

A Brotherhood of Suffering

*Langston Hughes in the
Hispanic World and Haiti*
by Edward J. Mullen
Archon Books, 1977. $12.50

MANUEL DURAN and
NICOLAS SHUMWAY

Although North American critics have shown until recently an appalling ignorance, if not indifference, regarding Hispanic letters, North American writers, in a few notable cases, have been an entirely different story. Langston Hughes, like Washington Irving, Waldo Frank, and Ernest Hemingway, was early affected by the Spanish-speaking cultures, first in Mexico, which provided a picturesque backdrop for several of his pieces, and later in Cuba, where he recognized in the plight of black Cubans a brotherhood of suffering that transcended both national and linguistic frontiers. Finally, like other Western intellectuals of his generation, Hughes came to see in the Spanish Civil War a symbolic struggle between racist fascism and the true democracy which guided his dreams and informed his writing.

Hughes' extensive and sustained contact with the Hispanic world is a subject for several studies, and fortunately Edward J. Mullen's *Langston Hughes in the Hispanic World and Haiti* is an admirable beginning. The book begins with an informative, quasibiographical essay, "The Literary Reputation of Langston Hughes," in which the author supplies ample evidence of Hughes' contact with major Hispanic writers such as Carlos Pellicer, Xavier Villarrutia and Nicolás Guillén as well as the Haitian novelist Jacques Roumain, whose *Gouverneurs de la Rosée* he later helped translate. There follows a lengthy bibliography of translations of Hughes' works into Spanish. The next section supplies the bulk of the book and consists of an anthology of Hughes' writing, both in prose and poetry, on Hispanic and Haitian themes as they appeared in numerous North American publications. From the charming descriptions of life in Mexico to the intelligent commentaries on racism in Spain and the passionate outcries against the brutality of the Spanish Civil War, the anthology section is perhaps the most interesting part of the book, if only because it collects under one title a number of important pieces on related themes that were previously unavailable to anyone without a great deal of time and a good re-

search library next door. The last two sections consist of a perfunctory (four short pieces) selection in Spanish of Hispanic writers who wrote about Hughes, followed by a short bibliography of the same.

Despite the undeniable usefulness of Mullen's book, one feels that an important chapter has been left out. In his preface, Mullen states that "the purpose of this book is to bring [Hughes'] writings on the Hispanic world and Haiti together with an essay tracing his influence and literary contacts in the Spanish-speaking world and the Caribbean". In reality, little is said about Hughes' influence on Hispanic writing, although ample evidence is given supporting the existence of such influence. For example, Mullen documents Nicolás Guillén's reaction to Ramón Vasconcelos' xenophobic assertion that Guillén borrowed nothing from North America, but nowhere does he show the existence of Hughes' influence in Guillén's work. A textual analysis demonstrating two-way influences between Hughes and the *negritude* writers generally would round out Mullen's book.

MANUEL DURAN and NICOLAS SHUMWAY teach in the Department of Spanish at Yale and have each published widely on Hispanic literature.

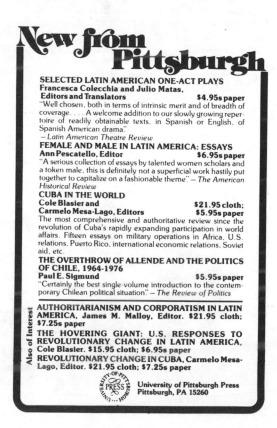

Review

Latin American Literature and Art

Fiction	Jorge Luis Borges
	Gabriel García Márquez
	Manuel Puig Octavio Paz
Art	Elena Poniatowska
	Ernesto Cardenal
Poetry	Pablo Antonio Cuadra
	Nélida Piñón Severo Sarduy
Reviews	Mario Vargas Llosa
	Rubem Fonseca
Film	Enrique Lihn Isabel Fraire
	Eduardo Gudiño Kieffer
News	Carlos Fuentes
	Alejo Carpentier

Review

Subscribe Now!

Rates for Review: $7.00 yearly within the United States;
$9.00 foreign; $10.00 institutions. Past issues available.

NAME

ADDRESS

680 Park Avenue New York, N.Y. 10021
Review is published in Spring, Fall and Winter
A publication of the Center for Inter-American Relations